The Governan
Hertie School c

OXFORD

The Governance Report 2016

The content for *The Governance Report 2016* was developed as part of a joint undertaking of the **Hertie School of Governance** and the **Organisation for Economic Co-operation and Development** (OECD) to inform and shape the debate on the governance of infrastructure.

OXFORD
UNIVERSITY PRESS

Great Clarendon Street, Oxford, OX2 6DP,
United Kingdom

Oxford University Press is a department of the University of Oxford.
It furthers the University's objective of excellence in research, scholarship,
and education by publishing worldwide. Oxford is a registered trade mark of
Oxford University Press in the UK and in certain other countries.

© Hertie School of Governance 2016

Chapters 1 and 8 © Organisation for Economic Co-operation and Development
and Hertie School of Governance

Chapters 3 and 5 © Organisation for Economic Co-operation and Development

The moral rights of the authors have been asserted

First Edition published in 2016

Impression: 1

All rights reserved. No part of this publication may be reproduced, stored
in a retrieval system, or transmitted, in any form or by any means, without
the prior permission in writing of Oxford University Press, or as expressly
permitted by law, by licence or under terms agreed with the appropriate
reprographics rights organization. Enquiries concerning reproduction outside
the scope of the above should be sent to the Rights Department, Oxford
University Press, at the address above.

You must not circulate this work in any other form and you must impose
this same condition on any acquirer.

British Library Cataloguing in Publication Data
Data available

Library of Congress Cataloging in Publication Data
Data available

ISBN 978-0-19-875743-6

Printed in Great Britain on acid-free paper
by Clays Ltd, St Ives plc

Managing Editor: Regina List
Book design: Plural | Severin Wucher
Cover illustration: Emilia Birlo
Information graphics: Plural | Kilian Krug
Typeset in Publico and TheSans

Links to third party websites are provided by Oxford in good faith and
for information only. Oxford disclaims any responsibility for the materials
contained in any third party website referenced in this work.

Table of Contents

Preface	7
Acknowledgements	9
List of Figures, Tables, and Boxes	11
List of Abbreviations	13

I. The Infrastructure Challenge: 15
    Changing Needs, Persistent Myths
    HELMUT K. ANHEIER *and* ROLF ALTER

II. Infrastructure Governance and Government Decision-making   31
    GERHARD HAMMERSCHMID *and* KAI WEGRICH

III. Subnational Infrastructure Investment: 55
    The Governance Levers
    DOROTHÉE ALLAIN-DUPRÉ, CLAUDIA HULBERT,
    and MARGAUX VINCENT

IV. Infrastructure Project Delivery and Implementation: 79
    Risk Management Across a Project's Life Cycle
    GENIA KOSTKA

V. Good Governance and Choosing the Right   103
    Infrastructure Delivery Model
    IAN HAWKESWORTH *and* JUAN GARIN

VI. Governance Innovations: Infrastructure   125
    HELMUT K. ANHEIER *and* SONJA KAUFMANN

VII. Governance Indicators: Infrastructure   149
    MATTHIAS HABER

VIII. Improving Infrastructure Governance: 175
    Implications and Recommendations
    HELMUT K. ANHEIER *and* ROLF ALTER

References	189
About the Contributors	207

Preface

The *Governance Report 2016* is the fourth in this annual series about the changing conditions of governance, the challenges and opportunities involved, and the implications and recommendations that present themselves to analysts and policy-makers.

The Governance Report is an interdisciplinary effort to examine state-of-the-art governance. In doing so, it enlists experts from the Hertie School of Governance in Berlin as well as from other institutions. Special attention is paid to institutional designs and approaches, changes, and innovations that both state and non-state actors have adopted in response to shifts that have been occurring–and, in this year's edition, in relation to infrastructure.

The results are available in an annual series that includes this compact report and an edited companion volume, both published by Oxford University Press, and a dedicated website at www.governancereport.org. Together, these various outputs and outlets are designed to provide both policy-makers and analysts with ideas, knowledge, and tools to consider and implement policies and programmes that lead to better solutions to public problems.

Launched in February 2013, the first edition examines the challenges of financial and fiscal governance, proposes a new paradigm of responsible sovereignty for tackling global issues, highlights selected governance innovations, and introduces a new generation of governance indicators. In the 2014 edition, the focus turns to administrative capacity in OECD countries and how governments and their public administrations coordinate branches of the state, regulate markets, deliver services, implement policy, and make sense of increasingly complex tasks through the use of knowledge and analysis. It questions how much 'muscle' is left during the current 'age of austerity' after waves of reforms that have changed the architecture of the state. The 2015 edition picks up many of these topics in the context of the European Union, especially since the onset of the eurozone crisis, to assess where the European integration project is now, where it should go, and alternatives for getting there, highlighting the practical and political trade-offs facing governance actors.

For the 2016 edition, we collaborated with the Organisation for Economic Co-operation and Development (OECD) to examine how governance can be brought back into the current debate on infrastructure. Though all agree that infrastructure is a fundamental driver of economic growth and social development, unmet investment needs coexist with 'white elephants' and 'bridges to nowhere', and major construction projects face huge cost overruns and citizen protest. Drawing on novel survey data and case studies from around the world, *The Governance Report 2016* highlights the complexity and trade-offs faced by decision-makers, project managers, private businesses, and the population at large in setting priorities, choosing projects, and implementing them.

Finally, the Governance Report series seeks to provide evidence to support decision-making processes by developing a new generation of indicators. The dashboards in which we present data on a variety of variables either taken from existing sources or collected by our indicators team provide a wealth of information for policy-makers and researchers that can be extracted and analysed according to the issue or question at hand. In the first edition, we offer the rationale for introducing a new set of indicators into a veritable 'indicators industry' and a sampling of the kinds of useful analyses that could be performed. For the 2014 edition, the set of dashboards is expanded to incorporate variables that focus on administrative capacity. The 2015 edition, focusing on EU member states, offers a dashboard of various economic and public opinion variables and suggests ways of tracing convergence or divergence on those variables and examining other key relationships. For the 2016 edition, we combine responses to the Hertie School-OECD expert survey and other data to analyse performance on and linkages among infrastructure planning, management, and outcomes. The dashboards and analytical tools described in the Report are also available at www.governancereport.org.

Work on future editions focusing on democratic innovation, metropolitan governance, and other topics has already begun. We invite your comments and suggestions at www.governancereport.org.

Helmut K. Anheier and Regina A. List
Berlin, February 2016

Acknowledgements

Many people have been involved in developing this edition of *The Governance Report*, in addition to the authors of the various chapters.

In the process of developing the Report, we joined the Organisation for Economic Co-operation and Development to convene a High Level Focus Group on Challenges and New Solutions for the Governance of Infrastructure, held at OECD headquarters in Paris in January 2015. We appreciate the thoughtful contributions of the participants, including Gordon McKechnie, who chaired the session, Mario Aymerich (European Investment Bank), Thomas Barrett (European Investment Bank), Luigi Carbone (Regulatory Authority for Electricity, Gas and Water, Italy), Howard Chernick (Hunter College, City University of New York), Juan Garin (NormannPartners), Dominique Gatel (Veolia), Klaus Grewe (Jacobs Engineering), Iztok Jarc (Permanent Delegation of Slovenia to the OECD), Bert Kuby (EU Committee of the Regions), Charles Lloyd (PricewaterhouseCoopers), Ferdinand Schuster (KPMG), and Thomas Wobben (EU Committee of the Regions).

We also thank the Hertie School community, especially Jobst Fiedler and other faculty members who contributed ideas and constructive criticism. This Report could not have come together without the work of the core Hertie School Governance Report team, which, in addition to authors Matthias Haber and Sonja Kaufmann and Managing Editor Regina List, includes Jessica Leong Cohen, Diego Fernández Fernández, Olga Kononykhina, and Christopher (CJ) Yetman. Additional thanks are owed to Christian Behrendt, Daniel Belling, Mihaly Fazekas, and Liam McGrath, who helped along the way.

The Chapter 2 authors thank Anca Oprisor, Matasha Mency Mazis, and Bruno Paschoal for their research assistance and Jacint Jordana (IBEI Institut Barcelona d'Estudis Internacionals), Carlos Oliveira Cruz (Universidade de Lisboa), and Alexander Wendler for their valuable expert advice on the country case studies.

The Chapter 3 authors thank colleagues from the OECD Public Governance and Territorial Development Directorate who provided comments on the draft, in particular Monica Brezzi, Isabelle Chatry, Claire Charbit, Ian Hawkesworth, Karen Maguire, Joaquim Oliveira, and William Tompson, and Bert Kuby, Andrea Forti and Pawel Zamojski from the EU Committee of the Regions (CoR), as well as the CoR for their support in organising the joint OECD-CoR survey in 2015 and having it translated into 24 EU-country languages.

The Chapter 4 author thanks Carolin Reiner and Niklas Anzinger for their help with collecting and writing up the case studies.

And the Chapter 5 authors thank Celine Kaufmann, Deputy Head of Division, Dorothée Allain-Dupré, Senior Analyst, and Rolf Alter, Director, for their contributions and comments, as well as all of the Public Governance and Territorial Development Directorate, OECD, Paris.

Thanks are also due to Zora Chan, Magriet Cruywagen, Andrea Derichs, Simone Dudziak, Doroteja Enčeva, Faye Freyschmidt, Stefanie Jost, Charlotte Koyro, Regine Kreitz, and Felicitas Schott at the Hertie School and to Andrew Davies, Katherine Poinsard, Sally Taylor, and Andrea Uhrhammer at the OECD.

We also wish to thank the Board of the Hertie School of Governance for encouraging this Report, and for providing critical feedback and direction. In addition, we would like to mention the members of the Report's International Advisory Committee: Craig Calhoun (London School of Economics), William Roberts Clark (Texas A&M), John Coatsworth (Columbia University), Ann Florini (Singapore Management University and Brookings Institution), Geoffrey Garrett (University of Pennsylvania), Mary Kaldor (London School of Economics), Edmund J. Malesky (Duke University), Henrietta Moore (University College London), Woody Powell (Stanford University), Bo Rothstein (Quality of Government Institute, University of Gothenburg), Shanker Satyanath (New York University), James Vreeland (Georgetown University), Kent Weaver (Georgetown University), Arne Westad (Harvard University), and Michael Zürn (Wissenschaftszentrum Berlin).

At Oxford University Press, we thank Dominic Byatt for seeing the promise in this enterprise and to Olivia Wells and Carla Hodge for guiding us through.

For the Report's look we are grateful to the team of Severin Wucher and Kilian Krug at Plural in Berlin, and to Emilia Birlo for the cover art work.

Finally, we are especially grateful to the Hertie Foundation for its support, to Evonik and Stiftelsen Riksbankens Jubileumsfond for their support in launching the Report series, and to the Berggruen Institute for providing the financial resources that made this Report's development and production possible.

List of Figures, Tables, and Boxes

Figure 1.1: Need vs. current infrastructure spending, as per cent of GDP
Figure 1.2: Infrastructure spending and productivity growth (2004-2013)
Figure 1.3: Infrastructure investment and quality (2004/6-2013)
Figure 2.1: Change of relative share of infrastructure investment in different sectors over the last 5 years
Figure 2.2: Comparing prioritisation and perceived change in investment of key infrastructure sectors
Figure 2.3: Extent of involvement of different actors in national public infrastructure planning/priority setting
Figure 2.4: Main coordination challenges with respect to strategic planning for public infrastructure
Figure 2.5: Level of coordination challenges with respect to strategic planning for public infrastructure
Figure 3.1: Subnational public investment in OECD countries as a share of public investment (GFCF), 2013
Figure 3.2: Public investment as a share of GDP in OECD countries (1980-2013)
Figure 3.3: Evolution of SNG expenditure in OECD countries (2006 = base 100)
Figure 3.4: Central and subnational government investment trends in selected OECD countries over 2005-2014 (2006 = base 100)
Figure 3.5: Overall public investment spending trends by SNGs since 2010
Figure 3.6: Trends in investment spending: share of SNGs reporting an increase of more than 10 per cent since 2010, by type
Figure 3.7: Sectors most affected by funding gaps in SNGs
Figure 3.8: Main challenges perceived by SNGs with respect to strategic planning and implementation of infrastructure investment
Figure 3.9: Practices that help the management of infrastructure investment in SNGs
Figure 3.10: Correlation between governance indicators and regional GDP growth in selected SNGs (2001-2011)
Figure 5.1: Decision tree for infrastructure delivery option choice
Figure 6.1: Step-wise WUMP process
Figure 7.1: Experts per country
Figure 7.2: Country performance in infrastructure planning, management, and outcomes
Figure 7.3: Infrastructure Governance Index
Figure 7.4: Infrastructure planning and infrastructure outcomes
Figure 7.5: Infrastructure planning and infrastructure management

Figure 7.6:	Infrastructure management and infrastructure outcomes
Figure 7.7:	Estimation of over- and underachievement based on expected performance
Figure 7.8:	Level of economic development and infrastructure planning
Figure 7.9:	Level of economic development and infrastructure management
Figure 7.10:	Level of economic development and infrastructure outcomes
Figure 7.11:	Estimation of over- and underachievement based on level of economic development
Figure 7.12:	Total investment in inland infrastructure as a percentage of GDP and infrastructure outcomes performance
Figure 7.13:	Change in infrastructure spending over the last 5 years and infrastructure outcomes performance
Figure 7.14:	Change in infrastructure spending and overall infrastructure quality over the last 5 years
Figure 7.15:	Infrastructure investment as a percentage of GDP and productivity growth (2004-2013)
Figure 7.16:	Transparency as relevant planning criterion of infrastructure management and infrastructure outcomes
Table 4.1:	The life cycle of an infrastructure project
Table 4.2:	Case studies examined across the four major project life cycle phases
Table 4.3:	Key governance challenges and solutions according to the project life cycle approach
Table 4.4:	Innovation toolbox
Table 5.1:	Setting a preferred sectoral approach
Table 5.2:	Country circumstances
Table 6.1:	Potential governance-related responses to key infrastructure challenges
Table 6.2:	Overview of selected cases
Table 7.1:	Selection of indicators on infrastructure governance
Box 5.1:	Modes of infrastructure delivery
Box 5.2:	Checklist for investigating relevant delivery mode

List of Abbreviations

ACP	Autoridad del Canal de Panama (Panama Canal Authority)
BFA	Bayesian factor analysis
BIM	building information modelling
BOT	build-operate-transfer
BRICS	Brazil, Russia, India, China, and South Africa
BRT	bus rapid transit
CoR	European Union Committee of the Regions
DAM	Day-Ahead Market
EU	European Union
FIFA	Fédération Internationale de Football Association
GDP	gross domestic product
GFCF	gross fixed capital formation
GIZ	Deutsche Gesellschaft für Internationale Zusammenarbeit
HVHR	High Value High Risk
IA	Infrastructure Australia
ISO	independent system operator
ITDP	Institute for Transportation and Development Policy
ITU	International Telecommunications Union
KPI	key performance indicator
MW	megawatt
NIMBY	'Not in my backyard'
O&M	operation and maintenance
OECD	Organisation for Economic Co-operation and Development
PAC	Programa de Aceleração do Crescimento (Growth Acceleration Programme in Brazil)
PPP	public-private partnership
PRG	partial risk guarantees
PwC	PricewaterhouseCoopers
RAKLI	Finnish Association of Building Owners and Construction Clients
RCF	reference class forecasting
RE	renewable energy
SADC	Southern African Development Community
SAPP	Southern African Power Pool
SNG	subnational government
SOE	state-owned enterprise
TSO	transmission system operator
VDC	Village Development Committee
WUMP	Water Use Master Plan

I. The Infrastructure Challenge
Changing Needs, Persistent Myths

HELMUT K. ANHEIER *and* ROLF ALTER

The *Governance Report 2016* deals with the governance of public infrastructure.[1] For a long time the near exclusive responsibility of governments and financed entirely from public budgets, infrastructure–like many other public and quasi-public goods–has come under increased scrutiny, with frequent calls for improved efficiency, more transparency, and better outcomes in terms of quality and sustainability. These goals are supposed to be achieved through risk and incentive models for better resource allocation, greater involvement of the private sector generally, and wider use of public-private partnerships (PPPs) in particular. Other public governance instruments such as integrity frameworks and procurement systems to curb corruption as well as ways to increase citizen engagement are to complement the drive for performance.

Infrastructure matters: it is an essential component of everyday quality of life and business environments.

Infrastructure matters. Mostly taken for granted by those living in developed market economies, infrastructure tends to be noticed when it is absent, declining, or decrepit. At the same time, it is an essential component of everyday quality of life and business environments. Indeed, infrastructure is seen as the engine for productivity growth and competitiveness and as a safeguard investment for future economic well-being.

Yet, as we will see in this Report, much of the conventional wisdom about infrastructure can be questioned. The evidence base is surprisingly weak and partially inconclusive: estimates of future infrastructure needs differ strikingly, and the essential link between infrastructure spending and productivity growth is less than clear cut. The same can be said, for example, about the financial investments required, the shares of public and private

---

The opinions expressed and arguments employed herein are solely those of the authors and do not necessarily reflect the official views of the OECD or of its member countries.

funding needed, or the influence citizen participation has on the planning process and, ultimately, the quality of infrastructure.

This Report argues that the governance[2] of infrastructure, long neglected by policy analysts and academics alike, is key to not only individual project success but also overall country performance and competitiveness. Bringing in the lens of governance readiness in terms of analytical, regulatory, coordination, and delivery capacities allows us to address responsibility and decision-making, needs for reform, citizen trust, and the future-proofing of infrastructure. Rather than considering the mobilisation of resources as the primary bottleneck for infrastructure investment, the governance perspective suggests that heightened attention be paid to the decision-making and administrative processes involved, and that this be done in the context of macroeconomic conditions that vary across countries and may involve different trade-offs.

What Are the Issues?

At their best, infrastructure policies deliver needed roads, energy grids, water systems, communication lines, internet access, airports, and train services within budget, on time, of high quality, and sustainably over time[3]–and are based on some degree of public consensus, including on how to allocate public funding. Ideally, such policies not only trigger economic growth and increase productivity but also improve quality of life and enhance environmental sustainability. At their worst, there is government silo mentality, pork barrel politics, waste, corruption, severe overspending, time delays, high sunk costs, and poor outcomes in terms of productivity growth, quality, and sustainability.

Indeed, investment in infrastructure is significant: on average in 2014, OECD countries spent 3.2 per cent of GDP on infrastructure investments and maintenance, including research and development. The public share of these expenditures makes it the fourth largest government spending area after social spending, compensation of employees, and goods and services used by government. However, since the 2008–9 financial crisis, government expenditures on investment have fallen in absolute and relative terms, decreasing in nominal terms from US$1,440 per capita in 2009 to US$1,288 per capita in 2014, and from 4.1 per cent to 3.2 per cent of GDP during the same time period (OECD 2016a).

While infrastructure spending has declined on average in recent years, the relative roles of the public and private sectors have been shifting, not only in terms of financing but also in wider perspectives. Especially the delivery and maintenance of infrastructure have become multi-actor systems that go well beyond government and public agencies to involve business corporations and organised civil society. With more stakeholders involved, there is also more debate about how much countries ought to spend, and for what, how, and by whom. Well-designed projects fail because of NIMBY, or 'not in my backyard', attitudes, and urgently needed projects suffer delays because of flawed planning procedures or corruption.

There are many successful infrastructure projects, to be sure, and infrastructure continues to be built, maintained, and upgraded. While most infrastructure projects are relatively small-scale and involve known technologies and procedures, others are massive and complex. Here, too, one finds successful examples. One prominent case is the Øresund Link between Copenhagen and Malmö, connecting Denmark and Sweden. Despite the scale of the project, which included a tunnel, an artificial island, and a bridge, it finished three months ahead of schedule. Although less demanding, the construction of the AVUS A115 highway, including a connection between two critical existing highways in Berlin, was finished ahead of schedule and below budget (see Case Study 5 in Chapter 4). The Bangkok Mass Transit System, commonly known as the Skytrain, was, despite an initial construction delay of three years, completed within budget and a month ahead of schedule.

Of course, failures attract public attention more than successes. The Central Artery/Tunnel Project in Boston, also known as the Big Dig, is almost legendary in all these regards. The Eurotunnel was six months delayed, followed by 18 months of unreliable service, while the Betuweroute double-track freight rail line in the Netherlands was delayed by over 1.5 years and was slow to pick up traffic. The new Berlin airport, originally scheduled to open in 2012, is some 148 per cent over budget and still unfinished (Kostka and Anzinger 2016; see also Case Study 1 in Chapter 4). Railroad projects like the High Speed 2 in the United Kingdom are sometimes years behind schedule, as is the high-speed rail link between Hong Kong and Guangzhou.

Behind these more or less notorious cases lies a sobering, long-standing pattern: already over a decade ago, Flyvbjerg, Bruzelius, and Rothengatter (2003) estimated that nine out of ten large-scale infrastructure projects face significant time delays and cost overruns, while benefit shortfalls of more than 50 per cent are not unusual. Flyvbjerg, Holm, and Buhl (2004) demonstrated that delays in transportation infrastructure implementation are very costly, increasing the percentage of construction cost overruns as measured in constant prices by 4.6 percentage points per year of delay incurred after the time of decision to build. More recently, Kostka and Anzinger (2016) reported average cost overruns of 30 per cent for Germany, 17 per cent for the Netherlands, 22 per cent in northern Europe, and 24 per cent in other western countries. Another analysis shows that cost overruns are not outweighed by benefit overruns (Flyvbjerg and Sunstein 2015) and hence constitute misallocations, even sunk costs. What is more, cost overruns are more frequent in newer infrastructure fields like IT than in transport or water projects (Kostka and Anzinger 2016).

This mixed performance record gains even more significance in the light of recent studies that foresee a growing gap in overall infrastructure investments over current levels, suggesting a two-fold conclusion: not only are there deficits in infrastructure delivery given current investment levels, but these investments seem insufficient to begin with given future demands. Yet available estimates differ significantly and are not directly comparable as they use varying methodologies and cover different time periods and countries. For example:

- According to McKinsey, global infrastructure investments until 2030 will amount to US$57.3 trillion measured in 2010 US dollars, leaving a significant gap of 73 per cent against the current baseline (Dobbs et al. 2013). The study estimates that 4.1 per cent of GDP would have to be spent worldwide on infrastructure to meet identified needs. This demand is already hardly met on a global scale, as only 3.8 per cent of GDP was being spent at the time of that report.
- Standard & Poor's (2015) estimates €1 trillion investment in European Union (EU) member states is needed for the next three years until 2018–9.[4]
- The American Society of Civil Engineers estimates that in order to update infrastructure in the United States, a total of US$3.6 trillion across sectors would be needed by 2020. However, if current spending trends prevail, the actual investment gap will amount to US$4.7 trillion by 2040 (ASCE 2013: 6).

Perhaps not surprisingly, such reports tend to focus on investment opportunities and lament the lengthy approval processes that are costly and risky for investors. In any case, there seems enough evidence of a mismatch between infrastructure needs and finance. However, there are significant differences across countries: While the EU, US, Brazil, India, and South Africa seem to underspend relative to estimated needs, China and Japan overspend. As Figure 1.1 shows, Japan is almost spending double the amount on infrastructure than it would actually need. This fiscal expansion is part of a larger strategy (under Prime Minister Abe) intended to jump-start the country's stagnant economic growth (McBridge and Xu 2015). Spending about 8.5 per cent of its GDP on infrastructure, China overinvests domestically and allocates significant funds to projects abroad. The recently established Asian Infrastructure Investment Bank, with a quarter of its US$100 billion founding capital from China, emphasises the country's interests in manifesting its role as the major regional power, not to mention an increasingly global one (see Deutsche Welle 2015). A recent example is the Addis Ababa Light Rail that opened in September 2015 and was mostly financed by the Export-Import Bank of China.

An initial conclusion could be that with the notable exception of China and Japan, most countries threaten to fall behind, a pattern that should be examined in the context of two economic aspects closely related to infrastructure investments: multiplier effects impacting GDP growth, and productivity gains.

That infrastructure spending has notable multiplier effects seems conventional economic wisdom. For the four largest eurozone economies, Broyer and Gareis (2013) found that increases in public infrastructure investment were associated with higher output, private investment, and employment rates in the quarters following the expenditure shock. Moreover, according to the authors, positive effects last twice as long in less developed economies as in mature ones (Broyer and Gareis 2013: 7). For 2015–17 infrastructure investments, Standard & Poor's estimates that the multiplier effect ranges between a high of 2.5 per cent of GDP for the United Kingdom and Brazil to 1.4 per cent for the eurozone and one per cent for Australia and Indonesia (Standard & Poor's 2015: 6). Again, the multiplier effects are greater

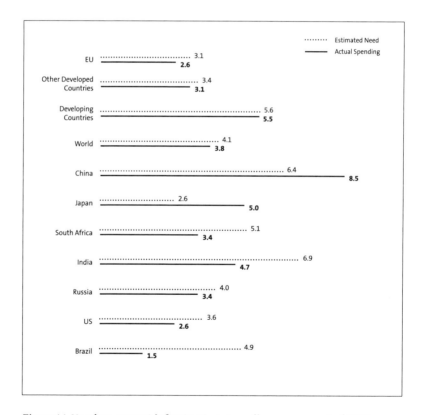

Figure 1.1 **Need vs. current infrastructure spending, as per cent of GDP**
Source: Adapted from Dobbs et al. (2013).
Permission to reuse granted by McKinsey & Company.

in developing economies than in developed market economies. China, India, and Brazil boost GDP growth rates of at least double the increase in investment. By contrast, multiplier effects in countries such as Australia, Germany, and Canada are smaller.

Regions in the periphery of Europe, i.e. southern Spain, Portugal, southern Italy, Greece, northern UK, and Ireland, have benefitted relatively more from EU infrastructure spending. EU structural and cohesion funds have also positively contributed to GDP per capita growth of region or country recipients (Fiaschi, Lavezzi, and Parenti 2011: 22). When those EU funds increased by one per cent (over the period 1990–2010), the GDP per capita of the eurozone grew by 0.9 per cent. These funds have favoured the less developed countries in the eurozone, which have in turn increased their GDP per capita (Maynou et al. 2015: 9). For the US, Cohen, Freiling, and Robinson (2012: 10) conclude that 'the most important take-away is that every type of public infrastructure spending in our study results in significantly positive returns to the government. These investments return some portion of the money initially outlaid by the government over a twenty-year time horizon, and, in several cases, more than pay for themselves.'

These are strong claims, but as we show below, observed patterns cast serious doubts as to the seemingly unconditionally positive relationship between infrastructure spending and economic returns. First of all, demand-driven effects of infrastructure spending depend on the economic cycle and are more pronounced at lower points. The multiplier has been lower in Germany, for example, because the country was impacted less by the 2008 crisis and is by 2015 close to full employment. What is more, given its highly globalised, export-driven economy, increases in infrastructure spending will have multiplier effects spread across major trading partners and are hence weaker domestically (Standard & Poor's 2015: 10).

Of course, multiplier effects and per capita income gains are temporary phenomena unless they lead to productivity growth and higher quality services. Almost unquestionably, economists and planners alike assume infrastructure investments to have a positive impact not only on GDP growth but also on productivity, but are these assumptions accurate? Figure 1.2 shows that the relationship between infrastructure spending and productivity growth is less than clear-cut and reveals an overall result quite different from the necessarily positive association suggested by Cohen, Freiling, and Robinson (2012) or Fiaschi, Lavezzi, and Parenti (2011). While the trend is estimated to be positive, the uncertainty in the data allows for a flat or even negative relationship, rather than expressing an undeniable positive relationship. Indeed, taking a longer-term perspective, i.e. a ten-year horizon, Figure 1.2 reveals four patterns between mean investment in infrastructure as a share of GDP and multifactor productivity growth at the country level:

- Investments are high, and productivity growth is high, which is in accordance with conventional wisdom, e.g. Japan and, as an extreme outlier, Korea;
- Investments are high, and productivity growth is lower than might be expected in light of conventional wisdom, e.g. Australia and Spain;
- Investments are low, and productivity growth is high, which is also not in line with conventional wisdom, e.g. US, Germany, and to a lesser extent Austria; and
- Both investments and productivity growth are lower than average, which is in accordance with conventional wisdom, e.g. Italy and New Zealand, as exceptional cases.

The point of Figure 1.2 is that the relationship between infrastructure spending and productivity growth is certainly not unconditionally positive, as surprisingly few countries fall into the category of higher infrastructure

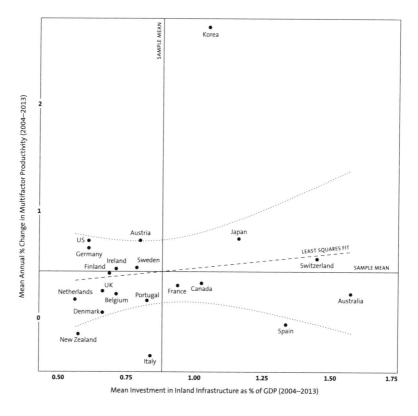

Figure 1.2 **Infrastructure spending and productivity growth (2004—2013)**
Source: OECD (2016b)

THE INFRASTRUCTURE CHALLENGE

investments and higher productivity growth. Apparently, in some countries, other factors mitigate that relationship in significant ways. What seems clear is that even Pereira and Andraz's (2013: 11) already cautious conclusion cannot be taken at face value: 'While there is little consensus about the magnitudes of the effects of public investment in infrastructures, there is also little doubt that they are positive and significant but substantially smaller than the earlier estimates.'

A similarly puzzling pattern emerges in regards to a second key issue, the relationship between infrastructure spending and change in infrastructure quality. As is the case with productivity growth, the relationship between expenditures and quality improvements is again less than clear-cut, as shown in Figure 1.3. Like before, four separate patterns emerge between mean investment in infrastructure as a share of GDP and quality improvement over a ten-year period at the country level:

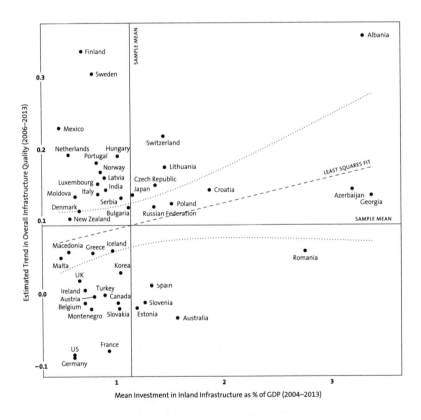

Figure 1.3 **Infrastructure investment and quality (2004/6—2013)**
Sources: OECD (2016b), World Economic Forum (2015)

- Investments are higher than average, and quality improvement takes place, which is in accordance with conventional wisdom, e.g. Albania, Georgia, Croatia, Azerbaijan, Poland, and several other transition economies, along with Switzerland;
- Investments are lower, and quality improvement is high, which is not in accordance with the expected pattern, e.g. Finland, Sweden, Mexico, Hungary, and the Netherlands, among others;
- Investments are higher than average, and infrastructure quality saw at best meagre improvement, if not decline, which again defies conventional wisdom, e.g. Romania, Australia, Slovenia, and Estonia; and
- Investments are lower, and quality suffers, which is in line with the standard expectation, e.g. US, Germany, and France, along with several other developed market economies as well as transition economies.

Taken together, these two empirical relationships reveal patterns more complex than and indeed somewhat more puzzling than economic textbooks might suggest.

Facts and Myths

From a macroeconomic perspective, we arrive at a perplexing picture: though investment in infrastructure is on the rise in many countries, actual spending falls behind substantially different assessments of future needs, and substantial plans remain exactly that. We also see underinvestment in some countries, overinvestment in others, a pattern of delays and cost overruns, and an unclear connection between productivity and quality. Indeed, the *ultimo ratio* of infrastructure investments, i.e. its tight connection with productivity growth and quality improvements, seems puzzling.

Kostka and Fiedler (2016) see infrastructure policies locked in systemic uncertainty, caught in an uneasy and contested triangle of assessed needs, financial and delivery capacities, and technology. Clearly, decisions about infrastructure, particularly large projects, are often political in nature and require some sort of wider public legitimation. Few governments can dictate such projects; usually, some form of collective decision-making, such as elections, public hearings, or administrative procedures, is required. Then, there are the financing and delivery of projects, often divided among different levels of government and within an increasingly complex interplay between public and private actors. Finally, infrastructure–be it the construction of communication lines, generation of energy, or treatment of water–is also about technology. Given changes in technology, there is the challenge of future-proofing, as today's technology may be suboptimal or even obsolete during the lifespan of an infrastructure asset, hence jeopardising productivity gains.

Note that all three—needs assessments, finance and delivery capacities, and technology—operate with different rationales, are often on different timelines in terms of their objective functions, and engage different expert communities, e.g. politicians, lawyers, administrators, investors, engineers, and technicians, that may not 'speak the same language'. Such divergences lead to the systemic uncertainty that Kostka and Fielder (2016) refer to and invite naming and shaming, as the authors' anatomy of project failures shows. They also encourage the search for generic fixes, for solutions that promise greater performance predictability in terms of risks and rewards. Over time, such search modes crystallise as persistent myths that characterise the field of infrastructure policy today. In our view, these myths stand in the way of a more profound debate on how to govern infrastructure effectively.

The first myth—about the determination and prioritisation of infrastructure needs and results in terms of quality, performance, or ownership—is that national infrastructure plans are unnecessary because they are top-down and have no local ownership. Hence, needs assessments are often the result of simply aggregating project proposals from different levels of government or relying on indicative estimates of underinvestment. Yet they involve no visioning exercises to put assumptions to the test and to challenge their implications. Few countries have coherent processes of evaluation and priority-setting across individual projects at the national level, nor do they have integrated approaches to infrastructure planning over time to identify impact, cost, or synergies and trade-offs for evidence-based decision-making. The lack of ex ante assessments is compounded by a lack of systematic ex post evaluations. McKinsey estimates that US$1 trillion—over one-third of the total investment amount of US$2.7 trillion needed—could be saved with effective infrastructure planning, suggesting that there is much room for efficiency gains (Dobbs et al. 2013).

The second myth is about the absence of trade-offs in infrastructure investment. Yet there are clear tensions between infrastructure for productivity and quality, e.g. better roads and faster internet connections, and resilience, e.g. better flood protection and improved national security. Both types of infrastructures involve different actors, and they likely require separate sets of policy and regulations, including those on how to handle overlaps, e.g. efficient water ways and flood protection. Investments in national security infrastructure are usually off the books, so to speak, as is their relation to other investments, even though military and non-military infrastructure investments are closely linked, for example in transport or communication. What is more, scale effects easily play into this tension: a more efficient use of renewable energy, e.g. wind turbines, may require large investments in smart grids, which in turn increases vulnerability, e.g. as a target for terrorism.

A third myth sees financial resources as the primary bottleneck, based on the rationale that if only more funds were available, infrastructure needs could be met. In reality, it is more a problem of channelling investment capital towards the right and well-managed projects through adequate risk and incentive systems. A related myth is about risk sharing between the public and private sectors and centres on the notion that such sharing is realistic and allows the public sector to shift risks to a private sector all too ready to shoulder the responsibilities entailed. Experience with PPPs, however, is mixed and has shown that this relationship is much more complex (da Cruz and Cruz forthcoming). While some see a tendency for profits to be privatised and losses made public, with failures becoming political rather than business liabilities, others point to successes and the wide range of instruments available such as revenue guarantees for private providers. In any case, effective risk sharing requires a level playing field for the public and private sectors in terms of expertise, experience, and space for decision-making. In reality, there are asymmetries in each, potentially provoking suboptimal outcomes of risk sharing agreements.

Another myth claims that, in the planning and realisation of infrastructure projects, inclusive participation of all stakeholders will necessarily resolve conflicts, bring about higher public acceptance, and lead to better outcomes in terms of quality. In reality, more participation can invite biases and conflicts, as does under-participation. It can ultimately mean cost increases and delays and may even lead to abandoning investments altogether at high social costs. There is neither a systematic assessment of current participation models nor a comprehensive search for effective voice mechanisms.

A final myth, although we could add others, relates to corruption.[5] The myth states that problems of corruption can be addressed by more and tighter regulation. In reality, such regulation can actually go hand in hand with higher levels of corruption unless adequate monitoring and enforcement capacities are in place. Despite some progress, with anti-corruption legislation in place and agencies to investigate allegations of corruption established in many countries, corruption in many places is attributed to the same failings identified more than a decade ago, namely weak political leadership, inadequate capacity and funding, a lack of independence, no clear reporting hierarchies, and the absence of government commitment to enact reforms that may be politically difficult (Heilbrunn 2004; see also Mungiu-Pippidi 2016a, 2016b). It is indicative that 60 per cent of the cross-border cases of corruption analysed by the OECD were found to be related to public procurement (OECD 2014c).

The argument here is not that the impact of corruption on infrastructure cannot or should not be reduced or that only highly participatory projects lead to quality outcomes. Nor is the argument that only public funds can fill the investment gap or that PPPs are good for infrastructure policies. Rather, we argue that it is more a matter of how infrastructure policy is governed that makes the difference.

Bringing Governance Back in

Using the governance lens allows us to unpack these myths and examine more closely the context for decision-making and implementation of infrastructure. Four governance capacities are central here: analytical, coordination, regulatory, and delivery. Specifically:

- 'Analytical capacity is about the organisation and type of advice that informs governmental policy-making' (Lodge and Wegrich 2014a: 44), as well as understanding 'how systems are performing' and 'what kind of future demands and challenges are likely to emerge' (Lodge and Wegrich 2014a: 42). It involves policy-related analytics, e.g. planning infrastructure requirements under conditions of uncertainty, as well as project-based analytics and reliable and comparative data, all of which contribute to the integration of policies to resolve trade-offs and achieve synergies.
- Coordination capacity is 'the ability to mediate between the need to specialise through dispersing functions within organisations and by creating new actors, on the one hand, and the need to keep a common interest among dispersed actors, on the other' (Lodge and Wegrich 2014a: 41). It also includes a reward system that emphasises collaboration in addition to pure outputs (see also OECD 2014d).
- Regulatory capacities 'are about control and oversight. They entail the presence of regimes that combine standards . . . with an apparatus that detects and enforces compliance' (Lodge and Wegrich 2014a: 39; see also OECD 2014d).
- Delivery capacity, or 'the capacity to "make things happen" refers to the way in which states [and other actors] execute policy at the street-level' (Lodge and Wegrich 2014a: 36), which 'relies on a structure that is sufficiently resourced to give life to policy objectives' (Lodge and Wegrich 2014a: 37).

These capacities resonate in four of the main issues where governance matters most in the field of infrastructure:

First, there is what we term '**allocation**' to refer to how responsibilities, risk, and decision-making are assigned to or shared among stakeholders in order to achieve efficient, effective, and equitable outcomes. Whereas infrastructure was once considered a prototypical state-provided public good, wielded as a tool for development and security, it today includes a range of private actors: businesses as well as non-governmental organisations, special interest groups, lobbyists, and citizens as voters and activists. Decision-making takes place at various levels of government, including the supranational level, increasing complexity and uncertainty; allocation must reflect this at the policy, programme, and project levels. Put differently, governance needs to ensure a functioning allocation in terms of the optimal costs and benefits of infrastructure investments from a macroeconomic perspective.

Second, there is the need to ensure that the resulting arrangements among stakeholders are properly regulated, overseen, and implemented. Good governance arrangements can be institutionalised by setting appropriate standards and enforcement mechanisms. In this sense, **reform** may take place by changing formal policies and regulations or by establishing best practices, including informal norms, within a sector or industry. This includes coordination between national and subnational units of government and between governments and private stakeholders, including businesses and civil society organisations.

Third, there is the issue of public trust on the part of the population at large and those affected by infrastructure projects more directly. Central here is the role of civil society in decision-making processes about infrastructure, especially when those decisions involve large amounts of public resources and entail developments likely–or at least assumed to be likely–to significantly impact citizens' daily lives, even in their own backyards. Here, **trust-building** is about more than boosting popular support for previously made decisions or previously taken actions; rather, it is about finding ways to engage civil society groups at the level appropriate to the scale of the investment that improve resource allocation, ensure the best possible decisions, and ideally (re)establish legitimacy and transparency for those decisions. This requires rethinking the role of civil society relative to the public interest.

Fourth, there is **future-proofing**, or the need to ensure that existing infrastructure assets as well as those still in development are resilient and adaptable to future needs, technological advancements, and events such as natural disasters or systemic risks. Future-proofing, however, requires flexible governance structures to accommodate different possible pathways and truly unleash its potential. Future-proofing becomes a core component of infrastructure planning and management. To this end, governance actors should take a proactive approach and learn from best practices as well as adapt innovations from other regions, stakeholders, and sectors.

Overview

In this Report we explore these four issues of infrastructure governance while debunking the various myths *en passant*. The Report first addresses the analytical and regulatory capacity for decision-making under conditions of complexity and uncertainty, and how decision-making can be improved. In Chapter 2, Wegrich and Hammerschmid focus on why making good decisions is so difficult. Based on the results of a joint Hertie School-OECD expert survey and combining approaches of bounded rationality with institutional perspectives of political analysis, they argue that one first has to understand the underlying existing mechanisms leading to particular decision-making practices before institutional design recommendations can be usefully made. In other words, infrastructure planning and projects rarely start as some tabula rasa but come embedded in institutional practices and routines that may determine the nature and performance of projects even before they start. Their chapter clearly points to the importance of prior deep visioning.

The often complex and politicised links between national, regional, and local infrastructure planning, financing, and implementation are picked up in Chapter 3 by Allain-Dupré, Hulbert, and Vincent, who focus on subnational government (SNG) actors such as regions, states, and municipalities. SNGs are responsible for 60 per cent of public investment in the OECD on average (OECD 2015d). The role of SNGs poses specific challenges for both the financing and governance of infrastructure. Building on recent OECD work in this area and on the results of the 2015 OECD–Committee of the Regions (CoR) survey conducted in the EU, this chapter explores these challenges in greater detail and proposes good practices and recommendations to address them. The authors call for better coordination capacities among national and subnational actors and for greater analytical capacity for SNGs in particular.

In Chapter 4, Kostka takes up the topic of risk management across the project life cycle and proposes an approach that is adaptable to changing circumstances and intended to evolve throughout four project phases: planning, procurement, construction, and operation and maintenance. A life cycle approach can help to understand risks in all stages of the value chain more systematically by tracking risks and management challenges throughout the entire life of a project. Summarising common pitfalls and best practices in each of the four project life cycles and with a particular focus on governance issues, the chapter shows that choices and actions in earlier phases inevitably affect infrastructure delivery and quality in later phases.

Hawkesworth and Garin write in Chapter 5 about infrastructure delivery options and the governance challenges and trade-offs involved, offering an infrastructure decision tool to guide countries in assessing and balancing their specific needs. They introduce a decision tree framework that suggests that countries (i) set a preferred sectoral approach by assessing infrastructure objectives and the characteristics of the sector; (ii) assess how the country circumstances, e.g. macroeconomic parameters, public administration capacities, private sector capacities, and the legal environment, impact the sector; and (iii) choose a delivery model based on the project characteristics and overall approach.

The question of governance innovations and best practices across countries and fields, also in ensuring appropriate participation for building trust, is the topic of Chapter 6 by Anheier and Kaufmann. They offer a framework for studying governance innovations and offer six case studies to showcase how different stakeholder groups try to overcome challenges. The framework guiding the analysis of selected cases follows the four issues above–allocation, reform, trust-building, and future-proofing–in the context of the four governance capacities–analytical, coordination, regulatory, and delivery–required to facilitate or ensure the beneficial aspect of the infrastructure governance innovation.

Chapter 7 by Haber on governance indicators seeks to improve the evidence base of infrastructure policies in terms of planning, funding, implementation, and monitoring for 36 countries. Introducing the Infrastructure Governance Indicators Suite, which compares the countries' performances according to their inputs, throughputs, and outcomes, the chapter follows up on the perplexing patterns displayed in Figures 1.2 and 1.3 above in regards to the relationships between infrastructure investments, productivity growth, and quality improvements.

Finally, in a concluding chapter, we focus on the implications and recommendations that follow from the Report. Specifically, we assert that any attempt to improve decision-making on infrastructure needs to take into account the scale and the inherent complexity and risks of the field, and accept that political logics, rather than mere needs assessments and financial or technical aspects alone, can be the main drivers. When this Report advocates bringing governance into infrastructure policies, it also means acknowledging rather than denying their inherent political nature. Furthermore, we observe the relative under-development of some governance capacities, especially coordination and analytical capacities, compared to the over-institutionalisation of others, namely regulation. Rather than lamenting these realities, we propose building institutions that bring political influence into the open and confront it with economic, administrative as well as technical expertise, thereby also remedying weaknesses in coordination and analytical capacity. Our intent here is to extend the debate on the governance of infrastructure and contribute not only to the success of individual projects but also to overall country performance, competitiveness, and well-being.

> *Any attempt to improve decision-making on infrastructure needs to take into account the field's inherent complexity and risks and accept that political logics can be the main drivers.*

Endnotes

1. Infrastructure covers the facilities, structures, networks, systems, plants, properties, equipment, and physical assets—as well as the institutions and organisations that plan, finance, build, run, and maintain them—that provide public and quasi-public goods and services such as transport, energy, water, and communication. This Report will focus on civil infrastructure, i.e. will not address infrastructure relating to military needs and national security.

2. By 'good governance' we mean an effective, efficient, and reliable set of legitimate institutions and actors engaged in a process of dealing with a matter of public concern, be it in the field of financial markets, health care, security, or migration, at and across the local, national, and international levels. In other words, governance is about how we approach and solve a recognised collective issue or problem (Anheier 2013: 13, 16; Zürn, Wälti, and Enderlein 2010: 2).

3. A look at indicators from the World Bank (2016) reveals that in four fields—electricity, mobile phones, improved water sources, and improved sanitation facilities—improvements have taken place across all countries since 2005, especially in the number of fixed and mobile telephone subscribers and in access to improved water sources in low-income countries.

4. Aware of this shortfall, the European Commission introduced the European Fund for Strategic Investments (EFSI) to attract €240 billion private investment in infrastructure between 2015 and 2017 (European Commission 2014a).

5. PwC and Ecorys (2013: 16) found that, taken together, 'the overall direct costs of corruption in public procurement in 2010 for the five sectors studied in the 8 Member States constituted between 2.9 per cent to 4.4 per cent of the overall value of procurements in the sector published in the Official Journal, or between EUR 1 470 million and EUR 2 247 million.'

II. Infrastructure Governance and Government Decision-making

GERHARD HAMMERSCHMID *and* KAI WEGRICH

The governance of infrastructure is shaped by a somewhat paradoxical situation. On the one hand, infrastructure governance is no longer only about the state planning, financing, and delivering of infrastructure. Instead, delivery and increasingly planning and financing are often delegated to private parties. On the other hand, state action is a necessary precondition for any private engagement. Without the financial, regulatory, and coordinative role of the state, infrastructure investment would not happen. The state might be less visible in the delivery of infrastructure but still remains critical, and hence the way governments decide about infrastructure continues to be crucial. High quality decisions are important in order to prevent poor infrastructure from becoming a roadblock for economic development and to avoid choices that lock the economy and the state into inefficient, expensive, or dispensable infrastructures.

Are governments doing a good job in making decisions about infrastructure governance? A quick glance at media reports would suggest that they are not. For one, governments are accused of underinvesting, leading to a decline in quality and foregone economic benefits. They are accused of myopic decision-making, not taking into account the long-term economic, social, and environmental needs and impacts of infrastructure investments. And they are accused of statism, failing to engage the private sector. However, for any of these criticisms, the opposite can also be found. Governments are said to be guilty of waste and overinvestment in infrastructure for which there is no matching demand, of being captured by private interests, and of being inflexible in adapting to rapid change. When it comes to investment in infrastructure, it is obviously not easy to make the right decisions; matters can go wrong in two opposite ways.

These critiques are echoed by think tanks and consultancies. According to a report from the Institute for Government, strategic decision-making on infrastructure in the United Kingdom suffers from '. . . short-sightedness and lack of forward-looking strategy; failure to secure cross-party agreement, translated into high political risk; [and] serious weaknesses in the evidence base' (Coelho, Ratnoo, and Dellepiane 2014: 5). Nothing suggests that the practice of infrastructure decision-making in the UK is particularly problematic–some would say that it is particularly advanced–and similar critiques can be found relating to many other countries.[1] A comment from McKinsey consultants suggests that there is a general problem: 'Despite the fact that many governments face increasing constraints on their resources, they still continue to allocate them badly in the case of infrastructure' (Garemo and Mischk 2013).

Evidently, political decision-making on infrastructure investment and governance is hard to get right. Hence think tanks and consultancies recommend adopting the latest economic policy analysis, coordinating decisions better, insulating decision-making from fickle and myopic politicians, and in general learning from the good practices of other countries and especially the private sector. This chapter argues that any attempt to improve a government's capacity to make good decisions about infrastructure governance requires a prior analysis and thorough understanding of the patterns of decision-making. Before prescribing a treatment, we must first examine the symptoms for an accurate diagnosis. Hence this chapter addresses the following fundamental questions:

- What makes decision-making about infrastructure particularly difficult?
- How do governments decide about infrastructure?
- How do different national institutions shape infrastructure decision-making?
- To what extent are different institutional arrangements able to improve coordination towards more sustainable and less politicised infrastructure decisions?

The analysis presented in this chapter is based on the 2015 joint Hertie School-OECD Global Expert Survey on Public Infrastructure, which offers insights into practices, challenges, and innovations in 36 countries, both in the OECD and beyond. As described in more detail in Chapter 7, the survey involved experts across diverse infrastructure fields and from various types of organisations, including academic and research institutions, national governments, and the private sector.

Before presenting the survey results, we explore the challenges of complexity inherent in decision-making about infrastructure. An analysis of broad patterns of decision-making on infrastructure based on the survey results is followed by four case studies that explore how national governmental structures, political and administrative traditions, and situational contexts shape decision-making styles in the infrastructure domain. These styles exhibit the strengths and weaknesses of different governmental systems that should serve as a note of caution regarding 'best practice' advice for improving decision-making. The chapter closes with recommendations.

The Challenges of Complexity and Uncertainty in Infrastructure Governance

How should decisions about infrastructure investment be made? A widely shared view is that good decisions follow the logic of planning by first identifying societal demands, developing options across sectors and types of investments, and then comparing the costs and benefits of the various options. On this basis, priorities about investments should be defined, implemented, and later evaluated (see, for example, Chapter 5). And indeed, governments across the world apply various forms of economic analysis to analyse and prioritise options. However, the use of analytical tools alone for improving decision-making seems to bear limited effects, given the widespread criticism of decision-making practices. Conceptually, the two core aims of such tools–the deployment of objective information as a base for decision-making, and the de-politicisation of choices of infrastructure governance–face major obstacles.

The major obstacle for supposedly rational decision-making on infrastructure investment is the high degree of complexity and uncertainty characterising this field. This complexity is first of all the result of the generic nature of infrastructure governance, which obliges governments to commit large amounts of resources for long time periods under conditions of limited and conflicting evidence concerning the demand and effects of individual investments. As discussed in Chapter 1 of this Report, the relation between investments and their effects on economic growth and other expected benefits is often unclear, and this uncertainty cannot be easily reduced by making use of more or better evidence, because evidence to support such decisions is not simply and objectively 'out there'. Since different infrastructure sectors compete for funding, any evidence in support of spending should always be considered as manufactured, i.e. the production of evidence is part and parcel of the decision-making process about who gets what and when.

Given the implications of infrastructure investment decisions for industries, regions, and localities that benefit from investment, a number of players seek to influence those decisions. Politicians want to make sure that their constituents benefit; organised interests seek to defend and expand their fair share; and ministerial bureaucrats seek to defend their turfs and budgets. Such behaviour can be best understood by using the model of 'bounded rationality' (Simon 1955), in which actors do not seek to find the optimal solution for a problem but instead 'satisfice' with merely good enough results. Moreover, they do not take on the view of a great coordinator but rather pursue their preferences from the 'selective perception' of their particular position. A higher civil servant responsible for roads, for example, assesses policies only from the perspective of implications for this sub-area; other areas of spending, possibly particularly those related to other modes of transport, will be considered as competitors. Interest groups mobilise knowledge to support claims for their fair shares from the investment budget and closely cooperate with executive actors and politicians to do so.

The higher the complexity of a field, the more actors involved, and the more contested the evidence base of policy choices, the more difficult and unrealistic it is to use rational strategies of decision-making. In the field of infrastructure, bounded rationality is not a human weakness that can be corrected by smart 'choice architecture' design, as the nudge agenda suggests is possible for decision-making biases and blunders of individuals (Thaler and Sunstein 2008). Rather it is inherent to the complexity of the field; there is simply no baseline rationale for behaviour that can be easily identified.

This generic complexity of the infrastructure field has been further amplified by political and institutional change over the last decades. First, the cast of actors has expanded as a result of the dispersion of authority upwards, e.g. to the European Union or international organisations, and downwards to regional and local actors as well as sideways as a result of privatisation and the proliferation of public-private partnerships (PPPs). Involved actors now include various ministries, regulatory and executive agencies, local and regional governments, private providers, and hybrid organisations at the various levels of decision-making. These organisations pursue different goals and follow different institutional logics, often compete for funding, for example between different regions, and may possess formal or informal veto powers in decision-making. Orchestrating this diversity of actors is a challenge for the coordination capacity of governments (Lodge and Wegrich 2014b; Wegrich and Štimac 2014).

> *Orchestrating the diversity of actors is a challenge for the coordination capacity of governments.*

A second source of complexity is the changing policy context due to increasingly ambitious objectives. The development of a carbon-free economy, for example, requires not only the switch towards renewable sources of energy production but also very different technical and institutional solutions for energy transmission and storage. It requires keeping up with long-term commitments as well as adapting to changing technical solutions and risks. In the field of telecommunications, for example, quick fixes to bottlenecks in internet broadband provision can result in more problems a few years down the line (Lodge and Wegrich 2014b). The reforms of the 1980s and 1990s that resulted in the corporatisation and often privatisation of infrastructure providers have created the need to rely on regulation as the main tool of governance. However, complex and hybrid ownership structures, for example in the area of train services (see Bach and Wegrich forthcoming for Germany), undermine the regulatory capacity of governments (Lodge 2014).

The complexity of infrastructure governance translates into various challenges for government decision-making. Jordana (2014: 163 f.) identified three major challenges to the governance of infrastructure, which are essentially challenges for decision-making under uncertainty: (i) identifying the appropriate level of infrastructure provision, (ii) identifying the appropriate combination of public and private involvement, and (iii) providing democratic legitimacy in the process. And while these challenges can be distinguished analytically, in practice they have to be managed simultaneously.

Concerning the appropriate level of infrastructure provision, the challenge for decision-making is to avoid the two opposing types of failure: under-provision and over-provision. Such decisions are particularly difficult to make since they involve comparing options not only within one sector but also across sectors. Politicians have to make choices between competing spending claims, such as those between social spending and spending for investments. As Pereira and Melo (forthcoming) show for the case of Brazil, a particular political agenda might not allow for securing the amount of infrastructure investment that is required for economic and social development.

From a political economy perspective, investment in infrastructure might not be particularly attractive, given that the benefits will materialise in the future and will be dispersed across a range of stakeholders–for example, among all car drivers instead of specific recipients of a tax cut or subsidy. Infrastructure is one of the policy fields in which the time dimension poses a political challenge: costs are imposed in the short term and uncertain benefits will only be realised in the future (see Jacobs 2011). On the other hand, infrastructure investment can be made politically attractive when it comes with jobs and economic stimulus. Hence the political business cycle and the logic of constituencies are said to be more influential in shaping decisions than some general logic of economic development and welfare gains. Also, politicians might be inclined to support particularly visible, catchy projects rather than bread-and-butter investments. Investments in new projects therefore tend to be more popular than those in maintenance work, and new high-speed train lines often find more support than the capacity expansion of existing train lines, which would be more important from a transport policy perspective (see Coelho, Ratnoo, and Dellepiane 2014 on the HS2 high-speed train line between London and Manchester).

But choices have to be made not only between the broad categories of social versus investment spending but also between investing in different sectors of infrastructure (see also Chapter 3 on cross-sectoral coordination at the subnational level) and between different projects within one sector. Making fully rational decisions that take into account direct and indirect costs and benefits of different projects in one sector in addition to the relative value of investment in different infrastructure sectors poses extremely high demands on decision-makers. To base these decisions on the results of tools such as cost-benefit analysis would overload the information processing and conflict resolution capacity of the decision-making system (see Scharpf 1997 on these categories). Hence we should expect to find actors aiming to reduce complexity by deploying strategies of simplification not unlike those that were identified by scholars of incrementalism in the field of budgeting 50 years ago (Wildavsky 1964), such as taking past investment levels as a basis for negotiating minor adjustments between different sectors and programmes.

Concerning the combination of public and private involvement, the challenge is to balance between overcoming the limits of a pure public investment strategy by leveraging private investment on the one hand, and managing the risks of delegation to private agents on the other. These risks include potential state liability for failed private infrastructure projects and the question of benefit-risk distribution in PPPs and related arrangements. As da Cruz and Cruz (forthcoming) show, the sharing and transfer of risk is a challenging governance task for the public sector. A balance has to be found between keeping all risk with the public sector and trying to shift risk to the private sector, which comes with downsides such as increasing the costs of PPPs and undermining their value for money. In general, the track record of PPPs shows that the stereotype of more efficient, i.e. lower cost, delivery of private projects has not been confirmed (Hodge 2010). More often than not, PPPs are more expensive than pure public provision, but well-managed PPPs come with the advantage of higher levels of project control and higher quality of infrastructure. Decisions about private delivery and PPPs are not only driven by the scarcity of financial resources of the public sector and the limits of its delivery capacity (see Hupe and Hill 2014; Hertie School of Governance 2014). Budgetary rules in many countries incentivise politicians to hide expenditures for PPP contracts from the general budget or to explicitly use them to substitute short-term budget for less transparent grey debt.

Concerning democratic legitimacy and accountability, a key problem relates to the territorial dimension of infrastructure policy. As Jordana (forthcoming) shows, there is often a mismatch between the negative effects of infrastructure projects being highly concentrated locally–the proverbial road in the backyard–and the benefits being widely distributed. This poses another challenge for decision-making because negatively affected parties can make use of their legal rights to resist projects. More importantly, this challenge of democratic legitimacy also introduces another layer of complexity for the governance of infrastructure.

In summary, complexity is inherent to infrastructure governance and will not cease with the application of more advanced tools of economic analysis or more rational planning cycles. Decisions under conditions of complexity and uncertainty require political choices. This does not mean that decisions will always be, or should be, made without efforts to analyse impacts and attempts to coordinate across levels of government, between different sectors, and with private sector organisations. But it calls for an exploration of how governments deal in practice with these challenges and what the role of politics and institutions is.

How Do Governments Decide about Infrastructure? Findings from an International Expert Survey

The Hertie School-OECD Global Expert Survey on Public Infrastructure asked infrastructure experts to evaluate the planning, coordination, and funding of public infrastructure at the national government level and to assess overall funding trends as well as comparisons among the different infrastructure sectors in their countries. We also inquired about the role of planning instruments such as national infrastructure plans and about the challenges identified in the literature. We were particularly interested in the reality of decision-making: what rationales drive decisions about funding and investment at the national level?

Infrastructure investment and funding

Concerning the development of funding, infrastructure experts perceived a slight increase on average, with the majority having perceived either increases (35.9 per cent) or decreases (41.9 per cent) over the last five years. In other words, and confirming the assessment in Chapter 1, we see contrasting developments in different countries. The perception of increased spending is stronger in non-OECD countries such as China, Indonesia, and Nigeria, suggesting a 'catching up' type of development, but it is also rather high in rich OECD countries such as Canada, Denmark, Norway, and Switzerland. In other OECD countries, the perceived decrease in spending may have been affected by the aftermath of the financial crisis, since five of the six countries in which over two-thirds of the experts perceived declining infrastructure spending–namely, Greece, Iceland, Ireland, Italy, and Portugal–have been strongly affected by the financial or the eurozone crisis.

In terms of sectoral investment patterns, we find clear differences between OECD and non-OECD countries. In the OECD countries, experts perceived the strongest growth of infrastructure investment in IT/communication and energy, a decrease in investment in defence, and a rather stable share of investment in all other sectors. For the non-OECD countries, we find growth perceived in all infrastructure areas: highest in transportation and energy, with buildings being the only exception (see Figure 2.1).

Overall, this trend is in line with what respondents perceived as sectors prioritised in their countries for public infrastructure investments. Both transport and energy were seen as clear priority areas by 66.5 per cent of infrastructure experts in OECD countries and 59.7 per cent in non-OECD countries. A first insight comes from comparing the prioritisation of sectors with the perception of changes in investment. As shown in Figure 2.2, for

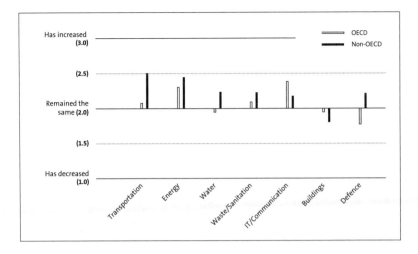

Figure 2.1 **Change of relative share of infrastructure investment in different sectors over the last 5 years.**
Note: On a 3-point scale, with 1=has decreased, 2=remained the same, and 3=has increased.

both transport and energy perceived growth clearly lags behind prioritisation, whereas for most other sectors, especially IT/communication, perceived investment growth clearly surpasses sector prioritisation. Aligning infrastructure investment to needs and priorities seems to be especially challenging for transportation and, to a lesser degree, energy. In contrast, investment in IT/communication and waste and sanitation was often perceived to be higher than prioritisation.

This finding is also confirmed by survey respondents' observations of funding gaps, i.e. lack of sufficient financial resources to undertake investment or maintain infrastructure, in their countries. In non-OECD countries, experts perceived major funding gaps for all sectors, with 48.3 to 60 per cent perceiving severe gaps, with the exception of IT/communication and defence. In OECD countries, major funding gaps were reported only for transportation and buildings, with 58.5 per cent and 46.6 per cent, respectively, having observed severe gaps. For transportation, perceived funding gaps are highest in Australia and the United States, as well as in Egypt, Greece, Nigeria, Romania, Slovenia, and Sweden, all with more than 80 per cent of experts having reported severe gaps. For IT/communication, only 15 per cent of all surveyed experts considered there to be a severe funding gap, compared to 30.6 per cent having seen no funding gap at all.

With regard to the funding sources for infrastructure investment, the survey results show that there has been very little change in the relative weight of different funding sources over the last five years, with only taxes

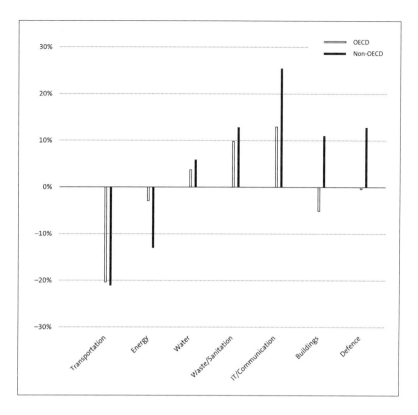

Figure 2.2 **Comparing prioritisation and perceived change in investment of key infrastructure sectors**
Note: Per cent of experts seeing it as priority area minus per cent of experts perceiving increasing investment over the last 5 years.

and especially user fees showing a moderate increase: 42.4 per cent of experts reported an increase for taxes, and 52.1 per cent for user fees. In non-OECD countries, experts observed an increasing dependence on bank loans and loans from multilateral banks. Private sector funding does not seem to have increased overall, with 27.8 per cent of respondents having reported an increase and 26.1 per cent a decrease, despite the high attention PPPs are given in academic and public debates. A closer look at the country level, however, shows clear differences: over 60 per cent of infrastructure experts in countries such as Greece, Hungary, Ireland, and Italy saw a clear decrease of private sector financing, while over 60 per cent in other countries such as Australia, Germany, and the US saw a clear increase.

Criteria for decision-making and involvement of different societal actors

Turning to infrastructure planning and decision-making patterns and, more specifically, what the surveyed experts regard as the most relevant criteria, political priorities and considerations were assessed as the most important criterion by far in all countries (mean of 4.4 on a 5-point scale, from 1=to a small extent to 5=to a large extent). Affordability (mean of 3.6) and economic benefits (mean of 3.5) were viewed as also rather important, followed by value for money (mean of 3.3) and environmental impact (mean of 3.1). In contrast, transparency/accountability (mean of 2.8) and sustainability (mean of 2.9) were considered less relevant. This general pattern was somewhat stronger in non-OECD countries, where political priorities stand out even more so as the most important criterion (mean of 4.6). We can thus conclude that decision-making about infrastructure is mainly about realising political preferences within given budget constraints. The complexity of multiple objectives and decision criteria is coped with via a clear ranking of objectives and rationales.

The survey results concerning the involvement of various societal actors in the process of national infrastructure planning and priority setting were somewhat surprising (see Figure 2.3). Overall, infrastructure experts considered the involvement of different types of actors outside central government to be rather low, with the notable exception of subnational government levels (see Chapter 3 for more on subnational governments). In particular, non-governmental organisations, citizens, and academics were seen to play only peripheral roles, a trend that was significantly stronger in non-OECD countries. As expected, the involvement of international funding institutions was seen as considerably more important in the context of non-OECD countries (mean of 3.4), since they represent a major funding source. Decision-making about infrastructure seems to be more insulated from the variety of stakeholders than expected, with central governments continuing to play a key role.

Whereas the involvement of private sector enterprises was considered by survey respondents to be only moderate on average, substantial differences were reported with regard to countries and infrastructure sectors. In countries such as Australia, the US, Chile, Switzerland, and the Slovak Republic, the surveyed experts observed rather high levels of involvement of private enterprises–in the US, private sector involvement was reported to be even higher than subnational governments or any other actor. With regard to infrastructure sectors, the experts observed a much higher involvement of private actors in the planning of infrastructure for IT/communication (mean of 3.9) and energy (mean of 3.6), in stark contrast to defence where, perhaps not surprisingly, private sector involvement was seen as very low (mean of 1.9).

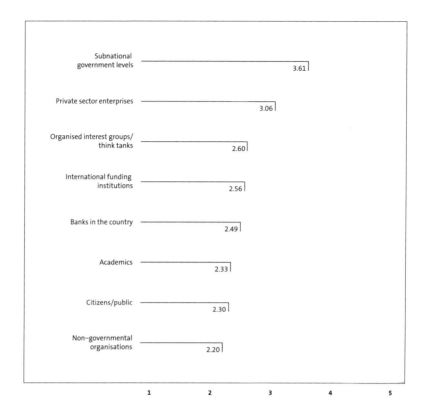

Figure 2.3 **Extent of involvement of different actors in national public infrastructure planning/priority setting**
Note: On a 5 point-scale, from 1=not at all to 5=to a large extent.

So far, so normal: infrastructure governance is about implementing political priorities. From a democratic perspective, it would be problematic if that were not the case. However, when we turn to the assessment of major challenges for strategic planning of public infrastructure, a more problematic aspect of this prerogative emerges: tension between political business cycles and the need for sustainable infrastructure planning was considered the most important challenge for strategic planning in both OECD and non-OECD countries (see Figure 2.4). While this is consistent with the responses regarding important criteria of decision-making–that is, political priorities as the most important criterion–it shows that this short-term political rationale is perceived as a major problem. Other substantial challenges include coordination across infrastructure sectors and coordination between central and regional levels, i.e. those dimensions of the sector that were identified above as drivers of complexity (see Chapter 3 for more on coordination challenges). Interestingly, none of the ten challenges was on

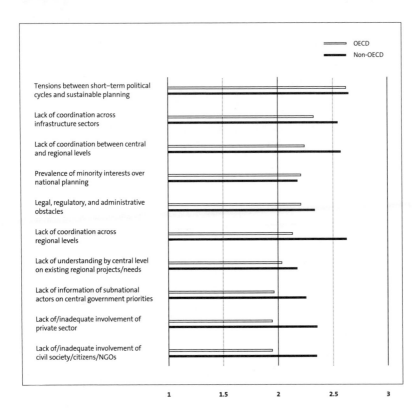

Figure 2.4 **Main coordination challenges with respect to strategic planning for public infrastructure**
Note: On a 3-point scale, with 1=not a challenge, 2=somewhat a challenge, and 3=major challenge.

average regarded by infrastructure experts as irrelevant, confirming the overall difficult nature of infrastructure governance. Comparing OECD and non-OECD countries, we find an overall higher relevance of most challenges in the non-OECD countries, where the lack of coordination across regional levels as well as between central and regional levels stands out.

One commonly recommended and increasingly implemented approach to cope with such coordination challenges is the development of national strategic plans to set out infrastructure priorities and thereby introduce higher rationality and transparency in infrastructure decision-making processes. The results of our survey reinforce earlier points about the prevalence of a political logic in decision-making. According to our expert respondents, such national plans or strategic guidance documents exist in the large majority of countries, although to a slightly higher degree in non-OECD countries, and in many countries these documents cover all relevant infrastructure sectors. However, when asked about the relevance of such plans for decision-making, the results are sobering: only 18.0 per cent of the experts surveyed considered such plans as very relevant, and another 26.2 per cent as rather relevant. In contrast, 26.8 per cent regarded such plans in their countries as not relevant at all or rather irrelevant. The differences between OECD and non-OECD countries were minimal, with a slightly higher relevance in the non-OECD countries, where such plans tended to be more prevalent.

Federal and unitary states

Comparing federal and unitary countries, no differences emerged on a number of dimensions: changes in investment levels, the importance of different sectors of infrastructure, the existence of funding gaps, and the involvement of private actors in infrastructure planning. There was also no major difference related to the criteria for decision-making, which reinforces the point that the complexity of the field is not artificially induced by institutional structures, but generic.

However, when it comes to coordination practices and challenges, we can identify some interesting differences. First, national plans/guidance documents for infrastructure planning have a slightly higher relevance in unitary states. Without overstating this result, it suggests that coordination with the subnational entities in federal states takes place outside the venue of the national strategic plan. However, that does not mean that subnational governments are not involved in the planning of infrastructure investments.

The strongest difference between federal and unitary states relates to the involvement of subnational levels of government, which is more intensive in federal countries. This result is also plausible since in federal countries, decision-making authority is more often decentralised or shared. And even if formal authority rests with the national level, there is often dependence on information coming from the subnational levels of government, as analytical capacities tend to rest here (for a case study on transport planning in Germany developing this argument, see Garlichs 1980). At the same time, the challenge of coordination between central and regional levels and across regional levels is considered higher in federal as opposed to unitary countries. Again this result is in line with the expectation that in federal systems the subnational level has some form of veto position, which makes coordination more difficult since it depends on cooperation and consent in an area which is essentially about distribution of benefits and costs. As we know from the scholarship on federalism in Germany and the European Union, the need for consensus-based decision-making can eventually lead to a 'joint-decision trap' (Scharpf 1988) in which policies are based on the lowest common denominator and changing institutional rules is difficult.

Coordination challenges: Examining outliers

Widely perceived problems and challenges seem to be better managed in certain countries than in others. Turning first to the tension between short-term political cycles and the need for sustainable investment, in which countries is this problem less pronounced?

China, not surprisingly, was assessed to have one of the lowest levels of tension between short-term political cycles and sustainable infrastructure planning (1.75, on a 3-point scale, from 1=not a challenge to 3=major challenge). The Netherlands (1.67) was assessed to be even better than China, with Japan (2.0), Switzerland (2.0), and Germany (2.27) following. While the results for China are plausible given the absence of competitive popular elections at the national level, the other four countries' political systems share strong elements of consensus-based decision-making, i.e. decisions require agreement among diverse actors. These countries did not score low regarding the relevance of political priorities as a criterion for decision-making; indeed, infrastructure experts from Switzerland (5.0) unanimously considered political priorities to be the most important criterion for decision-making. Arguably, consensus-based decision-making and high stability correct for the short-term nature of political attention spans. Federalism alone is not a guarantee for such an effect: Australia (2.8), Canada (2.9), and the US (2.8) are among the countries in which experts saw rather high tensions between political short-termism and the need for sustainable infrastructure. Considering that the UK (2.9) also scores rather high, one might argue that Anglo-Saxon democracies share certain characteristics that accentuate these tensions.

Taking an aggregate look at all coordination challenges (calculated as the mean of the 10 challenges used in the survey; see Figure 2.5), we again find the Netherlands and Switzerland, followed by France and Estonia, as countries reported to have better coordination of strategic planning for public infrastructure. Scandinavian countries were consistently assessed rather well, whereas reports on other country groups were less consistent. Australia stands out among the Anglo-Saxon countries; Germany was assessed to be much better in terms of coordination than Austria; and China and South Africa were considered much better than the other non-OECD countries, with the large countries Mexico, Indonesia, and Nigeria at the bottom end of the spectrum.

The survey also asked respondents to assess their countries' overall performances in the management of public infrastructure projects in different infrastructure sectors. The overall assessment is rather moderate, with means for the various sectors varying between 2.8 for defence and 3.2 for water (on a 5-point scale, from 1=low performance to 5=high performance). Infrastructure experts in non-OECD countries reported lower overall performances in the management of public infrastructure than experts in OECD countries. In non-OECD countries, public infrastructure for waste and sani-

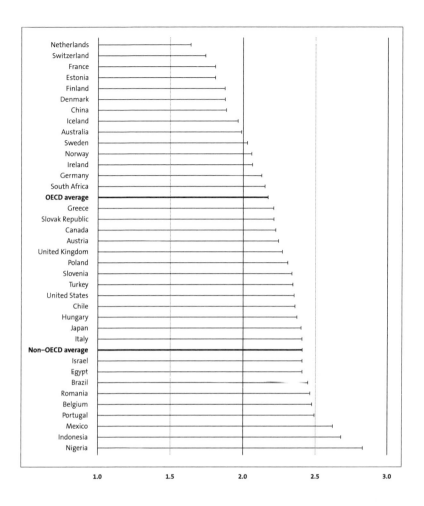

Figure 2.5 **Level of coordination challenges with respect to strategic planning for public infrastructure**
Note: Mean of all 10 challenges; on a 3-point scale, with 1=no challenges, 2=moderate challenges, and 3=major challenges.

tation (mean of 1.9) and water (mean of 2.2) were perceived to perform especially poorly. On the other side, countries such as the Netherlands, France, and Sweden were again assessed to perform significantly better in the management of public infrastructure projects in most sectors.

When looking for commonalities among these positive outliers–France, Netherlands, Sweden, and Switzerland, as well as Australia and China–we highlight that these countries have national plans for infrastructure in most areas and that, with the exception of France, these plans were assessed as more relevant than similar plans in other countries. Furthermore, higher levels of involvement of subnational actors, private sector, and citizens in policy-making were perceived in all these countries, except Sweden. Also, surveyed experts saw value for money and sustainability in public infrastructure planning and decision-making as more highly relevant in these countries.

Different Institutional Arrangements for Coordinating Infrastructure Decision-Making

While our expert survey revealed important similarities in decision-making about infrastructure governance, in particular concerning the role of political forces, it also pointed out major differences in cross-country comparison. In particular, national institutional systems and traditions such as state structure, i.e. federal versus unitary, and political culture, i.e. consensus versus competitive, were identified as key drivers of national patterns of decision-making. In this section, we further explore this link between national institutional structures and patterns of decision-making. Using selected country cases, we analyse how different institutional arrangements–independent bodies, centralisation, decentralisation, and private sector involvement–influence the practice of decision-making on infrastructure and especially the prevalence of political factors.

Australia: Establishing Infrastructure Australia as an independent expert body

Australia is frequently mentioned as an example of a country that successfully adopted a key reform approach, i.e. the establishment of an independent expert body that rationalises the planning of long-term infrastructure investments. Infrastructure Australia (IA) was set up in 2008 in response to inadequate coordination in infrastructure planning. Granted statutory independence in 2014, IA consists of an independent, 12-member board that appoints its CEO. IA's chief purpose is to provide advice to the national government through the relevant minister on Australia's infrastructure needs.

IA's key responsibility is the development of the Australian National Infrastructure Plan, a 15-year roadmap of infrastructure investment priorities that is revised every five years on the basis of audits aimed at assessing the value added, or 'Direct Economic Contribution', of infrastructure to the Australian economy. IA's audits look at future demands, establish an evidence base, and identify priorities for investment both in terms of regions and projects. The ranking of regions according to the Direct Economic

Contribution of infrastructure is, as might be expected, contested by regions that are ranked lower, e.g. due to low population and/or low growth, which eventually triggers government responses such as the establishment of regional development programmes.

Taking into account these assessments of regions, IA also develops an Infrastructure Priority List (see Infrastructure Australia 2013) to provide a pipeline of infrastructure projects by which to guide investment decisions. The Australian Infrastructure Plan should then take into account IA's audits, evaluations, and lists. Whereas the focus previously lay on the assessment of individual projects, the 2015 audit was the first comprehensive effort to define overall infrastructure needs and requirements.

While IA has established itself well over the past years, the extent to which it has achieved the goals of de-politicising and actually changing the way infrastructure decisions are made is debatable. For one, IA is a statutory body advising the Commonwealth Government. However, much of the responsibility for infrastructure provision in areas such as roads, public transport, electricity, ports, and dams lies with the state governments. Even if IA's analyses influence federal decision-making on financing contributions, they are not driving decisions at the state level. Second, the government is not legally obliged to finance projects identified by IA as priorities, and in fact, many infrastructure projects in Australia–such as those for regional development as well as discretionary programmes for sporting, recreational, and other local infrastructure needs–are funded by the federal government although they do not qualify for the Infrastructure Priority List. Third, the government continues to make decisions regarding nationally significant infrastructure projects despite contrary or lacking information from IA, which is not the only institution offering evidence and advice to the government.

Concerning the independence of IA's advice, the Minister for Infrastructure and Regional Development must not give directions about any content or advice that IA provides. However, the Minister may direct IA to evaluate proposals for investment 'as determined by the Minister'–including those that may not be nationally significant. While the enabling legislation sets out a consultative process of nominations to the Board and requires the Minister to be satisfied regarding proposed members' experience, appointments are ultimately made by the Minister. In practice, there is nothing to stop successive governments from stacking the IA board with political appointees. In a report on public infrastructure (Australian Government 2014), the Australian Productivity Commission–the Government's review and advisory body on microeconomic policy–suggested further strengthening the IA, in particular the independent cost-benefit assessment of projects for increased transparency. Furthermore, recent legislative changes emphasise a stronger role of cost-benefit analysis, which should also broaden its focus to include social, environmental, and economic concerns. However, the practice of infrastructure decision-making suggests that even in this arguably highly developed case of Infrastructure Australia, political rationality and influence can trump rational and independent decision-making. What can be deduced from the Australian experience is that the creation of an 'independent' body for infrastructure planning and rational assessment of projects will not automatically de-politicise the process. Tensions between the logic of rational planning and political decision-making will remain.

Spain: Mismatch of a centralised planning system

Another tension in infrastructure decision-making is between centralised and decentralised decision-making. As discussed above, coordination with regional and local institutions is critical for good infrastructure decision-making (see also Chapter 3), but how this coordination plays out depends on national institutional patterns, e.g. federal versus unitary states. The case of Spain shows how centralised decision-making can lead to imbalances. In the field of transport planning, decision-making has been shaped for centuries by the desire to centralise transportation around the country's political capital (Bel 2011). Even today, responsibility for key areas of infrastructure–major airports and commercial ports, most railways, and the majority of motorways–is concentrated at the central government level. Coordination with the regional level usually takes the form of a bilateral negotiation of sectoral plans between the central and regional governments, which co-finance some of the projects. This relation is, however, very asymmetric and often involves party political channels, i.e. regional governments lobbying for projects in Madrid using party political connections. In Spain, one can observe a shortage of governance capacities that take into account the political, social, and economic complexities of a country that is comparatively multi-polar in its socioeconomic geography.

This centralisation reflects to some extent the significance of infrastructure policy for Spain's economic and social development, especially over the last several decades. Having received financing from the World Bank between 1963 and 1977 and EU subsidies a decade later, the country has significantly improved its infrastructure, which was ranked 13th best in the world in 2013– with railroads ranked 4th (Schwab 2014: 342)–and boasts twice as many international airports and 10 per cent more highways than Germany (Bel, Estache, and Foucart 2013: 130).

The central/regional government imbalance is reflected in initiatives such as high-speed train connections and highways developed over the last two decades with the aim to strengthen the political centre. This centralised structure is even visible in air transport, with a fragmented airport network essentially providing feeder connections to the Madrid hub. In particular, when key political actors developed the ambition to turn Madrid into first, the economic centre of the Iberian peninsula and second, a global city, a range of projects were implemented that are today considered to lack an economic rationale. The central government was able to implement a centralised infrastructure network that, while based on a consensus among national political parties, is disconnected from regional economic and social needs. Albate, Bel, and Fageda's finding that 'investment programmes in network modes (i.e. roads and railways) are negatively related to distance from the capital city' (2012: 2) illustrates that allocation of investment resources for transport infrastructure in Spain has been guided by political goals rather than investment needs, demand analyses, or economic impact.

Regional governments in Spain lack the capacity and funds to develop regional and/or local transport infrastructure as well as political or managerial control over vital regional infrastructure such as ports and airports. This contrasts with strong technical capacities at the central government level, with the national Ministry of Public Works and Transport as the administrative backbone and political promoter of the centralist approach to infrastructure development. A classic iron triangle of the ministerial bureaucracy, politicians, and the construction industry reinforces the view of infrastructure development as key for developing the Madrid region into an economic centre. While current debates about transport infrastructure have realised the limitations of earlier approaches favouring the centre and are raising the question of how to develop a more capillary infrastructure network, efforts to take action face the obstacles of a strong political coalition favouring the centre and a strong alliance between political actors and the construction industry (Bel, Estache, and Foucart 2013).

Germany: Tensions of joint decision-making in a federal system

Tensions between centralised and decentralised decision-making also shape infrastructure governance in Germany, but in very different ways. Here, setting priorities is inherently problematic because the system favours an equal distribution of resources due to the pattern of joint decision-making that gives the *Länder*, i.e. the federal states, a strong voice in federal decision-making. In the case of transport planning, this pattern is still evident despite a distribution of powers that would suggest otherwise. Adopted for the first time in 1973, with new versions developed by the Federal Ministry of Transport every 10 to 15 years and revisions appearing every five years, the federal transport plan aims to define investment priorities in roads, railways, and waterways for the medium term. And while the federal transport plan is not legally binding in itself, subsequent development laws formally deciding transport infrastructure investments are firmly based on it.

The case of transport planning is unusual within the peculiar system of joint decision-making in German federalism, which in general divides responsibilities between levels of government according to functions, not policy fields (Scharpf 1988). This functional division of responsibilities concentrates decision-making power at the federal level but delegates implementation powers to the *Länder*. As a result, the *Länder* are heavily involved in federal law-making and have strong veto powers in the Federal Council (*Bundesrat*). This type of federalism has created a negotiation system between levels of government that usually follows principles of equal treatment of all *Länder* and a status quo orientation when it comes to the distribution of resources (see Scharpf 2009). However, the standard division of labour in Germany's joint decision-making system does not fully apply to transport infrastructure planning: decision-making power and control of implementation are in the hands of the federal government, but infrastructure planning and building still resides with the *Länder*, which act under a model of delegated 'federal contract administration' that gives the federal level strong formal oversight competencies.

As Garlichs (1980) showed, despite the strong position of the executive branch of the federal government in the area of transport infrastructure planning, patterns of joint decision-making remain: the principles of equal treatment of the *Länder* and status quo orientation still apply, and the planning process is very much a bottom-up process in which the *Länder* submit project proposals as input to the federal plan. Garlichs argues that the absence of administrative delivery capacity makes the federal level in general and the transport ministry in particular dependent on information coming from the *Länder*. And despite the significant advantage of local knowledge, this information is based on the selective perception of each *Land*, resulting in a bias towards projects that are considered relevant for individual *Länder* but do not necessarily reflect nationwide priorities. The continued prevalence of this pattern, first diagnosed 35 years ago, is evidenced by current debates calling for a more integrated planning system, both in terms of spatial and sectoral planning (Heuser and Reh 2015). In its coalition agreement from 2013, the two governing parties of the federal government pledged to develop a 'national priority concept' to address exactly this concern (CDU, CSU, and SPD 2013).

Another increasingly voiced criticism is that the actual implementation of the federal transport plan consistently lags behind schedule. In the state of Brandenburg, surrounding Berlin, less than 30 per cent of the 2003 transport plan had been completed by 2012: of the 236 investment projects included in the plan and the 2004 development law, 62 had been completed and three were under construction. For 47 per cent of the projects, no planning activities had been initiated at all (Vogelsänger 2012). Such delayed and partial implementation is widespread across Germany. According to expert interviews within the *Länder* administration, this pattern of unrealistic planning is mostly due to the influence of politicians, i.e. individual members of parliament (*Bundestag*), lobbying for projects benefiting their constituency. The political influence results in an imbalanced distribution of resources between the *Länder* by favouring larger *Länder* and those with strong political footing in the transport ministry.

To overstate our critical assessment to some extent: the planning regime does not allow for systematic top-down planning due to the absence of administrative delivery capacity at the federal level, and bottom-up planning is subject to political influence and bias, despite the increasing sophistication of planning systems and tools. Indeed, as Garlichs points out, quoting a country comparison report, the German system has from the start been considered to be one with high technical sophistication (Garlichs 1980: 77). However, the logic of political influence and bargaining finds its way to influence decision-making despite seemingly more objective analysis in the form of cost-benefit analysis.

The reform debate recently culminated in proposals towards further centralisation of the system: in early 2015, an expert commission on infrastructure investment advising the federal Minister for Economic Affairs and Energy, besides calling for more PPPs and private investment, proposed the creation of an agency under the control of federal government that should take over the *Länder's* implementation role in highway planning (Expertenkommission 2015). Media reports (see, for example, Becker 2016, Funk 2016) have suggested that the federal ministers for transport and finance have agreed on a concept for a federal highway authority (*Bundesautobahn Gesellschaft*) in the form of a limited company (GmbH), as already existing in Austria since 1982. However, the prospect of this initiative remains uncertain, since such a reform requires constitutional change and hence the consent of a supermajority in the Federal Council. Such an institutional solution would not come without its own risks and potential downsides: as it is unlikely that political influence would stop being exerted on the planning process, such influence might possibly be exerted in an even less transparent and more biased way than is the case today. The risk is that such a regime, in addressing the recurring limitations of infrastructure planning in Germany, would come with other as yet unforeseen problems and limitations.

Brazil: Private sector involvement leading to new coordination challenges

A final example, Brazil, shows how coordination problems between levels of government can be amplified through the extensive involvement of private parties in infrastructure governance. An illustrative case is the Growth Acceleration Program (*Programa de Aceleração do Crescimento*, or PAC), begun in the mid-2000s in response to an infrastructure investment gap and an overall low quality of infrastructure in Brazil. The investment gap is the result of a long period of reduced spending for infrastructure since the 1990s. After high levels of investment–some five per cent of GDP–in the early 1980s, investment levels dropped to 2.25 per cent for two decades, reaching only 2.5 per cent in 2013 (Garcia-Escribano, Goes, and Karpowicz 2015). During those two decades, infrastructure investment levels were low compared to other Latin American countries and in other emerging markets (Calderón and Servén 2010; Frischtak 2008). Melo and Pereira (2015) identified the combined effect of commitment to high social spending with an emphasis on fiscal discipline as the main driver of low levels of infrastructure investment.

In the 2000s, political pressure to increase infrastructure investments grew, not only due to acute crises such as power shortages but also because of chronic problems such as decaying roads, overcrowded airports, and poor public transportation (Bielschowsky 2002). The government's ability to directly invest in public infrastructure was somewhat limited by the privatisation of state-owned companies in the 1990s and the subsequent build-up of regulatory agencies. However, the idea that a regulated market could provide the necessary infrastructure investments quickly proved disappointing, due in part to complex administrative and regulatory procedures (Frischtak 2008). PPPs were considered a potential way out of the quagmire, and new legal instruments for stimulating PPPs and balancing public and private engagements were established in 2004 (Câmara dos Deputados 2004).

The idea of PPPs gained traction when then-President Luíz Inácio Lula da Silva set up in 2007 the first PAC, which sought to combine the general aim of improving infrastructure with an emphasis on sectors neglected by the private sector, e.g. social housing, railways, and roads in remote areas (Ministério do Planejamento, Orçamento e Gestão 2007). But PAC also intended to use public spending as leverage for private investment and to create conditions for private investments: less than 15 per cent of the initial R$500 billion within the programme's scope was planned as direct public funding (Ministério do Planejamento, Orçamento e Gestão 2007). Hence, PAC mainly consisted of massive infrastructure concessions to the private sector and the creation of PPPs, with an offer of attractive loans from Brazilian public banks and funds. The federal government remained in charge of controlling and directing investments towards strategic targets and regions.

In the final year of Lula's second term, the follow-up phase of PAC was announced, and PAC II became part of the presidential campaign platform of Dilma Rousseff, then a minister in the Lula government who was regarded as the 'mother of PAC'. Under PAC II, the programme was expanded in terms of both budget, to nearly R$ 1 trillion for 2011 to 2014, and scope, by targeting more extensively the social component of the programme and local needs. Moreover, the programme was intended to address the challenges of hosting the 2014 FIFA World Cup and 2016 Olympic Games, in Rio de Janeiro. PAC II targeted six areas: transportation, energy, social housing, basic infrastructure, urban reforms, and health and educational structures (Casa Civil 2010).

However, implementation problems mounted with the programme's expansion. Many projects remained on paper, while others suffered major delays, price adjustments, and lack of proper funding mechanisms. Among the problems mentioned are poor planning and regulatory instruments, lack of coordination between government and controlling agencies, and corruption (Melo and Pereira 2015: 13 ff.). While administrative capacities were built up in the presidential office, similar capacities were lacking in line ministries dealing with infrastructure. The *Comitê Gestor do PAC*, an interministerial group responsible for monitoring and joint decision-making, developed several approaches to improve decision-making, but the programme remained overly complex. Moreover, the shift of emphasis in PAC II towards local investment projects strained the capacities of municipal and state governments: some 33,000 projects were under the responsibility of the municipalities, and 5,000 under state jurisdiction (Melo and Pereira 2015: 14). Since the federal programme requires co-funding via PPP financing, state and municipal governments set up their own PPP coordination bodies and launched a range of uncoordinated initiatives (Caldas and Vale 2014). The indirect and complex programme design, e.g. state and local government must propose projects to the federal government, which prepares the final project pipeline, contributed to poor planning through a 'first come, first served' style. Although PAC is still active and was extended for another round with Rousseff's re-election, its execution rate is lower than expected (Contas Abertas 2016), it remains troubled by constant conflicts between federal and state governments, which blame one another for delays and cost increases (Amora 2014), and both the nation's current fiscal crisis and corruption scandals have contributed to reducing investment and slowing the pace of implementation.

Concluding Recommendations

This chapter set out to provide evidence for and better understanding of the logics and practices of government decision-making in infrastructure. We summarise our findings and related recommendations in six points:

First, any attempt to improve decision-making on infrastructure needs to take into account the inherent complexity, uncertainty, and hence political nature of the field. This challenge cannot be dealt with by simply applying tools of rational decision-making, which work well for simple problems but not so well for complex ones. Political rationality will always be a key driver of decision-making, and the task of reforms is to increase the quality of political decision-making–not to replace politics with technocratic analysis or expert decision-making.

Second, and relatedly, the influence of independent bodies in infrastructure governance should not be overestimated. While independent bodies are only now becoming more influential and their role is very much evolving, it is unrealistic to assume that political forces will be displaced from the decision-making process. Such a naive institutionalism (Roberts 2010)–an understanding of institutional change as being limited to formal-legal changes–has troubled many fields of economic policy and became a fashion in infrastructure governance. Again, the criterion for evaluating such bodies should be whether analysis and evidence and the debates moderated by them have enhanced the quality of political decision-making, i.e. by requiring political actors to justify their decisions with evidence.

Third, exercise caution with generalisations and the proclamation of best practices. Considerable cross-national variation exists concerning governance arrangements, the most pressing governance challenges, and how–and how well–they are handled. Different countries display different patterns of strengths and weaknesses–for example, too much or too little central decision-making–and require different institutional arrangements.

Fourth, do not expect national infrastructure plans to be effective on their own. Such plans can be effective tools for high quality decision-making through transparency and evidence, but only if they are actually given significance in the decision-making process, i.e. key actors being involved and buying into the plan.

Fifth, high quality decision-making is driven by institutions, not instruments. Countries that manage the challenges of decision-making well are those that display features of consensus-oriented, inclusive decision-making. Reform debates in infrastructure display a problematic combination of naive institutionalism and a focus on instruments such as plans and analytical instruments. How institutions work and how they can be improved needs to be considered in light of the specific political and administrative context and tradition of a particular country.

Sixth, reconsider the across-the-board diagnosis of an infrastructure gap. We need more and better evidence for better diagnoses of where exactly–in terms of countries, regions and sectors–an infrastructure investment gap exists.

Endnotes

1   On Brazil, see Pereira and Melo (forthcoming). On Germany, see Fratzscher (2016).

III. Subnational Infrastructure Investment
The Governance Levers

Dorothée Allain-Dupré, Claudia Hulbert, and Margaux Vincent

Investment is a key determinant of economic growth. However, OECD countries are facing an investment gap (OECD 2015g). Both private and public investment levels are down compared to the period prior to the 2008 global financial crisis. At the same time, developed countries face huge maintenance costs associated with past infrastructure investments: estimated to be one per cent of GDP on a yearly basis in the United States, for instance (Standard & Poor's 2014). Infrastructure needs are even greater in developing countries, in particular for new investment. The global challenges of climate change and population growth exacerbate the need for renewed infrastructure. The cost of adapting to climate change could amount to several billion US dollars annually for each infrastructure sector, e.g. transport, water, and energy.

Assuming that public budgets across the OECD will remain tight for some time to come, governments need to diversify their sources of financing of infrastructure investment. Increased private financing might help address growing needs. While financing is one side of the problem, other constraints that impede effective investment in sustainable infrastructure are often underestimated. Several recent studies estimate that improvement in infrastructure management could lead to substantial savings and enhanced infrastructure productivity (OECD 2015g, 2013; IMF 2015; Rajaram et al. 2014; Dobbs et al. 2013). As shown throughout this Report, infrastructure projects with deficient governance result in cost overruns, delays, underperformance, accelerated deterioration due to poor maintenance, and occasionally, expensive 'white elephants' and 'bridges to nowhere'. They also contribute to undermining confidence in markets and private partners, which is a major issue at a time when governments are increasingly called upon to consider external sources of financing.

The opinions expressed and arguments employed herein are solely those of the authors and do not necessarily reflect the official views of the OECD or of its member countries.

National governments have an important role to play in establishing the framework conditions needed to better select and implement sound infrastructure projects. Subnational governments (SNGs) also play a specific role, although this is often neglected in the literature linked to infrastructure. SNGs–defined as all levels of government below the national one (regional and local),[1] i.e. administrative regions, states/provinces, counties, and municipalities–are responsible for a large share of public investment: on average, around 60 per cent in the OECD (see Figure 3.1). Most of this public investment goes to infrastructure. This particular role of SNGs poses specific challenges for both the financing and governance of infrastructure investment. This chapter explores these challenges in greater detail and proposes good practices and recommendations to address them.

This chapter builds upon recent OECD work in this area[2] and on the results of the 2015 OECD–Committee of the Regions (CoR) survey, in which 255 subnational governments from all European Union (EU) countries except Luxembourg participated.[3] We first draw on the survey's results as well as additional quantitative data to highlight the decline in subnational investment and the limited diversification of financing. We then focus on the critical governance challenges that are more specific to SNGs and the practices perceived by SNGs to be helpful in overcoming some of these challenges. Finally, we attempt to make a preliminary link between the effectiveness of subnational governance of infrastructure investment and outcomes in terms of regional growth before closing with a set of recommendations.

Decrease in Subnational Investment and Limited Diversification in Financing

Large variation in subnational infrastructure investment spending across countries

Investment in public infrastructure is a shared responsibility across levels of government. Fifty-nine per cent of public investment in OECD member states was carried out at the subnational level in 2013; 55 per cent on average in the EU (Figure 3.1). Whether through shared policy competencies or joint funding arrangements, public investment typically involves different levels of government at some stage of the investment process. Such shared responsibilities and tasks make the governance of public investment particularly complex.

A large share of subnational public investment, measured by gross fixed capital formation (GFCF), goes to infrastructure in areas of critical impor-

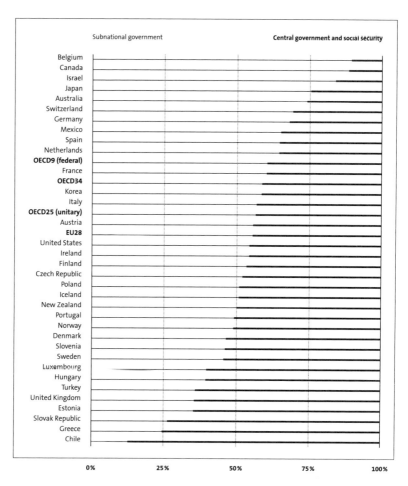

Figure 3.1 **Subnational public investment in OECD countries as a share of public investment (GFCF), 2013.**
Note: Data for Chile: 2012 instead of 2013;
Turkey: 2011 instead of 2013.
Source: OECD (2015e).

tance for future economic growth, sustainable development, and citizens' well-being. In terms of total investment by SNGs across the OECD, 37 per cent is allocated to economic affairs, e.g. transport, communications, economic development, energy, and construction. Approximately one-quarter of public investment is used for investment in the education sector, and a further 11 per cent is dedicated to housing and community amenities, e.g. community development, water supply, and street lighting. The remaining investment is allocated to general public services, environmental protection, healthcare, and other activities.

Subnational spending for public investment varies significantly across countries. The ratio of subnational to national spending tends to be higher in federal countries such as Belgium, Canada, the US, Germany, and Switzerland. In unitary countries, the role of subnational governments in public investment is somewhat less pronounced, although in several countries, including Japan, Israel, Netherlands, France, and Korea, subnational governments still play a crucial role.

Long-term and recent trends

Since the 1970s, public investment has progressively declined in OECD countries on average, from 4.5 per cent of GDP in 1980 to 2.5 per cent in 2013 (see Figure 3.2). This long-running downward trend is due to the fact that many OECD countries have well-developed infrastructure and have therefore focused mainly on operation and maintenance of existing assets.[4]

After having been relatively stable in the OECD from the mid-1990s to the mid-2000s, the decrease in public investment was amplified after the economic crisis of the late 2000s. At first, local investment was stimulated during 2008–9 due to investment recovery packages launched by national governments in the wake of the global economic downturn. After 2010, fiscal consolidation policies adopted at the national level led to a sharp decline in subnational investment. In many OECD countries, current expenditures, in particular social benefits, have grown more rapidly than revenues and hence have reduced the fiscal space left for investments.[5] This is especially true for subnational public investment, which has been consistently used as an adjustment variable in fiscal consolidation strategies (see Figure 3.3) (OECD 2014d).

Because revenues have grown more slowly than expenditures, and because SNGs have faced declining transfers from national governments in many countries, subnational debt has increased rapidly over recent years. Many SNGs have increased the share of debt in the funding of infrastructure investments. However, additional funding for SNGs through debt may be limited by the recent evolution of SNG fiscal rules. Many countries have introduced balanced budget requirements that may affect expenditure or debt-brake provisions that do not include exemptions for funding investment expenses.

The decline of subnational public investment has been particularly marked in the EU, continuing through 2014 (see Figure 3.4). In the EU, public investment conducted by SNGs decreased by more than 20 per cent between 2009 and 2013, i.e. five per cent per year in real terms. Many EU countries, especially those hit hardest by the eurozone crisis, continue to have negative public investment-to-GDP gaps compared to their pre-economic crisis levels, e.g. −2.4 per cent of GDP in Ireland and −1.8 per cent of GDP in Spain

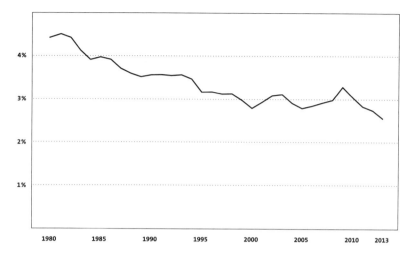

Figure 3.2 **Public investment as a share of GDP in OECD countries (1980–2013)**
Note: Since 1995, all OECD countries except Chile, Greece, Iceland, Mexico, Slovenia, and Turkey.
Australia: 2007 instead of 2008–13.
Canada: 2010 instead of 2011–13.
Israel, Korea, and the US: 2011 instead of 2012–13.
New Zealand and Switzerland: 2012 instead of 2013.
Sources: OECD National Accounts for 1995–2013
(Data from SNA93, see OECD 2016a); Sutherland et al. (2009).

(Allain-Dupré, Hulbert, and Vincent forthcoming). While public investment at the central government level seemed to be slightly recovering in the EU in 2014, public investment at the subnational level did not seem to be recovering as quickly as GDP and revenues (see again Figure 3.3). All sectors were hit by the decrease, in particular transport, housing, and education and health infrastructure.

Financing challenges vary greatly across the different categories of SNGs

Behind the aggregate data, the results from the OECD–CoR survey reveal a great deal of variation across the different categories of SNGs in the EU, confirming the need to look beyond national averages. While 44 per cent of SNGs surveyed reported a decline in investment since 2010, 24 per cent reported having increased investment by more than 10 per cent since that time (see Figure 3.5). In fact, the survey results show that most of the cuts

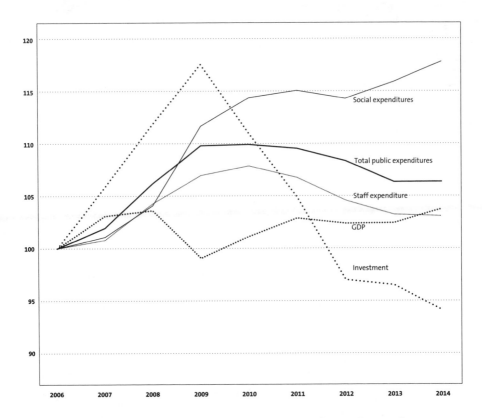

Figure 3.3 **Evolution of SNG expenditure in OECD countries (2006 = base 100)**
Note: All OECD countries except Australia and Chile.
Turkey: 2011 instead of 2012–13.
Source: OECD National Accounts (data extracted in 2015, see OECD 2016a).

in public investment were reported by large SNGs, in particular administrative regions and large cities. By contrast, 30 per cent of small municipalities– those with fewer than 50,000 inhabitants–and 28 per cent of medium-size municipalities reported having actually increased their overall spending by more than 10 per cent since 2010 (Figure 3.6). This variation might indicate that the cuts in public investment were made by large SNGs, which devote a higher share of spending to investment, and that it is easier to cut large-scale projects than small-scale ones. In turn, these results might indicate that not only the level but also the type of investment was affected by tight fiscal constraints, and that adjustments on the part of SNGs have targeted larger and probably more strategic infrastructure investment projects.

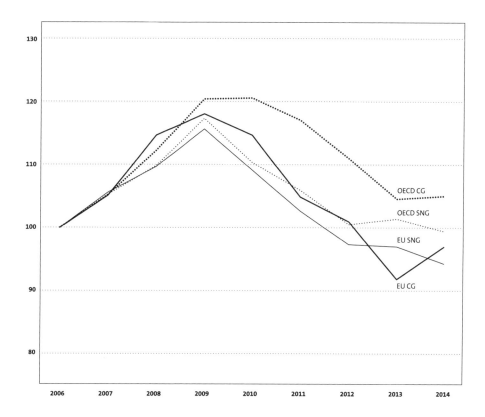

Figure 3.4 **Central and subnational government investment trends in selected OECD countries over 2005–14 (2006 = base 100)**
Note: CG=central government; SNG=subnational government.
All OECD countries except Chile, Iceland, and Slovenia. Australia, Israel, Japan, Mexico, New Zealand, Switzerland, and the US:
2013 instead of 2014.
Mexico: 2003 instead of 2000–2.
Greece: 2006 instead of 2000–5.
Turkey: 2006 instead of 2000–5 and 2011 instead of 2012–14.
Data from SNA 08.
Source: OECD (2016a) and Eurostat.

Diversification of financing remains limited

While the main reasons for the aggregate decline in investment spending at the subnational level are connected with the increase in current expenditure and the reduced fiscal space left for investment, 53 per cent of SNGs reported a decrease in grants from their national government. The OECD–CoR survey results also reveal that the recourse to borrowing appears to have rather

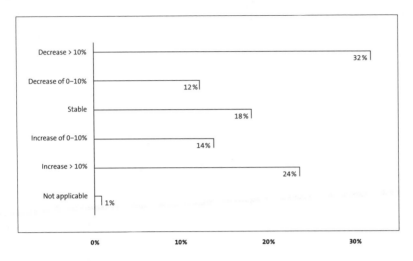

Figure 3.5 **Overall public investment spending trends by SNGs since 2010**
Source: OECD (2015d)

been reduced. Thirty-nine per cent of SNGs mentioned a reduction or stabilisation in borrowing to finance investment since 2010, with only 12 per cent reporting an increase; the remaining 49 per cent did not express an opinion on the issue. Only four per cent of SNGs have increased their recourse to bonds, a finding that is not so surprising since SNG recourse to bond financing is not permitted in many EU countries, especially for municipalities.

In this context of tight fiscal constraints and a decrease in more traditional sources of funding, e.g. transfers or bank loans, along with increases in social expenditures and reduced fiscal space for investment, diversification into external sources of financing would be needed to be able to invest in new infrastructure. However, the survey results show that diversification –for instance, through private funding, public-private partnerships (PPPs), or funding through financial markets via inter-municipal borrowing agencies–remains very limited at the subnational level. Only seven per cent of SNGs, mostly regions and large cities, reported having increased their private sources of financing for infrastructure investment since 2010. This lack of interest in adding private sources of financing might be explained by the complexity of using PPPs, especially the extensive technical and legal capacities that they require and that most SNGs below a certain size do not have. This may also reflect a lack of knowledge within SNGs of the variety of financial mechanisms available, as well as a lack of coordination across SNGs to pool financial resources in order to engage in innovative financing mechanisms.

The limited diversification of funding combined with the decrease in more traditional sources of financing result in financing gaps. Almost all SNGs surveyed reported perceiving gaps in overall public investment spend-

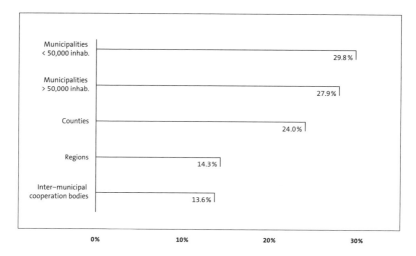

Figure 3.6 **Trends in investment spending: Share of SNGs reporting an increase of more than 10 per cent since 2010, by type**
Source: OECD (2015d)

ing, i.e. insufficient resources to meet demand. This is especially true for the building of new infrastructure, with 55 per cent of SNGs reporting perceived gaps, as well as for the operation and maintenance of existing infrastructure, reported by 41 per cent. The extent of gaps, shown in Figure 3.7, vary greatly across the different sectors of infrastructure and reflect the allocation of competencies across levels of government. Gaps in financing roads, for example, are reported by 85 per cent of small municipalities, whereas gaps in financing public transport and infrastructure for education are mostly mentioned by large SNGs, i.e. regions and large municipalities.

Critical Governance Challenges Specific to SNGs: Diagnosis and Possible Solutions

Increasing local infrastructure investment efficiency is crucial for compensating for large investment gaps in recent years, in particular at the subnational level, and for promoting output growth while limiting increases in public debt. As noted at the outset, the public governance dimension is just as important as the financing aspect in contributing to public investment and growth outcomes at both the national and subnational levels (OECD 2013, 2015a, 2015d). By scaling up good practices in selecting and delivering new infrastructure projects, SNGs could deliver sig-

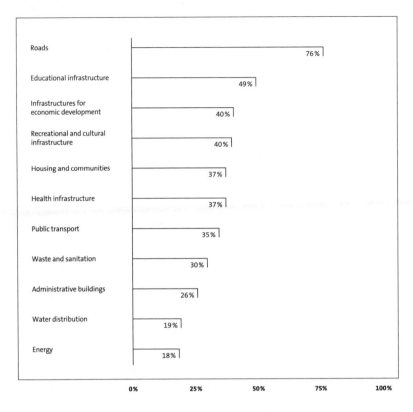

Figure 3.7 **Sectors most affected by funding gaps in SNGs**
Source: OECD (2015d)

nificant improvement in infrastructure productivity (see Chapters 4 and 5 in this Report).

Clearly, some governance challenges are more specific to SNGs, which by their nature are inherently fragmented and diverse in their management capacities and resources. Coordination across levels of government for effective infrastructure investment is necessary but difficult in practice. Many SNGs, in particular small jurisdictions, lack the capabilities to design and run infrastructure investment. In 2014, the OECD adopted a 'Recommendation of the Council on Effective Public Investment Across Levels of Government', which focuses on multi-level governance challenges and ways to overcome them (see OECD 2014d). The results of the OECD–CoR survey provide a comprehensive picture of the governance challenges reported by SNGs (see Figure 3.8) as well as the practices that were reported as effective solutions.

While the challenges are numerous, the results of the survey show that many SNGs are implementing a panoply of strategies to improve the management of infrastructure investments (see Figure 3.9). Improved medium-term planning, external support for designing projects, and improved cooperation with neighbouring SNGs were reported as the most important practices by all categories of SNGs. When looking in more detail, slight variations across SNGs may be observed. Small municipalities see external support for designing infrastructure strategies and simplification of procurement as the most important practices, while 70 per cent of large municipalities–with more than 50,000 inhabitants–have a greater interest in increased stakeholder engagement. Regions emphasised increased external support for designing infrastructure strategies and more rigorous selection criteria for investment projects.

Below we explore the issues flagged by SNGs as top challenges and ways to address them, in particular by i) better designing and planning infrastructure using a long-term perspective; ii) better coordinating across levels of government, jurisdictions, and infrastructure sectors; iii) improving performance monitoring and evaluation; and iv) improving framework conditions, notably regulatory and procurement frameworks.

Designing and planning infrastructure using a long-term perspective

The lack of capacity to adequately design and plan infrastructure investment using a long-term perspective was seen as a key challenge by the majority of survey respondents. Two-thirds of SNGs reported that the capacity to design long-term infrastructure strategies was lacking in their locality. A dearth of sufficient in-house expertise to design infrastructure projects, perceived by 56 per cent of SNGs, especially small municipalities and inter-municipal structures, hinders their ability to turn strategies into viable projects. Furthermore, although ex ante appraisals, analyses, and tools such as cost-benefit analysis, environmental impact assessment, and territorial impact assessment had been implemented, two-thirds of SNGs lamented that results were not consistently used in decision-making. A similar proportion of SNGs reported failure to take into account the full life cycle of infrastructure investment when designing projects, a lapse that most often leads to fiasco (see Chapter 4 for selected cases). Finally, two-thirds of respondents reported insufficient or inadequate involvement of civil society representatives, citizens, and non-governmental organisations in the choice of infrastructure projects as a challenge, with one-quarter of respondents considering this a major challenge that can lead to acceptance and support problems.

Improvements in multi-year planning for infrastructure investment were considered by all categories of SNGs as the most important practices for improving the governance of investment. In-depth multi-year planning of subnational investments is especially essential for improving outcomes.

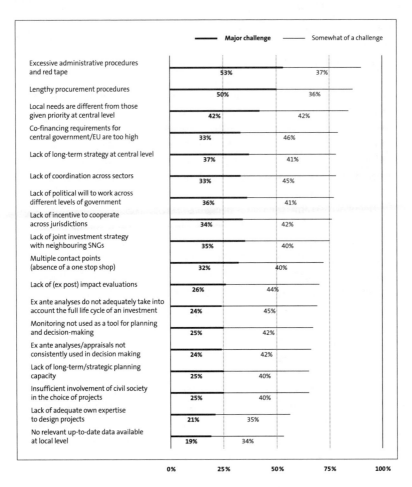

Figure 3.8 **Main challenges perceived by SNGs with respect to strategic planning and implementation of infrastructure investment**
Source: OECD (2015d)

This approach has been used extensively in New Zealand, where all SNGs are required to adopt plans that lay out spending and investment intentions for the coming 10 years. The plans are designed to ensure that investment decisions by SNGs are integrated and linked to each community's desired outcomes. France now recommends that SNGs use multi-annual investment plans more systematically.

A comprehensive, multi-year view of costs, benefits, and risks is also important, but the survey results show the challenges in obtaining such a view. Increasingly, this means evaluating value for money and the combination of quality, features, and price over the life cycle of an investment (OECD 2008). Comprehensiveness also means a broad view of benefits and

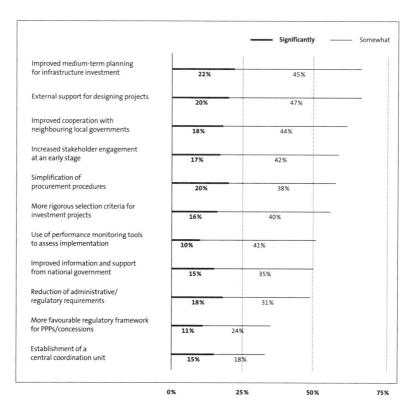

Figure 3.9 **Practices that help the management of infrastructure investment in SNGs**
Source: OECD (2015d)

costs, including 'accounting for the benefits if new infrastructure generates cross-jurisdictional spillovers' (Sutherland et al. 2009: 19). It is also essential to construct a detailed analysis of long-term costs entailed by each option. Toward this end, the London Infrastructure Plan 2050, for instance, aims to improve infrastructure planning and delivery through systemic assessment of needs and consideration of different types of infrastructure, as well as their total cost and possible methods of funding and financing.

While growth objectives are crucial, an exclusive focus on growth may overlook important social or environmental costs or benefits of an investment. Governments should assess different types of risks and uncertainty associated with public investment, including those pertinent to a particular region or locality, as part of an appraisal. In the Australian state of Victoria, for example, strong ex ante monitoring mechanisms are in place, especially through an innovative High Value High Risk (HVHR) process that is used for investments with values above a defined threshold or for those that entail high risk. Under the HVHR process introduced in 2010, such investment projects undergo rigorous scrutiny and approval processes, with increased oversight over various stages of investment development, procurement, and delivery. The process also includes the development of performance indicators that serve as the basis for monitoring infrastructure performance after implementation (OECD 2015a).

Involving private and public actors in planning as well as later stages of public investments can have substantial benefits, such as reduced costs, better decisions, and greater support for projects. The involvement of civil society and businesses may also lead to precious information gains. For instance, the London Infrastructure Plan 2050 was elaborated in an inclusive way with involvement and feedback from businesses, government, and infrastructure providers. In Germany, the decision to build a new runway at Frankfurt Airport was accompanied by a mediation process initiated by the state government of Hesse with the goal of reconciling concerns about noise and other environmental impacts with the economic case for the new runway. The process was initiated prior to the decision to build the runway and included extensive consultations with project proponents and opponents. Most recommendations made by the mediators were implemented in the planning process, and after the end of the mediation process, a regional forum contributed to the dialogue among stakeholders until the planning process was completed and construction had started (OECD 2014a).

Coordinating across levels of government, jurisdictions, and infrastructure sectors

Another set of key challenges reported by more than three-quarters of SNGs relates to coordination across levels of government, jurisdictions, and infrastructure sectors. This finding among SNGs echoes the opinion of specialists responding to the Hertie School–OECD expert survey (see Chapter 2) who considered all three types of coordination to be among the main challenges to infrastructure planning and management.

Vertical coordination among levels of governments

The results of the OECD–CoR survey confirm that challenges in vertical coordination between SNGs and national governments are prominent. The most common vertical coordination challenge, mentioned by 84 per cent of SNGs, is a mismatch between local or regional needs and those given priority at the national level. This is particularly marked for large SNGs: regions, counties, and metropolitan areas with more than 500,000 inhabitants. Furthermore, the lack of long-term infrastructure strategy at the national level was reported by 78 per cent of respondents as a challenge, and by 37 per cent as a major one. It is particularly problematic for regions and small municipalities. Added to these challenges is a lack of political will or administrative culture needed to work across different levels of government–particularly noticeable for inter-municipal structures, possibly because this type of structure tends to be weaker from a political perspective, especially when not elected, thus reducing the will to cooperate.

Coordination between levels of governments is needed to reduce asymmetries of information regarding investments, help reduce funding gaps, and ensure alignment of strategic priorities for infrastructure development. Platforms for vertical coordination have been established in several OECD member states, in particular federal countries. In Australia, for instance, the independent statutory authority Infrastructure Australia works with sub-federal states, territories, local governments, and the private sector on the basis of rigorous cost-benefit analysis to identify investment priorities and the policy and regulatory reforms necessary to enable timely and coordinated delivery of national infrastructure investment. It also advises Australian subnational governments on how to manage infrastructure gaps and bottlenecks that hinder economic growth (see Chapter 2 for more on Infrastructure Australia). In Canada, the federal government is represented in the provinces via structures such as regional federal councils and regional development agencies, whose interests lie not only in representing the federal, or national, government's priorities in the provinces but also in conveying provincial preferences to the federal authorities. The result is tripartite agreements, i.e. formal contractual arrangements among federal, provincial, and local authorities that support the implementation of infrastructure policies. In France, territorial strategies are formalised as contractual arrangements across levels of government through state-region planning contracts (*contrat de plan État-région*) that stipulate co-decision and co-financing of interventions.

Horizontal cooperation for economies of scale

Though the potential benefits of coordination across jurisdictions may seem obvious, this type of coordination was perceived as a significant challenge by most SNGs surveyed. More than three-quarters of SNGs reported the absence of a joint investment strategy with neighbouring cities or regions. Nearly the same percentage of SNGs considered the lack of incentives, including financial, to cooperate across jurisdictions to also be a problem.

Horizontal cooperation between SNGs is critical for reaching economies of scale, in particular through the pooling of some infrastructure investments. Moreover, horizontal coordination allows SNGs to share information about their current and forthcoming investments and may help limit problems linked to duplication of investments. Such coordination may take place in dialogue platforms, through the consolidation of several SNGs' plans, or through financial incentives from the national government. For instance, Switzerland relies on three major mechanisms to promote cooperation across regions: cantonal conferences, inter-cantonal agreements, and cross-border cooperation. The federal government provides up to 500,000 Swiss francs annually over three to six years for innovative multi-jurisdiction projects (OECD 2014b).

Horizontal cooperation may also imply the mutualisation of capital funding toward facilitating access to finance. In several countries, local government funding agencies have been created to pool the borrowing needs of local authorities and to issue bonds in capital markets. The Scandinavian countries and the Netherlands have had funding agencies for a long time, and the trend is quickly spreading across other parts of Europe. In France, a local government funding agency (*Agence France Locale*) was created in December 2013 to raise cost-efficient resources in capital markets by pooling together the funding needs of its members. New Zealand has established a Local Government Funding Agency as a debt vehicle that raises bonds on the local and international markets. Discussion is underway in Australia as well. Such agencies may also contribute to strengthening local capacities. For example, the Swedish Kommuninvest also operates as a knowledge hub, providing research, advice, and training for local authorities.

Coordinating investments across several sectors

SNGs experience various types of difficulties linked to different forms of coordination, e.g. between levels of government, jurisdictions, or infrastructure sectors. One-third of SNGs consider the lack of coordination between sectors, e.g. between transportation, housing, broadband, water, and spatial planning, as a major challenge. For another 45 per cent, it is 'somewhat a challenge'. This is particularly the case for large SNGs. When infrastructure investments are planned while taking into account other sectors, complementarities that may save time and financial resources can be exploited.

Cross-sectoral infrastructure investment is challenging but, when implemented correctly, may be a major source of economies of scale and can avoid duplication costs. Many OECD countries seek to enhance coordination across sectors for investments through the use of broad strategic investment plans, financial incentives, or specific contracts for cross-sectoral investments. In Austria, for instance, integrated territorial strategies for public investment are key instruments to encourage cross-sectoral coordination and multi-year planning.[6]

Performance monitoring and evaluation

Monitoring and evaluation are crucial but often neglected elements of any strategic or project process. Unfortunately, even when monitoring systems exist, they are frequently pursued as administrative exercises, as opposed to tools for planning and decision-making, as reported by 66 per cent of SNGs surveyed. In the case of ex post impact evaluations of infrastructure projects, the challenge seems even greater. A majority of respondents–71 per cent–reported the lack of ex post impact evaluations as a challenge, and for 32 per cent it was reported as a major problem. However, only 19 per cent of small municipalities cited the lack of ex post evaluations as a challenge, possibly due to the fact that evaluation of large projects is more complex.

Previous OECD work has also identified the lack of ex post evaluation as a challenge, including at the national level (OECD 2011). For example, in the United States, the absence of ex post evaluation was identified as a major challenge for the implementation of the investment recovery programme in 2008–9. The only requirement for performance monitoring was based on inputs, such as kilometres of roadway or level of expenditures, rather than outcomes or long-term objectives (US GAO 2010). Ex post evaluations are clearly lacking in the majority of OECD countries. In the United Kingdom, the Parliament's Public Accounts Committee and the National Audit Office recently criticised the Department for Transport for its lack of ex post evaluation, especially for rail projects (Finch 2015).

Careful monitoring of infrastructure investments not only helps track progress but also contributes to decision-making regarding the direction of current as well as future projects. However, as the OECD–CoR survey shows, many SNGs face difficulties in conducting proper monitoring and consider it to be an administrative burden. In order to harness the productive value of information gained through monitoring and evaluation, governments should produce information that is timely, relevant, and actionable and should use it in a meaningful way (OECD 2014d).

In Spain, the region of Galicia participated in a European Commission pilot project based on using outputs and outcomes indicators as a central mechanism for managing public investment funded by the EU. Certain principles of performance budgeting were implemented by the regional government in order to use the outputs and outcomes as input for 2013 budget negotiations. The ultimate goal was to reorient the management of public investment toward results as opposed to expenditures (Hulbert 2012). In Italy, the Basilicata region has a Public Investment Evaluation Unit within the Department for Structural Funds that is responsible for monitoring and evaluating all public investments in the region, checking the consistency of strategic projects with respect to the regional development and annual financial plans, and performing impact evaluations of public investment projects on employment and production.

As noted above, ex post evaluations are crucial for assessing the outcomes of infrastructure investment, but such evaluations remain a challenge for SNGs. Where physical infrastructure is concerned, the primary task is to identify real economic impacts.

Regulatory and procurement frameworks

The large majority of SNGs respondents–90 per cent–considered excessive administrative procedures and red tape to be a challenge, and for more than half of the respondents, a major one. The existence of lengthy procurement procedures and the delays caused by such systems also ranked high among the hurdles faced by SNGs in implementing infrastructure projects. Furthermore, the existence of multiple contact points for completing these administrative procedures was seen as a problem by three-quarters of SNGs.

Even when procurement rules are set at the national level, SNGs have a role in facilitating their implementation. Collaborative procurement across levels of government, e.g. purchasing alliances, networks, framework agreements, and central purchasing bodies, can also help improve procurement capacity. For example, in France, many SNGs are seeking to reach economies of scale through the creation of agencies that regroup their purchases (Cour des Comptes 2015). In 2014, several regions–including Aquitaine, Centre-Val de Loire, Lorraine, Île-de-France, Pays de la Loire, and Rhône-Alpes–created an association to pool their purchases related to information systems. The central purchasing body can support the local level with market analysis, procurement strategy, and negotiation of framework contracts with economic operators. This ensures coverage of, for example, the costs of storage and logistics involved in purchasing goods, an often overlooked problem at the subnational level. SNGs can also seek to develop electronic procurement. For instance, Galicia, in Spain, has developed a web platform for public procurement procedures for all public entities, including municipalities.

In most unitary countries, regulatory frameworks are established at the national level, whereas in federal countries they may be imposed at the sub-federal state or provincial level. However, even when frameworks are designed at the national level, SNGs should be involved in setting up these conditions, for example through regular consultation of new norms that may impact SNGs. Regulatory coherence is of particular importance in infrastructure sectors such as energy, ICT, and water, owing to the greater degree of regulation to which such activities are typically subjected (OECD 2015b). Even relatively basic public works projects may be impeded by a lack of regulatory clarity or coherence. In Australia, through the Council of Australian Governments, governments agreed to revise their regulatory impact assessment procedures to consider whether an existing regulatory model outside their jurisdiction would efficiently address a policy issue in question and whether a nationally uniform, harmonised, or jurisdiction-specific model would be best for the community.

Improved Subnational Governance of Infrastructure Investment Matters for Growth and Well-being

The results of the OECD–CoR survey have allowed for the elaboration of indicators to measure the degree of governance challenges faced by SNGs (see Chapter 7 for a similar effort based on the Hertie School–OECD expert survey). These indicators are based on 20 variables related to the governance challenges cited by survey respondents, from the design of strategic planning to the implementation and monitoring of infrastructure investment projects (for more details see OECD 2015a). Final scores summing the responses of each respondent are based on a total of 100 points. A high final score is associated with a lower degree of perceived challenges and a more effective governance of infrastructure investment.[7]

Final scores summing the responses of respondents range from 6 to 86. The average score of the 255 SNGs surveyed is 39.3. For the entire EU, 16 per cent of SNGs surveyed have a very high score; 30 per cent a high, above average score; 38 per cent a below average score; and 16 per cent a very low score. Considerable variation occurs within each of the different categories of SNGs, and interestingly, no single category of SNGs emerges as having much better results for governance indicators than others. At the national level, variation across SNGs is also very important: for example, in Germany, 27 per cent of SNGs have a very high score, 40 per cent a high score, 24 per cent a medium score, and 8 per cent a low score.

The governance indicators also allow testing of associations with socioeconomic indicators connected with regional growth and well-being. Regions with the highest scores for the governance indicators experienced higher growth rates over the period of 2001–11. This correlation was made for the 47 SNGs that responded to the OECD–CoR survey at the level of administrative regions or counties and for which data are available (Figure 3.10). Preliminary correlations also show positive relationships between these subnational governance indicators and other indicators of access to infrastructure such as roads and railways, access to the internet, and better environment in terms of air quality. The governance indicators for the administrative regions surveyed also appear to be positively associated with indicators of citizens' perceptions about the quality of governance as developed by the University of Gothenburg (Charron, Dijkstra, and Lapuente

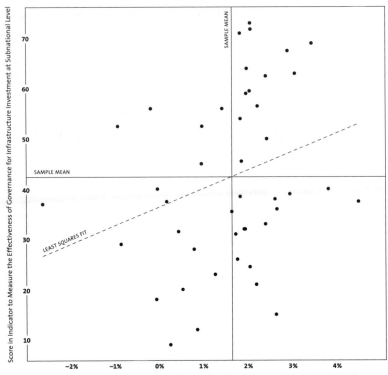

Figure 3.10 **Correlation between governance indicators and regional GDP growth in selected SNGs (2001–2011)**
Note: TL2 and TL3 are regions based on the OECD classification. They correspond to NUTS2 and NUTS3 in the EU.
Source: OECD (2015d).

2015). For the regions covered by both data sets, those with the highest scores for the governance indicators are perceived by citizens as having better public service quality and less corruption.

These results seem to confirm that improving the governance of infrastructure investment at the subnational level could have positive effects that not only imply improved transparency and accountability processes but are also directly connected to overall regional growth and well-being.

Conclusion and Recommendations

This chapter aimed to show that many of the governance and financing challenges for infrastructure investment have specific implications for SNGs, hence the need to focus more systematically on this angle of analysis. Various innovative practices are being put in place to meet the many challenges reported by SNGs and therefore improve the results of infrastructure investment at the subnational level. Such practices need to be shared more broadly to promote learning across SNGs, both within countries and at the international level. In order to implement the 2014 'Recommendation of the Council on Effective Public Investment Across Levels of Government', the OECD developed a toolkit that provides more detailed guidance to policy-makers and includes a set of indicators and good practices (OECD 2015a). In 2015, the OECD also endorsed the 'Governance of Infrastructure Framework', explained in Chapter 5, which identifies a set of preconditions for effective infrastructure investment and provides concrete guidance on the choice of modalities to deliver infrastructure projects (OECD 2015g).

Subnational and national solutions should complement each other to foster effective subnational infrastructure investment. For SNGs, some priorities are to:

- Focus on improving medium-term planning as a top priority and better connect planning and budgeting frameworks to enable a multi-year approach to investment;
- Foster integrated cross-sectoral investment strategies at the local level to benefit from complementarities across sectors;
- Seek to mutualise resources, both financial and human, to invest at the relevant scale and thereby achieve economies of scale;
- Seek to mutualise procurement and develop electronic procurement, in particular in small municipalities and at the metropolitan level;
- Assess operations and maintenance costs of infrastructure investment and plan for future financing;
- Consider the full life cycle of infrastructure investment when designing projects; and
- Better connect monitoring and evaluation to budgeting and policy-making.

In order to promote sound subnational investment, national governments should:

- Encourage the development of medium-term expenditure frameworks at the subnational level and foster greater connection between planning and budgeting;

- Strengthen multi-level governance arrangements to ensure alignment of investment strategies and priorities across national governments and SNGs;
- Provide formal incentives to foster cross-jurisdictional cooperation; and
- Focus on subnational capacity building for infrastructure investment, especially the use of complex financial tools, through a differentiated approach targeting different needs in different types of regions and localities.

Appendix: OECD–CoR Survey of Subnational Governments

The consultation was conducted between 31 March and 15 July 2015 in all official EU languages. To encourage more objective answers, respondents were told that their answers would remain strictly confidential. The survey targeted representatives of subnational governments (SNGs)–that is, regions, provinces, counties, and municipalities–in charge of investment planning, financing, monitoring, and implementation. In total, 295 respondents from all EU countries except Luxembourg participated in the survey. Out of these respondents, 255 are SNGs in the 27 EU member states, i.e. administrative regions, counties, and municipalities–the focus of the analysis in this chapter.

The number of respondents per country was relatively consistent:

- Countries with more than 10 SNG respondents: Germany, Spain, Estonia, Romania, Greece, Austria, Poland, Finland, and Italy.
- Countries with five to 10 respondents: Hungary, UK, Denmark, Portugal, Croatia, France, and Sweden.
- Countries with fewer than five respondents: the Netherlands, Ireland, Czech Republic, Cyprus, Slovakia, Lithuania, Latvia, Belgium, Slovenia, Bulgaria, and Malta.

Although not constructed with a quota system, the responses for the different countries and SNG categories (regions, counties, large municipalities, small municipalities) were relatively balanced, with a slight over-representation of small municipalities: regions and provinces (25 per cent); intermediary entities, e.g. counties and departments (10 per cent); municipalities under 50,000 inhabitants (33 per cent); municipalities between 50,000 and 500,000 inhabitants (22 per cent); large municipalities with more than 500,000 inhabitants (2 per cent); and inter-municipal cooperation structures (8 per cent).

More information on this survey and the methodology used to develop governance indicators is available on the OECD web site: http://www.oecd.org/effective-public-investment-toolkit/oecd-eu-survey.htm

Endnotes

1. The definition of SNGs may differ throughout the chapter since the concept used by the System of National Accounts on which much of the quantitative data is based is slightly different from that used for the OECD-CoR survey. Furthermore,

in countries where counties are not just an administrative entity but also have a political mandate, they are considered to be SNGs.

2   See in particular OECD (2015g) and OECD (2013). A longer version of this chapter will be available as an OECD Working Paper in 2016 (see Allain-Dupré, Hulbert, and Vincent forthcoming).

3   The OECD conducted a survey (OECD 2015d) in cooperation with the EU Committee of the Regions on infrastructure investments at the subnational level in EU countries. The survey targeted representatives of subnational governments (SNGs) in charge of investment and focusing on financing and governance challenges and good practices. For more details see http://www.oecd.org/effective-public-investment-toolkit/oecd-eu-survey.htm.

4   Public-private partnerships (PPPs), which account for less than 10 per cent of public sector infrastructure investment in most OECD countries (Burger and Hawkesworth 2011), are also often not recorded in public investment.

5   The ratio of the gap between subnational revenues and expenditures-to-GDP worsened during 2007 and 2013 in 17 of 33 OECD countries.

6   Since 1971, the Austrian Conference on Spatial Planning (ÖROK) has served as a common platform for spatial planning coordination. It involves all federal ministries, the *Länder*, and the umbrella associations of municipalities and social partners and also manages EU Structural Funds programmes in Austria. Its executive body is chaired by the Federal Chancellor and includes all federal ministers and state governors, the presidents of the Austrian Union of Towns and the Austrian Union of Communities, and the presidents of the social and economic partners as advisors. Decisions are consensus-based. Thematic committees and working groups, formed by senior officials of the territorial authorities and social and economic partners, were set up at the administrative level to achieve ÖROK's tasks and projects.

7   The results of this exploration should be considered with a clear understanding of the potential caveats, since these indicators are based on perceptions. Like all surveys based on perceptions, it makes the problem of endogeneity unavoidable when linking institutional quality to performance (Rodríguez-Pose 2010; Ugur 2010).

IV. Infrastructure Project Delivery and Implementation
Risk Management Across a Project's Life Cycle

GENIA KOSTKA

Although previous chapters in the Report have pointed to declining levels of investment on average among OECD countries, an infrastructure investment boom seems to be underway in many parts of the world. According to PricewaterhouseCoopers (PwC 2014), nearly US$78 trillion will be spent globally on infrastructure between 2014 and 2025. McKinsey & Company has estimated that 9,100 infrastructure projects comprising over US$1 billion in volume are currently in the pipeline worldwide (Beckers et al. 2013). In the wake of the 2008 financial crisis, many western nations committed to massive new infrastructure projects as stimulus investments despite skyrocketing national debt levels (Flyvbjerg 2009). In Canada, for instance, infrastructure spending rose from 2.5 per cent of GDP during 2000–6 to 3.3 per cent during 2007–12 (The Economist 2015), an increase partly triggered by low interest rates and spare capacity in the construction industry. New investments are also on the rise in many emerging economies. According to PwC (2014), close to 60 per cent of global infrastructure spending will be in the Asia-Pacific market alone by 2025, as the region is still saddled with deficient infrastructure despite becoming the world's growth engine. For instance, India's recent Five Year Plan (2012–17) targets new infrastructure investments of US$1 trillion (Teo 2015).

Despite the apparent investment boom in many countries and regions, policy-makers in the European Union and many other advanced economies also face large backlogs of sorely needed infrastructure upgrades. In the United States, bridges are on average 42 years old; dams, 52 years old. In Germany, every third bridge is more than 100 years old (The Economist 2015). European Union member states invested less than €400 billion in infrastructure in 2013: a decline of 11 per cent compared to infrastructure investments in 2010 (Ammermann 2015). In view of this gap between actual investment and the amount of investment reportedly needed to maintain economic competitiveness by international standards, the European Commission introduced the European Fund for Strategic Investments (EFSI), an ambitious plan to attract €240 billion in private investment in infrastructure between 2015 and 2017 (European Commission 2014a).[1]

Table 4.1 **The life cycle of an infrastructure project**

Project Phase	Description
Selection, planning, and design	Public purpose, strategy, design, budget, and implementation time frame are defined. Forecasting feeds into the process.
Procurement and contract design	The legal basis is established, and tasks including project management, construction, and operation and maintenance are allocated. Partnerships between private and public stakeholders are often established via tendering processes.
Construction delivery	Engineering and construction contractors take over responsibility for the project until its final delivery.
Asset operation and maintenance	The project's functioning is sustained via operation and maintenance until decommissioning.

Source: Beckers et al. 2013

To capture the benefits of infrastructure spending, improved project delivery is necessary. Delivery of such projects often falls short because risks are systematically underestimated while benefits are overestimated (Flyvbjerg 2014). As noted already in Chapter 1, Flyvbjerg, Bruzelius, and Rothengatter's study (2003) of 258 transport infrastructure projects in 20 countries found that nine out of ten large-scale infrastructure projects faced significant time delays and cost overruns, while benefit shortfalls of more than 50 per cent were not unusual. A recent study covering 165 large infrastructure projects in Germany found that the average cost overrun per project was 52 per cent (Kostka and Anzinger 2016a). As a result of such delivery problems, many fiscally constrained countries risk a spiral of slow growth and accumulating debt levels. McKinsey has estimated that a lack of sufficient risk management of large infrastructure projects may lead to direct value losses of US$1.5 trillion globally between 2013 and 2018 (Beckers et al. 2013). Good governance is crucial for on budget, on time, and sustainable delivery of large infrastructure projects, as well as for fiscal responsibility of large public funds locked in such investments.

Improving the governance of large infrastructure projects is not a straightforward task. It requires understanding the nature of the problem as well as typical pitfalls in order to find solutions. What constitutes good governance of infrastructure, and how can policymakers improve the delivery performance of large infrastructure projects? How can the delivery process be improved to systematically address cost and time issues as well as other political obstacles while still ensuring high quality? One starting point is to understand governance issues systemically across the life cycle of projects (Beckers et al. 2013; Miller and Hobbs 2005; OECD 2015g).

Life cycle analysis

Large infrastructure projects are typically difficult to manage. Their long-term nature and large numbers of stakeholders–often with conflicting agendas–only increase uncertainty and risk. Considering also the overall complexity of large infrastructure projects, a systematic and forward-looking risk analysis can significantly improve project delivery. This chapter proposes a state-of-the-art life cycle-based approach to risk management that is adaptable to changing circumstances and intended to evolve throughout four project phases: planning, procurement, construction, and operation and maintenance (Beckers et al. 2013). A life cycle approach can help to systematically understand risks in all stages of the value chain by tracking risks and management challenges throughout the entire life of a project (Beckers et al. 2013).

Case selection

This chapter summarises common pitfalls and best practices in each of the four project life cycle phases and with a particular focus on governance issues. While the case studies below (see Table 4.2 for a summary) were chosen in order to illustrate typical problems and potential solutions related to each individual phase, the analysis will show that choices and actions in one phase inevitably affect infrastructure delivery throughout the life cycle.

Project Phase 1: Selection, Planning, and Design

The first phase of a project's life cycle involves questions regarding purpose, design, budget, and time frame of implementation, which are usually based on forecasts. An especially important task is for project planners to identify, assess, and quantify the risks that a project will be exposed to across its life cycle (Beckers et al. 2013). This initial planning phase is also an opportunity to introduce the project to the public and essentially sets up the framework for future decision-making processes.

Common pitfalls

The planning phase of large infrastructure projects is particularly challenging. Among the mistakes that typically lead to significant delays and cost overruns in infrastructure projects, those made in the planning phase weigh most

Table 4.2 **Case studies examined across the four major project life cycle phases**

Phase	Case Study	Performance	Key Governance Issues
Selection, planning, and design	BER Airport, Germany	−	• Insufficient planning in detail prior to the contracting and construction phases • Failure to appoint a general contractor, leading to faulty risk allocation during construction • Insufficient supervision and expertise deficiencies
	Laibin B Power Project, China	+	• Sufficient risk allocation and an appropriate governance setup • An open and competitive bidding process • Consistent support from relevant authorities
Procurement and contract design	Elbe Philharmonic Hall, Germany	−	• Inappropriate governance setup, leading to poor management decisions • Insufficient planning, resulting in ad hoc contractual design and additional costs
	Phu My 2.2 Power Plant, Vietnam	+	• An efficient bidding process, competitive pricing, and partial risk guarantees
	AVUS A115 Highway, Germany	+	• An innovative penalty and reward system to incentivise good planning
Construction delivery	Nordsee Ost Offshore Wind Park, Germany	−	• Interface complexity between grid connection and park construction • Complications related to pioneer technology at an early stage of development
	La Yesca Hydroelectric Power Plant, Mexico	+	• Comprehensive project life cycle management • State-of-the-art monitoring and performance assessment techniques • Risk management that allowed for optimal contractor selection and supervision
Asset operation and maintenance	St. Pauli Elbe Tunnel, Germany	−	• Insufficient institutional knowledge about asset maintenance needs
	Panama Canal, Panama	+	• Governance reform through corporatisation for operational independence • A holistic operation and maintenance strategy

heavily. When project size increases, the likelihood of stakeholder fragmentation, conflicts of interest, and coordination and complex interdependency problems also increase, and decision-making and comprehensive planning become more complicated (Aaltonen and Kujala 2010; Van de Graaf and Sovacool 2014; see also Chapter 2). Risks are often insufficiently allocated across a project's life cycle, leaving planners and managers with little ability to detect miscalculations during subsequent phases. During competitive bidding processes, for example, bidders have an incentive to overestimate benefits while underestimating risk factors in order to win contracts (Flyvbjerg 2009, 2014; Flyvbjerg, Bruzelius, and Rothengatter 2003). Yet without comprehensive planning, public entities cannot crosscheck the cost and time feasibilities of proposals. Another common pitfall is a so-called uniqueness bias that prevents learning from other, potentially similar projects due to the desire for a unique design (Budzier and Flyvbjerg 2013; Flyvbjerg 2014).

Project outcomes are also hampered when planning processes are incomplete, typically leading to rent-seeking behaviour, principal-agent problems, and contested information when large amounts of money are at stake (Eisenhardt 1989; Flyvbjerg, Garbuio, and Lovallo 2009; Stiglitz 1987). For the construction of the Berlin Brandenburg (BER) Airport in Germany (see Case Study 1), premature tendering and contracting resulted in the need to manage the planning and execution phases simultaneously. As a consequence, the project spiralled out of control: coordination flaws, frequent change requests, and planning mistakes multiplied, and the supervisory board lacked the capacity to regain control over the project.

Faulty project governance arrangements often result from a combination of expertise deficiencies and insufficient supervision. Early in the run-up phase of projects, inexperienced planners and managers, unwilling to rely on established processes and organisational forms, often lose control over projects but hide poor performances (Kostka and Fiedler 2016). In the case of the BER airport, the failure to appoint a general contractor led to assumption of that role by the state-owned enterprise that, while experienced in airport operation and maintenance, was wholly inexperienced in construction and therefore completely overwhelmed with managing the multitude of tenders. Without existing construction expertise, the airport's supervisory and control bodies lacked the knowledge to detect bad performance and scrutinise project developments, and purchasing missing skills externally only increased complexity. The combination of a lack of adequate planning and insufficient supervision has set the delivery date back by at least four years and increased costs by a projected €2.5 billion.

Case Study 1 **Berlin Brandenburg (BER) Airport, Berlin, Germany**
Insufficient planning, faulty risk allocation, and lack of supervision

After reunification in 1990, the federal German government and the states of Berlin and Brandenburg decided in 1996 to develop a new airport that would eventually replace two older ones. Now already more than four years behind schedule, with projected costs almost double the initial amount, Berlin's flagship transport infrastructure project has become a high profile failure.

Insufficient planning prior to the contracting and construction phases: Planners gave in to political pressure from government authorities and, in order to target unrealistic completion and opening dates, started the complicated tendering processes and awarded contracts prematurely. This resulted in the need to continue planning during execution, and frequent change requests and planning mistakes were the consequences.

Failure to appoint a general contractor, leading to faulty risk allocation: Though appointment of a general contractor was foreseen in the original project plan, the state-owned airport development firm, Flughafen Berlin Brandenburg GmbH (FBB), assumed that role instead and was ultimately responsible for coordinating some 50 smaller subcontractors. The lack of a general contractor that would take on the technical and financial risks of implementation and handling the subcontractors in an adequate way left FBB and its government shareholders managing all risks.

Insufficient supervision and expertise deficiencies: The board of the project developer was composed of members who lacked expertise in large infrastructure projects and were therefore unable to adequately scrutinise developments, challenge project management, or exert cost oversight. Furthermore, because the project developer's shareholders provided full debt guarantee, the lenders had no incentive to conduct the processes, e.g. feasibility assessments and contract oversight, usually applied by banks for arm's-length commercial loans. The flow of information was faulty, and independent oversight and transparency were absent. Parliamentarians and the public were mostly kept uninformed.

Source: Fiedler and Wendler (2016)

Best practices

Good planning is indeed possible. Ideally, an infrastructure project should be embedded in a strategy linked to broader development goals (Beckers et al. 2013). Williams and Samset (2010) emphasise the importance of front-end planning, i.e. comprehensive planning from beginning to end before construction starts. In international surveys conducted in 2015, subnational government representatives and infrastructure experts ranked improved comprehensive and medium-term planning processes as most helpful for enhancing the planning and procurement of public infrastructure (see also Chapters 2 and 3). The case studies of the BER airport and the Elbe Philharmonic Hall, a signature building in Hamburg (see Case Study 3), illustrate how early planning mistakes can catalyse inexorable cost spirals. While a more extensive and detailed planning process is costly in itself and does entail the possibility of a project's cancellation, adequate planning can mitigate risks before they occur and avoid expensive ad hoc change requests (Fiedler and Schuster 2016).

McKinsey stresses the importance of professional risk management during early planning (Beckers et al. 2013). Practices can include state-of-the-art forecasting techniques, evaluation of adverse scenarios, stress tests, and the establishment of monitoring processes. One such forecasting technique used to estimate project risks and calculate budget contingencies is reference class forecasting (RCF), first suggested by Kahneman and Tversky (1979). With RCF, planners place the proposed project in a statistical distribution within a set of similar, already completed projects and choose a level of security, e.g. a factor of risk aversion, from which a contingency sum can be calculated.

Expertise and private sector knowledge should also be included in both the coordination and supervision of projects at an early stage (Flyvbjerg 2014). According to the Global Expert Survey on Public Infrastructure conducted for this Report, infrastructure experts ranked 'reliance on experienced project coordinators' as most helpful for improving the construction and monitoring of public infrastructure (see Chapters 2 and 7 for additional survey results). In many cases, supervisory bodies, including those for the BER airport and the Elbe Philharmonic Hall, lack experts with first-hand experience in designing large projects (Kostka and Fiedler 2016). Without expertise, it is difficult to assess the credibility of plans and cost estimates, or to efficiently and effectively run and control projects. Supervisory bodies need to be staffed with experts in the project matter. Aside from possibly knowledgeable civil servants, this mainly means the inclusion of private sector knowledge at the highest level of project management—whether through consulting contracts, officially recognised honorary work, or the informal participation of experts, who ideally would understand the mechanics and constraints of the public sector and be able to roam freely between the pro-

Case Study 2 **Laibin B Power Project, Guangxi Province, China**
An appropriate governance set-up, enabling sufficient allocation of risks

---

Laibin B is a 720-MW coal-fired power plant, initiated in 1996 with the intention to attract foreign capital and technology to southwest China. The project involved full foreign ownership by a consortium throughout its life cycle, with an estimated total cost of about US$600 million

Sufficient risk allocation and an appropriate governance setup: Three separate contracts stated the rights and obligations of the project company and of the Guangxi government in regards to the full life cycle of the project. The Guangxi government provided guarantees on power purchase, fuel supply, transportation, and dispatch. The provincial utility and the government had only limited roles in the ownership and operation of the power plant, thereby reducing the risk of conflicts of interest.

An open and competitive bidding process: With both foreign and domestic firms involved, a consortium of Électricité de France and GEC Alsthom (now known as Alstom), financed by creditors such as HSBC, Barclays, and Crédit Agricole Indosuez, won the concession contract, which mandated a tight completion schedule at a regulated rate of return.

Consistent support from relevant authorities: Laibin B was approved at the State Council level, with the active participation and full backing of the State Planning Commission and the Ministry of Power Industry, especially during the project's planning and contracting phases. Key government ministries issued repeated statements of support to clear up uncertainties and strengthen the provincial government's ability to implement the project.

Sources: Bellier and Zhou (2003); Wang et al. (1998)

---

cess-oriented world of civil service and the solution-oriented private sector (Kostka and Fiedler 2016).

Furthermore, planners should take pre-emptive measures to prevent public opposition as well as potential damage to communities and the environment (GIZ 2015). Such measures include publishing up-to-date information about project progress and involving the public through referendums or auctions, as well as making use of compensation laws that regulate potential externalities (GIZ 2015; Olsen 2010). One initiative to enable better planning is the Major Projects Authority[2] in the United Kingdom, which publishes information about major public projects, including infrastructure, on an annual basis, monitors and evaluates such projects, and has a mandate to intervene if deemed necessary (Her Majesty's Government 2015). The establishment of a comprehensive, detailed, and publicly available database of large-scale infrastructure projects can be a basis for sector-based benchmark analysis and can also allow for a democratic process of public scrutiny.

One example of how good planning can result in a suitable governance set-up and enable appropriate allocation of risk is the Laibin B Power Project (see Case Study 2), China's first state-approved build-operate-transfer (BOT)[3] project. Specific, clear rights and obligations of both the contracted party and the provincial government provided certainty, and an open and competitive bidding process was coupled with strong support from and coordination between key government stakeholders at multiple levels. As a result, the project has been considered a success story in a market that may be especially complicated for foreign enterprises.

Project Phase 2: Procurement and Contract Design

The second life cycle phase follows once all plans about a project's key characteristics have been laid out. If a project is conducted via public procurement, tasks across the life cycle will be allocated to partners through a competitive auction. For a project based on public-private partnership, this phase determines the concession periods, stakeholder responsibilities, and mechanisms for accountability. Contracting establishes the legal basis for smoothly functioning partnerships.

Common pitfalls

Procurement and contract design present distinct challenges as well. If critical steps in the first project phase are missed or botched, those missteps will continue to hamper project delivery during the second phase. For example, failure to select an appropriate project design and ownership structure during the planning phase, e.g. too many subprojects, and missed efforts to quantify risks and returns beforehand will make the procurement phase significantly more challenging (Beckers et al. 2013). But even if planning is sufficiently thorough, planners can still miss critical milestones at this time. The key risk lies in the complexity of the governance structure. With many individual contracts, failure to anticipate interdependencies of complex portfolios may lead to suboptimal risk-return trade-offs (Beckers et al. 2013; Fiedler and Schuster 2016). In the case of the Elbe Philharmonic Hall, the planners chose three governance pillars that were, taken on their own, appropriate for the project: central project management, parallel processing[4], and a forfeiting

> *Case Study 3* **The Elbe Philharmonic Hall, Hamburg, Germany**
> Ad hoc contractual design and inappropriate governance set-up
>
> With construction begun in 2006, the Elbe Philharmonic Hall will be Hamburg's tallest building upon completion, although its date of completion has been delayed until at least 2017. In 2011, construction stopped for over 18 months until the governance set-up was renegotiated.
>
> **Inappropriate governance set-up, leading to bad management decisions:** The city selected a privately run, publicly owned project development agency as the main interface between the architects and the construction company. Little parliamentary or other supervision was incorporated into the governance set-up. An unwieldy coordination effort resulted, leading to the construction firm taking advantage of information asymmetries and a destructive work relationship between the planners and the contractors. To finance construction, the city chose a forfeiting model, whereby the city of Hamburg rather than a private investor (in this case Hochtief) would take the largest share of ownership (see also endnote 5). Though this model promised the city cost savings and greater control over construction and operation, delays in project completion meant that Hamburg had to begin making costly loan interest payments before any revenues had been generated.
>
> **Insufficient planning, resulting in ad hoc contractual design and additional costs:** Early on in the project the city signed a lump sum agreement with the private builder, Hochtief: A single price of €352 million was agreed. This unrealistic agreement stemmed from four major factors: incomplete planning for the design of the building, insufficient risk management, overly ambitious tender schedules, and public pressure. Numerous post-contractual change requests by planners and government actors that led to further coordination challenges altered the entire scope of construction, the heart of the contractual agreement. The unfinished planning status of the project enabled Hochtief to demand additional financial compensation by claiming that the new plans deviated from the initial construction scope.
>
> Source: Fiedler and Schuster (2016)

model[5] (Fiedler and Schuster 2016). However, planners underestimated the interdependencies among the pillars, and there was little outside supervision over the project development agency, resulting in an unmanageable coordination burden (see Case Study 3). A rushed procurement and contract design phase, partly due to the parallel processing approach, resulted in a premature contract with unreasonably low cost assumptions, and a high number of complex change requests increased the scope of the construction and therefore the overall costs. As of mid-2015, the Hall's completion had been delayed by seven years, and estimated costs had risen by 150 per cent. Further factors that can negatively affect the contracting phase are limited transparency of cost and risk ownership and leadership voids. The latter can result, for example, from frequent changes among top management actors and insufficient expertise on the supervisory board, as in the BER airport project (Case Study 1; Fiedler and Schuster 2016; Fiedler and Wendler 2016; Flyvbjerg 2014).

Best practices

In the planning phase prior to procurement, focus on customised design and ownership structures can ensure optimal risk-ownership allocation (Beckers et al. 2013; OECD 2015g). Then, the key milestone in the procurement and contract design phase is to align financing sources with expected cash flows (Beckers et al. 2013). For example, in order to ensure the feasibility of a build-operate-transfer (BOT) scheme, Vietnam's Phu My 2.2 Power Project needed a competitive financing structure of private lenders. Through the project's efficient, open, and competitive bidding process, which was supplemented by partial risk guarantees from the World Bank, a sufficient finance structure was ensured throughout the project's life cycle (Matsukawa and Habeck 2007; see Case Study 4).

Relationships between contractors and clients should be carefully managed both before and during the procurement and contract design phase. In addition to due diligence with contractors before selection (Flyvbjerg 2013), central contract-writing units at the regional or national levels can establish more balanced power relationships between contractors and clients (Flyvbjerg 2009). Proper risk allocation and the allocation of clear responsibilities and decision-making in the design of procurement can offer incentives for experts to scrutinise projects and for construction firms to ensure on-budget and on-time delivery (Miller and Hobbs 2005). Penalties and rewards may (dis)incentivise project planners to improve forecasting accuracy (Flyvbjerg 2014; Taleb 2007). The AVUS A115 highway project in Berlin, Germany employed an innovative bonus-malus scheme that entailed financial penalties for the contractor for delays, and rewards for early completion (see Case Study 5). This model led to successful delivery ahead of schedule and below the planned cost. The contracting entity should further anticipate any risks of delays in construction or defaults of contractors and hence mandate that contractors agree on reasonable penalty payments and liability charges in such cases (del Río and Linares 2014).

Contracting often involves competitive auctions and rounds of bidding. The governmental body in charge of a project should ensure the independence of the auctioneer and the contractual partner, as well as low prequalification requirements and easy procedures for reduced barriers to entry (del Río and Linares 2014; Maurer and Barroso 2011). The contracting entity also

Case Study 4 **Phu My 2.2 Power Project, Phu My, Vietnam**
Partial risk guarantee scheme to obtain sufficient funding

A 715-MW natural gas-fuelled power plant, Phu My 2.2 was planned as a 20-year BOT project under a consortium headed by Électricité de France and including Sumitomo and Tokyo Power Co. The first tender was launched in 1997 and Phu My 2.2 began commercial operation in 2005. With projected construction costs of US$480 million, the plant's construction was completed at a cost reduction of approximately 15 per cent.

An efficient bidding process, competitive pricing, and partial risk guarantees: The World Bank Group provided private creditors with partial risk guarantees (PRG), which insured against the risk that the government might fail to meet its payment obligations. Once the project's risk potential was reduced, more private bidders became involved, which in turn enhanced competition.

Sources: Matsukawa and Habeck (2007), Asian Development Bank (2011)

Case Study 5 **AVUS A115 Highway, Berlin, Germany**
Delivery success through an effective incentive scheme

AVUS A115 is a 9km-long city highway around Berlin. Construction was initially scheduled to take place over 30 months, between June 2011 and November 2013. Estimated costs amounted to €28 million and were financed by the city. In the end, the highway was completed in 18 months and at a reduced total cost of €24 million.

An innovative penalty and reward system to incentivise good planning: The AVUS A115 project used a simple yet effective bonus-malus scheme: For every day of delay, the construction company had to pay a fine, and for every day that the project was finished before the due date, they gained €20,000. As a result, the company worked long hours and used innovative technology such as specialised asphalt-paving machinery. The construction company made an extra €1 million of profit and finished ahead of schedule with no additional costs for the municipality.

Sources: Senatsverwaltung für Stadtentwicklung und Umwelt (2012), Hauptverband der Deutschen Bauindustrie e.V. (2013)

needs sufficient administrative capacities to carry out the auction effectively and ensure timely issuance of required permits and transparency and fairness of the overall procurement procedure (GIZ 2015). Additionally, the government should provide a high level of information to prevent a so-called winner's curse, in which the value of the auctioned asset is less than the bidder anticipated and, as a result, the winner overpays or has a smaller net gain than expected. If the government provides only limited information about the auctioned asset, the resulting information asymmetries may lead to underestimation of costs and the selection of non-feasible projects (del Río and Linares 2014). Finally, to foster social acceptance of new projects, auctions can facilitate engagement by involving citizens as operators or investors, or by including them in the decision-making process (GIZ 2015). In order to encourage smaller actors and citizen initiatives to join auctioning processes, policymakers can lower barriers for entry by altering prequalification requirements for bidders (GIZ 2015).

Project Phase 3: Construction Delivery

After all stakeholders have been selected and contracts and responsibilities mandated, the third phase of the project life cycle, the actual construction of the asset, takes place.

Common pitfalls

During the construction phase, state-of-the-art risk management is key. It is unlikely, however, that even an optimal construction phase can save a project that was already faulty at the planning and contracting phases: the previously determined governance set-up of a project is often a core determinant of (un)successful construction outcomes. For example, in the case of the Nordsee Ost offshore wind park, located off of the German coast in the North Sea, the division of tasks between the private developer and the regulated transmission system operator led to unclear liabilities that ultimately delayed construction and increased project costs (see Case Study 6).

Typical traps endangering infrastructure projects during the construction phase include governance issues such as a lack of coordination and poor working relationships among key stakeholders, as in the case of the Elbe Philharmonic Hall (Fiedler and Schuster 2016; see Case Study 3), as well as weak leadership, e.g. frequent top management changes and unclear instructions that result in loss of efficiency (Flyvbjerg 2014). A lack of standardised performance measurement can also complicate projects (Beckers et al. 2013). Lastly, there may be gaps between contractual obligations and

Case Study 6 **Nordsee Ost Offshore Wind Park, North Sea, Germany**
Separation of construction tasks complicated technological and financial challenges

In recent years, Germany has generously subsidised offshore wind as part of the country's *Energiewende*, an ambitious plan to increase the share of renewable energy in its electricity mix. Offshore wind parks in Germany typically operate under a 'semi-private' governance set-up in which park construction and energy generation are private, with developers incentivised by feed-in tariffs. Grid connection, on the other hand, is regulated by the government and handled by private transmission system operators (TSOs).

The 295-MW Nordsee Ost offshore wind park began operating in 2015 after being completed 18 months behind schedule and with a 30 per cent cost overrun due to regulatory uncertainty as well as gaps in both the private developer's and the private TSO's abilities to deliver.

Complex interdependencies between grid connection and park construction: The private developer, German utility RWE, and the regulated private TSO, Dutch state-owned TenneT, were faced with very different technological and financial challenges with unclear liabilities and risk allocation. When TenneT experienced shortages that drove the firm to halt construction on grid connections, RWE demanded compensation for foregone revenue. According to RWE, a lack of centralised planning on the part of the German government had created uncertainty in the supply chain and regarding liabilities. After ongoing legal disputes, the Federal Minister of Economics and Technology initiated a meeting of industry and government experts that included members of the Federal Network Agency and the Federal Maritime and Hydrographic Agency and was moderated by the German Offshore Wind Energy Foundation. The resulting 2013 reform established that wind park developers should be compensated for time delays by the TSO with 90 per cent of foregone revenue from electricity generation, an extra cost to be ultimately passed on to consumers by way of surcharges.

Complications related to pioneer technology at an early stage of development: Delays in construction delivery only increased due to the cutting-edge technology being deployed in the North Sea. Both grid connection and park construction faced extraordinary supply chain risks and bottlenecks because of insufficient specialised maritime infrastructure. Planners underestimated that converter platforms and transmission technology required pioneer effort.

Source: Kostka and Anzinger (2016b)

the contracted party's ability to deliver, e.g. insufficient finance, as well as material or personnel shortages. In the Nordsee Ost case, the use of pioneer technology mandated specialised equipment and materials that were in short supply due to underestimation of construction needs, and construction was significantly delayed as a result.

Best practices

The most common pitfalls in project construction are best addressed early on during the planning phase. A flexible governance regime for large infrastructure projects can lead to risk-aware cost engineering and sufficient stakeholder management that mitigates social and environmental risk. Planners should have also already integrated the following into the initial planning phase: a project risk manager with overarching risk responsibility; clear rules for information collection and flow between owner and supplier during construction; and metrics to measure contractor performance, e.g. a detailed schedule with key performance indicators (KPIs) linked to the contract, allowing continuous monitoring (Beckers et al. 2013).

One method to measure performance and allow continuous cost engineering throughout the project life cycle is building information modelling (BIM), a set of tools that can envisage virtual construction of an infrastructure facility prior to physical construction[6]. Among construction projects that had used BIM, 60 per cent reported cost reduction or control, and 34 per cent reported time reduction or control (Bryde, Broquetas, and Volm 2013). The construction of the Shanghai Tower is an example of BIM use for managing costs and achieving high sustainability performance (McGraw-Hill Construction 2010). During planning and construction, BIM assisted with testing more than 20 design options, clarified feasibility and additional costs arising from proposed changes, identified planning clashes, helped coordinate subcontractors, and supported energy analysis–resulting in the use of 32 per cent less materials than a conventional tower (Autodesk 2012).

In addition, milestone payments and contractor compliance monitoring can help manage financial risk and incentivise on-time and on-budget delivery (Beckers et al. 2013). Using such a milestone payment system reduced costs significantly in the construction of the AVUS A115 highway in Berlin (see Case Study 5).

Effective life cycle management of the La Yesca hydroelectric power plant in Mexico entailed detailed planning, regular performance assessments, thorough reporting, and effective contractor supervision (see Case Study 7). While hydroelectric dam projects are usually extremely challenging, with a worldwide average of 2.3 years in time delays and 96 per cent cost overruns, La Yesca was delivered on time and at roughly 55 per cent above planned cost, far less than the average cost overrun (Ansar et al. 2014; Lopez 2013).

Case Study 7 **La Yesca Hydroelectric Power Plant, La Yesca, Mexico**
Successful delivery through comprehensive life cycle management

Construction of the 750-MW La Yesca hydroelectric power plant, part of the hydrological system of the Santiago River at the border of Nayarit and Jalisco states, was sponsored by Mexico's state-owned utility, Comisión Federal de Electricidad, under the country's public works scheme. Construction began in January 2008 and was completed in November 2012 at a final cost of US$1.2 billion.

Comprehensive project life cycle management: Following an open bidding process, the Mexican company ICA was contracted in 2007 to lead a construction consortium that included Promotora e Inversora Adisa, La Península Compañía Constructora, and Constructora de Projectos Hidroeléctricos. The developer ensured relative cost-effectiveness coupled with adherence to social and environmental standards, including regular impact assessments and annual sustainability reports.

State-of-the-art monitoring and performance assessment techniques: Risk management for La Yesca included precise and transparent planning of the construction phases—diversion, containment, power generation, spillway, and other associated works—complemented by the use of standardised integrated management systems. ICA inspectors conducted random monitoring of each phase and process to detect possible deviations and intervene on a timely basis as necessary and documented the results in Agreement, Follow-Up and Closure books.

Risk management that allowed for optimal contractor selection and supervision: The project was monitored externally to increase accountability and public awareness and to reduce the potential for corruption. Transparencia Mexicana, a subsidiary of Transparency International, monitored the call for tender process by contributing to the drafting and reviewing of documents and later attended clarification meetings and visited the construction site as a so-called social witness.

Sources: Verduzco Chávez and Sánchez Bernal (2008), Lopez (2013), Water Integrity Network and Transparency International (2010), ICA (2014)

Project Phase 4: Asset Operation and Maintenance

This is the last phase of a project's life cycle. If the project at hand is a power plant, for example, then the asset operation phase would involve grid connection. More generally, this phase entails getting a newly constructed facility up and running and then keeping it running and maintained over the long term.

Common pitfalls

In this final phase of the project life cycle, mistakes made in earlier phases cannot be corrected easily. Most complications during the operation phase occur for the same reasons that complications arise during the construction phase: for example, insufficient planning, contracting problems, and faulty governance set-ups. If asset operation and maintenance (O&M) has not been previously integrated into a flexible governance regime and a comprehensive risk management strategy, there may be a lack of monitoring of O&M contractors to ensure on-time, on-budget, and high quality service delivery and financing (Beckers et al. 2013). This in turn may result in failure to meet contractually agreed upon performance indicators for service quality or availability, assuming the performance metrics were determined in the first place.

Another pitfall that may not always be considered, especially in maintaining, upgrading, or renovating infrastructure, is the absence of institutional learning and institutional memory. The restoration and renovation of the historic St. Pauli Elbe Tunnel in Hamburg, Germany has gone massively over budget largely due to a lack of knowledge about seemingly straightforward engineering issues: specifically, the maximum load that the tunnel could withstand and the construction material that would be most appropriate to meet conservation standards for an historic landmark (see Case Study 8).

Best practices

The pitfalls most often encountered in the asset operation and maintenance phase are again best addressed much earlier, during the planning and contracting phases. Planners should have already incorporated state-of-the-art techniques and risk management practices for operation. Asset management systems and tools such as real-time reporting, ex ante modelling, and ex post analytics can help O&M actors leverage data for improved O&M decision-making (WEF 2014). Planners should consider outsourcing monitoring to avoid in-

> **Case Study 8 The St. Pauli Elbe Tunnel, Hamburg, Germany**
> Insufficient institutional knowledge to maintain a historic landmark
>
> The 427m St. Pauli Elbe Tunnel, also known as the Old Elbe Tunnel, has been considered a landmark since opening in 1911. Despite the opening of a new tunnel under the Elbe, the St. Pauli Elbe Tunnel remains a highly trafficked passenger link that in 2012 was still used by 750,000 pedestrians, 100,000 cyclists and 120,000 vehicles. Although the tunnel has been continually modernised for decades, a five-phase restoration project was launched in 1994. As of mid-2014, the project was expected to cost nearly €100 million, in comparison to an initial forecast of €15-17 million and a revised estimate of €31 million in 2013. Completion has already been delayed by at least five years.
>
> **Insufficient institutional knowledge about asset maintenance needs:** Restoration activities increased steadily in both scope and complexity—resulting in higher costs and more time than initially planned—because original estimates were based on cursory spot checks that did not show the full extent of leakage and damage to the tunnel, or necessarily take into account conservation regulations. A lack of specialised knowledge of statics and a lack of awareness of the original construction's properties have continued to result in frequent changes to the project.
>
> Sources: Hamburg Port Authority (2013), Spiegel Online (2014), Hamburger Abendblatt (2014)

house manipulation and make available the option of replacing unsuccessful contractors (Beckers et al. 2013), while outsourcing operations and maintenance activities themselves may significantly reduce costs (WEF 2014).

The need for thorough planning does not end after asset delivery. In the case of the Panama Canal (see Case Study 9), central corporate planning efforts target not only measures of financial performance but also human resource, client experience, and operations metrics to drive efficiency (WEF 2014).

Case Study 9 **Panama Canal, Panama**
Enabling best practices in operations and maintenance through strategic governance reform

Since 1914, more than one million vessels have passed through the 80km Panama Canal. Approximately five per cent of the world's cargo is transported through the Canal, which is operated and maintained by Autoridad del Canal de Panamá (ACP, or the Panama Canal Authority), an autonomous government agency. After handover from the United States in 1999, the Government of Panama strategically developed the ACP as a commercial canal operator and established optimal enabling factors for effective O&M.

Governance reform through corporatisation for operational independence: Instead of privatisation, the Government of Panama chose to corporatise the ACP, which is now a legal entity under government ownership but with independent assets, finances, and operations. The ACP has remained accountable to the public, while taking advantage of private sector practices such as emphases on efficiency and productivity; streamlined, state-of-the-art financial management processes; and independent, qualified leaders selected on the basis of competence. As a result, the ACP is able to plan on a long-term basis without political interference, while the government receives profits totalling eight per cent of its budget.

A holistic O&M strategy: On the operations side, the ACP maximises asset utility, having reduced the average transit time from 27 hours in 1999 to 24 hours, decreased total costs, and expanded into ancillary services. The maintenance side appears to be no less important and is a key component in planning and procurement processes. The standardisation of O&M processes, significant investments in systematic upgrades, and detailed planning for overhauls—a full year before the scheduled start—embedded within a comprehensive maintenance schedule have reduced the amount of time needed to complete repairs while extending the life of the Canal.

Source: WEF (2014)

3 Key governance challenges and solutions according to the project life cycle approach

Phase	Challenges	Solutions
Planning	• Larger project sizes, increasing complexity and the likelihood of conflicts of interest • Incomplete front-end planning and insufficient risk management • Uniqueness bias and optimism bias • Rent-seeking behaviour, principal-agent problems, and contested information • Expertise deficiencies and insufficient supervision • Lack of commitment and leadership beyond political election cycles	• Linking projects to development goals and/or national strategies • Comprehensive front-end planning processes • Reference class forecasting (RCF) • Evaluation of adverse scenarios, stress tests, and establishment of monitoring processes • Experts, including those from the private sector, on supervisory boards • Comprehensive, up-to-date, and publicly available information • Public auctions and referendums, and use of compensation laws • Optimal, tailored governance set-ups • Public planning units for monitoring large projects • Impact assessments
Procurement	• Overly complex or inappropriate governance set-ups, leading to bad management decisions • Complex interdependencies between contracts • Insufficient planning, rushed contractual design, and/or poor risk allocation • Limited transparency of cost and risk ownership • Leadership voids	• Open and competitive bidding processes • Consistent support from authorities • Appropriate financing tools, e.g. partial risk guarantees (PRG) • Public contract-writing units • Clear allocation of responsibilities and decision-making powers • Stage-specific contracts, including rewards and penalties for performance, e.g. bonus-malus schemes • Sufficient government administrative capacity, independent actors, low barriers to entry, and a high level of information • Citizen involvement

Phase	Challenges	Solutions
Construction	• Lack of coordination and/or poor working relationships among key stakeholders • Weak management and conflicting instructions • Lack of standardised performance measurement • Gaps between contractual obligations and contractors' abilities to deliver • Complex interdependencies between contracts and/or firms	• A flexible governance regime • Appointment of an overarching risk manager • Clear rules for information flow • Standardised performance measurement, e.g. KPIs • Continuous cost engineering, e.g. via Building Information Modelling (BIM) • Milestone payments and contractor compliance monitoring • An independent coordination office to facilitate communication between stakeholders
Maintenance	• Lack of monitoring of operation and maintenance contractors • Contractual default risk • Insufficient institutional learning and memory • Lack of performance measurement for service quality • Lack of coordination with external stakeholders	• Systems for regular monitoring and reporting • Continuation of state-of-the-art risk management techniques • Asset management systems and tools • Outsourcing O&M monitoring and/or actual operations and maintenance • Long-term planning with targets based on financial performance as well as operations-related metrics • Choice of an optimal O&M governance regime, such as corporatisation • Incorporating maintenance function in all phases of life cycle

Conclusion

This chapter analysed typical problems of and potential solutions for the governance of large infrastructure projects. Table 4.3 summarises some of the most critical challenges across the project life cycle, as well as potential solutions–many of which were discussed or illustrated by the case studies above–based on a comprehensive risk management framework.

Three factors in particular enable successful project delivery over the course of an entire life cycle. First, comprehensive, front-end planning across all four phases–planning, contracting, construction, and operation–is necessary in order to determine strategy and incorporate effective risk management. Second, a flexible governance regime is a good choice to mitigate market risks, allow efficient stakeholder coordination, and reduce social and environmental risks. Third, risk management techniques including performance measurement, contractor monitoring, and supervision of the planners need to be incorporated within each of the major phases, too.

The planning and contracting phases are most important for setting up appropriate governance regimes. The cases of the Berlin Brandenburg (BER) Airport and the Elbe Philharmonic Hall in Hamburg, Germany, for example, show that insufficient planning and inappropriate contracting can lead to parallel processing of planning and construction–which risks immense coordination and management problems, delaying schedules and escalating costs. Other examples, such as the La Yesca hydroelectric power plant in Mexico, show that sufficient planning and stakeholder coordination, as well as a flexible governance regime and state-of-the-art risk management practices, are most likely to ensure on-time and on-budget delivery of large infrastructure projects. Other examples, such as the bonus-malus scheme for Berlin's AVUS A115 highway, illustrate innovative governance solutions. Table 4.4 offers a summary of the innovations that have been highlighted in this chapter. Many of these tools require different types of administrative capacities, including delivery, regulatory, coordination, and analytical capacities (Lodge and Wegrich 2014a). Additional infrastructure governance innovations can be found in Chapter 6 of this Report.

Challenges for project delivery are mounting, yet delivery can in fact be significantly improved.

With the current boom in infrastructure investment, challenges for project delivery are mounting, yet the case studies presented here suggest that delivery can in fact be significantly improved. Some of the recommendations presented in this chapter–including risk assessments over a project's life cycle, the inclusion of private sector expertise and capital, and the adoption of independent and external monitoring–are concrete solutions. Policy-makers and project planners need to be prepared to employ these solutions in order to meet the governance challenges involved.

Table 4.4 **Innovation toolbox**

Phase	Tool	Description	Examples
Selection, planning, and design	• Overarching risk management	• Using state-of-the-art techniques throughout the project life cycle	• La Yesca Hydroelectric Power Plant (Case Study 7)
	• Stakeholder coordination	• Mitigating political, social, and environmental risks	• Laibin B Power Plant (Case Study 2)
Procurement and contract design	• Partial risk guarantees (PRG)	• Providing private investors with financial security	• Phu My 2.2 Power Plant (Case Study 4)
	• Bonus-malus scheme	• Penalising time overruns, rewarding on-time deliveries	• AVUS A115 Highway (Case Study 5)
Construction delivery	• Regular performance assessment	• Developing metrics and random monitoring, e.g. through KPIs	• La Yesca Hydroelectric Project (Case Study 7)
	• Coordination offices	• Establishing clear rules about information flow	• Laibin B Power Plant (Case Study 2)
	• Building information modelling (BIM)	• Comprehensive value engineering	• Shanghai Tower (p. 93)
Asset operation and maintenance	• Outsourcing	• Ensuring independent external monitoring	• La Yesca Hydroelectric Power Plant (Case Study 7)
	• Systematic overhaul planning	• Planning upgrades and repairs in advance and embedded within comprehensive maintenance schedules	• Panama Canal (Case Study 9)

Endnotes

1. The EFSI includes a further €75 billion planned investment in small and medium enterprises and mid cap companies.
2. On 1 January 2016, the Major Projects Authority merged with Infrastructure UK to form the Infrastructure and Projects Authority.
3. BOT projects are when a public entity delegates to a private company the rights to design and build an asset, as well as the rights to operate and maintain it for a certain period, after which time the asset is returned to the public entity.
4. 'Parallel processing' is an approach in which planning and construction take place simultaneously.
5. Unlike an investor model, in which a private investor would finance and operate the commercial envelope and give the concert hall to the public upon completion,

a forfeiting model—suggested in this case by private construction company Hochtief—allowed the city to take ownership of most of the commercial envelope and thus maintain higher control over construction and operation. Hochtief received loans directly from the bank then billed the city for construction progress. However, after selling this claim back to the loan-giving bank, the city became the bank's creditor. As a public entity, the city received better interest rates than a private firm, and the resulting savings reduced projected costs by around €10 million (Fiedler and Schuster 2016).

6   Initially based on 2D computer-aided design (CAD) drawings for architecture, Building Information Modelling (BIM) instruments were later extended to 3D computer representations. In more recent years, BIM expanded to include time scheduling (the so-called fourth dimension), cost control (fifth dimension), possible design variations (sixth dimension), and sustainability analysis (seventh dimension).

V. Good Governance and Choosing the Right Infrastructure Delivery Model

IAN HAWKESWORTH *and* JUAN GARIN

OECD analysis[1] has shown that substantial benefits can be realised by better governance of public investment throughout its life cycle and across levels of government and that the quality of public governance correlates with public investment and growth outcomes (OECD 2013) as well as good budgetary governance (OECD 2015c). Conversely, and as we have seen in Chapter 4, poor governance is a major reason why infrastructure projects fail to meet their timeframe, budget, and service delivery objectives. The answer to this challenge will, in its broadest sense, focus on good governance in terms of planning, budgeting, assessment and evaluation throughout the project life cycle, transparency, accountability, and conducive regulatory frameworks. It will demand a strengthening of the entire institutional architecture of government in order to deliver the right strategic infrastructure on time, within budget, and in a manner that commands the confidence of all stakeholders. The elements and contours of a national governance framework for infrastructure are set out in this chapter.

The Infrastructure Decision Tree

The objective of good infrastructure governance is to make the right projects happen in a manner that is cost efficient, affordable, and trusted by users and citizens. The components of such a system could be broken down into a decision tree to guide policy and delivery choices and a set of general governance preconditions.

The choice of how infrastructure is delivered has implications for public sector discretionary control, value for money, and affordability. In many countries, however, the choice of modality is often based on habit and

---

The opinions expressed and arguments employed herein are solely those of the authors and do not necessarily reflect the official views of the OECD or of its member countries.

Figure 5.1 **Decision tree for infrastructure delivery option choice**

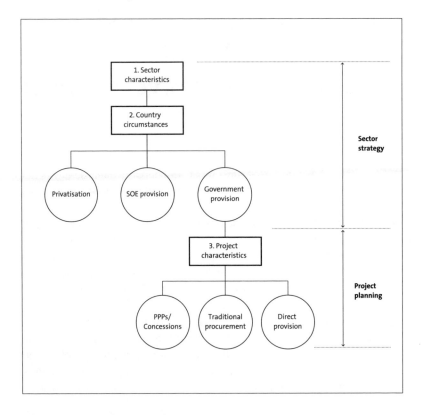

lacks specific criteria for both traditional infrastructure and private finance options (Burger and Hawkesworth 2011).

The decision tree (see Figure 5.1) and checklists presented here seek to raise issues that would need to be assessed by governments in order to make specific decisions as to how infrastructure can be best delivered. In line with the advice in Chapter 2 that we should be cautious about generalisations, they do not posit that one size fits all but rather emphasise that choices need to be conditioned by a country's unique circumstances.

This framework should enable countries to take a fresh look at their infrastructure delivery choices and identify where a change might add value given new priorities. For instance, if the challenge is to introduce greater cost efficiency, a greater use of market mechanisms might be beneficial insofar as the right country circumstances, such as a competitive market, are present. The framework's three-step process is based on sectoral criteria, country criteria at the national and subnational levels, and project criteria. It suggests that countries should:

1. Set a preferred sectoral approach by assessing reform objectives and the characteristics of the sector;
2. Assess how country circumstances such as political economy, government capacities, private sector capabilities, and the legal environment impact the sector; and
3. Choose a delivery model based on the project characteristics and overall approach.

Step 1: Setting a Preferred Sectoral Approach

First, countries should assess their sectoral objectives and sectoral characteristics. Considering these together and prioritising them should build a solid foundation for determining an optimal sectoral approach to infrastructure delivery.

Table 5.1 **Setting a preferred sectoral approach**

What are the prioritised sectoral policy objectives?	What characterises the market and how politically sensitive is the sector?
• Improving quality of services • Improving access to infrastructure • Improving efficiency • Reducing the need for government subsidies • Promoting innovation • Speed of delivery	What is the extent of market failure? • Potential for competition • Non-excludability • Network effects How politically sensitive is the sector? • Equity considerations • Land, environment, and health issues • National security considerations
↓ Optimal sector approach	

What are the prioritised sectoral policy objectives?

Decisions regarding investment strategies at both the sector and project level must be framed by an assessment of national and regional development goals as well as sector objectives (see Table 5.1). Moreover, since some objectives may be mutually exclusive, policy-makers should also establish a clear prioritisation of objectives ahead of making decisions regarding sectors (also examining potential complementarities and trade-offs), projects, and delivery modes. For example, the goal of providing universal access may not be consistent with the goal of achieving rapid roll-out of infrastructure. The following are some of the objectives that shape sector strategies and influence decisions relating to choice of delivery modes (see Table 5.1).

Improving quality of services. Decisions to invest in new infrastructure or to use an alternate delivery mode are regularly driven by considerations of service quality. Involvement of the private sector in the water and telecommunications sectors was often motivated by the objective of improving on the poor quality of service being delivered by state-owned enterprises (SOEs).

Improving access to infrastructure. A major motivation for infrastructure investment in developing countries in particular is improving access to basic services. Even in more developed economies, providing equitable access to essential infrastructure services irrespective of income level or location can be an important objective for policy-makers. Furthermore, disparities across regions or between urban and rural areas–very high even in OECD member countries–are sometimes higher within as opposed to across countries.

Improving efficiency. A key aim of infrastructure-related policy is providing high quality public services at the lowest possible cost to society. Efficiency considerations are thus often at the heart of decisions regarding infrastructure investment and modes of delivery. Inefficiencies such as overemployment, poor bill collection, system losses, and irregular maintenance practices by SOEs in infrastructure markets have been estimated to cost US$12 billion annually in Africa (Trebilcock and Rosenstock 2013).

Reducing the need for government subsidies. Many infrastructure sectors, even those dependent on user fees as a major source of funding, also rely on government subsidies in order to cover costs and ensure that service remains affordable for the majority of users. Inefficiencies in the delivery of services can thus be a heavy drain on government finances. The need to reduce the cost of providing a service can therefore be a major motivation for considering alternative delivery modes for infrastructure.

Promoting innovation. Ensuring that a particular public service continues to provide value for money over time requires infrastructure providers to adapt to evolutions in business models and technology. The capacity to innovate and develop new solutions can be an important consideration in the choice of modality and one motivation for pursuing private sector involvement. The choice of delivery option may also be shaped by a broader public sector reform process that seeks to streamline government and promote innovation in service delivery.

Speed of delivery. Setting aside the macroeconomic stimulus resulting from large construction projects, infrastructure only begins to have an impact once it is operational. Governments may therefore consider speed of delivery of an infrastructure project as an important objective that should inform decisions relating to mode of delivery and choice of provider.

What characterises the market and how politically sensitive is the sector?

The appropriate role for government in providing infrastructure and the optimal choice of delivery mode depend on a sector's economic and political characteristics. The need for government intervention should be dictated primarily by the extent of market failure in a sector. However, a degree of government intervention may also be necessary due to public expectations and the political sensitivity of certain sectors (see Table 5.1).

Extent of market failure

In sectors with multiple buyers and the potential for competition in the market, price signals may serve as accurate indicators of demand and supply. When market-based prices exist for a particular infrastructure good, the most efficient mode of provision is that of private firms operating in a competitive environment. Competitive forces ensure that consumers do not overpay, and price signals help guide firms' investment decisions. Under such circumstances, privatisation combined with effective competition policy would be the optimal mode of delivery. A number of infrastructure sectors in advanced economies, such as electricity utilities and telecommunications, exhibit such market-based pricing and are largely privatised.

In economies where conditions for market-based pricing do not exist a priori, prices will need to be regulated and will therefore not serve as a good guide for investment decisions. In such cases, privatisation may not be to the benefit of consumers and may even carry significant risks of creating a private monopolist. Instead, responses might include price and output regulation; vertical unbundling, i.e. separating retail, wholesale, and production operations; or provision by the government through an SOE, through a public-private partnership (PPP), or directly. Regardless of the specific approach taken, governments will play an important role in influencing investment levels in the sector, either through setting prices or selecting projects, and by providing financing directly or creating incentives for private finance.

Potential for competition. End users may benefit from the efficiencies generated by competition when a particular infrastructure good can be provided by multiple providers. When multiple providers offer an identical good simultaneously, competition is said to be 'in the market'. Under such circumstances, the most efficient solution and the one that will provide the greatest social benefit is private provision by multiple independent firms. However, because private firms will seek to create monopoly conditions for themselves, competitive markets are not naturally occurring. Competition therefore has to be policed and enforced in order to create the conditions for a free market.

Furthermore, there are circumstances in which it may be more efficient for a single provider to service the entire market. Such natural monopolies occur in sectors characterised by high capital costs and economies of scale. Left to their own devices, firms can exploit their dominant position to charge higher prices and provide poorer quality services.

When competition 'in the market' is not possible because a sector has features of a natural monopoly, privatisation may not offer the most efficient solution. Governments may nevertheless promote better outcomes for end users by organising competition 'for the market'. Firms will bid to be the natural monopolist, and if the auction is designed appropriately, they will relinquish some of their monopoly rents to the benefit of consumers or taxpayers. However, for such an approach to be successful a sufficient number of qualified bidders is essential in order to organise a truly competitive auction. Moreover, in order to retain as much bargaining power as possible once a contract has been awarded, governments should ensure that a credible threat of entry exists in the event of non-performance of the successful bidder.

Most vertically integrated infrastructure sectors contain mixtures of both market and natural monopoly elements. For example, in the electricity sector, the transmission and distribution system fits most closely with a natural monopoly given the cost and challenges that a competitor would face in seeking to duplicate it. Governments are therefore more likely to maintain public ownership of transmission assets or, at a minimum, ensure strong regulation of access costs and conditions. However, in-market competition may be feasible in the generation and retail aspects of the business, in which case governments might allow for the free entry and exit of private firms. A strategy for delivering infrastructure in a particular sector may involve a combination of approaches applied to different components of the sector's value chain. Privatisation should therefore be contingent on the structural separation of businesses in order to prise away those segments where there is a strong potential for in-market competition.

Non-excludability. A determining feature of public goods is their non-excludability, i.e. economic actors cannot be excluded from consuming the good. Goods that are non-excludable are typically under-provided when the provider is a private firm since payment for their use is voluntary. For this reason, goods that have important social values but are non-excludable are often, though not always, provided by the government.

A number of infrastructure sectors exhibit non-excludability to varying degrees. Street lighting is a classic example of a non-excludable public good since any passer-by or motorist will benefit from the presence of street lights. Road networks, with the exception of toll roads, are also traditionally non-excludable, though developments in technology are increasingly making it feasible to charge individual motorists for road usage. On the other hand, infrastructure sectors such as ports and airports are clearly excludable.

Network effects. Network effects reflect the change in value to a service with the participation of additional users. When an increase in the number of users makes a service more valuable, it generates positive network externalities. However, negative network externalities, often referred to as congestion effects, exist when additional users make a service less valuable for existing users. Traffic congestion, for example, is a common problem in road and rail transport. Congestion effects may also occur in telecommunications systems.

Complex systems featuring a high level of interdependencies may also contain chokepoints or be vulnerable to systemic failure. When multiple users or service providers share a common infrastructure platform with limited capacity, the owner or regulator of the platform must manage or regulate usage. Infrastructure that is vulnerable to congestion effects and systemic failure with the potential for widespread impact may require some form of government intervention, such as direct control through ownership or regulation such as congestion charging (Mello and Sutherland 2014).

Political sensitivity

In democracies, citizens seek to transmit their preferences and priorities by voting for representatives. This mandate provides legitimacy and feedback. Political sensitivity, or the importance attached to certain issues associated with infrastructure, therefore has a very legitimate role to play. Even if the characteristics of the market could guide decisions about the appropriate sectoral approach, political factors should and will also have influence, as pointed out in Chapter 2 on government decision-making.

Equity considerations. Many infrastructure services, such as water and electricity as well as social infrastructure such as health and education, are fundamental for human welfare and inclusive development. Access to such infrastructure is often viewed as a basic right in many countries and therefore carries considerable sensitivity. As a consequence, ultimate responsibility for the service is perceived by the public at large to lie with the government.

Moreover, because all members of a population are viewed as equally entitled to such infrastructure, considerations of equity are often at the heart of decisions around the provision of such infrastructure. Markets do not always provide equitable access to groups that are less able to pay for a service or that are more costly to supply because of their geographic location. The greater the importance attached to a particular infrastructure service, the more likely it is that governments will be perceived as the provider of last resort. Under such circumstances, governments will seek to exert influence either through direct provision, regulation, subsidies to increase affordability, or public service obligations.

Land, environment, and health issues. A feature of many infrastructure investments is the importance of land access and ownership issues to project development. A number of infrastructure sectors are highly land intensive. Being able to acquire rights to land at an acceptable cost and without undue delays is therefore critical to the success of a project. For example, a new rail line may require the acquisition of a continuous land corridor extending hundreds of kilometres. However, land is a finite resource and subject to numerous competing claims. Moreover, large infrastructure projects may have broader impacts on communities and ecosystems by creating obstacles that impede rights of way, alter a landscape, or impact land used for agriculture or hunting. For example, the construction of a large dam may require the relocation of entire communities. Land issues can be further complicated in countries where indigenous communities have ancestral claims to land or where property rights may not be formally assigned.

Given the sensitive nature of land, government intervention is essential for facilitating access to land for projects, compensating landowners and communities, and mediating disputes between developers, owners, and local communities. Governments' role in land planning cannot be delegated to the private sector because government participation is often essential for infrastructure investments to go ahead and for project implementation to proceed smoothly.

Large-scale infrastructure projects may also have significant environmental and health impacts that require government intervention. Communities living near highways may be exposed to high levels of air pollution and noise, large hydroelectric dams may have significant effects on natural ecosystems, and aviation is responsible for a significant amount of carbon emissions. When infrastructure has the potential to generate negative externalities, governments will need to intervene in order to minimise them and ensure that costs are internalised to the greatest extent possible.

National security. Certain categories of infrastructure that have national security implications, such as military installations, might be too sensitive to outsource to private firms. In such cases, governments are often directly responsible for the provision of infrastructure, or they might seek to exert a strong degree of oversight and control. Furthermore, perceptions of national security vary by country. For example, in certain countries, particularly non-democratic ones, the telecommunications sector is viewed as highly sensitive from the perspectives of security and political stability and is therefore increasingly subject to government intervention.

Step 2: Assessing How Country Circumstances Impact the Sector

A sectoral analysis applying the criteria described above should help to determine the most economically efficient and politically acceptable mode of delivery for a particular infrastructure category. However, this analysis may ignore the fact that achieving economic efficiency in the real world depends on having appropriate economic institutions, among other things, in place. Such an approach needs to be adapted to a country's circumstances. For example, in order for privatisation of infrastructure to be successful, there must be sufficient capacity in the private sector to deliver the infrastructure and create a credible threat of entry, as well as

Table 5.2 **Country circumstances**

Dimension	Components
Political economy	• Distribution of productive resources within an economy
Government capacities	• Public sector capacity for implementation, regulation, and monitoring
Private sector capabilities	• Skills and competences • The degree to which the market is competitive, and whether there is a level playing field between incumbents and newcomers, including those from abroad • Availability of finance
Enabling legal environment	• Clear and prudent legislation • Dispute resolution mechanisms • Legal enforcement

strong regulatory institutions to ensure that private firms do not gain excessive market power to the detriment of consumers and taxpayers. If these conditions are not in place, privatisation carries the risk of degenerating into a private monopoly that lowers welfare.

Thus, choices relating to sector approaches and delivery modes for infrastructure should be filtered by consideration of a country's political economy, its institutions, the capabilities of both government and private sector, and its openness to foreign investment (see Table 5.2). If the gap between a country's circumstances and the requirements of a particular mode of delivery is too wide, then pursuing that modality is sure to lead to failure.

Political economy

A country's political economy might predispose it to particular modes of delivery. In economies where a significant proportion of production remains in the hands of the state, as in China or Vietnam, the financial and technological resources for developing infrastructure may be concentrated within SOEs.

On the other hand, in market economies, productive resources and capabilities will be controlled for the most part by private firms, with the state having developed sophisticated regulatory tools for influencing and monitoring private sector behaviour. Choices relating to the development of infrastructure should therefore take into account the distribution of productive resources within an economy.

Government capacities

Different modes of delivery for infrastructure imply very different roles for the state. State involvement in infrastructure provision may thus span a range of activities, including planning, contracting, implementation, regulation, and monitoring. When governments deliver infrastructure through direct provision or traditional procurement, they are involved in the details of asset delivery and contract management. On the other hand, when infrastructure is privatised, the state plays the role of regulator and will delegate decisions relating to investment and production to the private sector. Both approaches entail a very different set of competences for governments (see Chapter 1 and Lodge and Wegrich 2014a for more on administrative capacities). As far as possible, government competences and capacity should be aligned with the choice of delivery mode (see also the section on governance preconditions below).

Private sector capabilities

One of the rationales for involving private firms in delivering infrastructure is to gain access to capabilities such as management skills or technological expertise that exist predominantly within the private sector. If those capabilities are not available within private firms, then private sector delivery may not generate efficiency gains and might even have a negative impact on value for money and impede competition in and for the market. Moreover, for private sector infrastructure delivery to deliver value for money, a sufficient number of capable firms in the market is needed in order to create the conditions for competitive supply or tendering. If a domestic market does not offer sufficient depth, authorities may need to include international firms in a tendering or privatisation process.

Enabling legal environment

Successful infrastructure development also depends on having in place a set of institutions that are adapted to the choice of delivery mode. Delivery modes that involve some form of private sector participation, such as privatisation or PPPs, require, as a fundamental precondition, the rule of law along with a set of legal institutions that ensure access to justice, impartiality, and enforcement of legal rulings. In the absence of these conditions, private firms are unlikely to even consider investing.

International companies can often contribute experience and technological leadership gained from having managed similar projects in other countries. This is particularly important when achieving efficiency gains and quality improvements that depend on applying state-of-the-art technology. An obvious precondition for the participation of foreign companies in infrastructure is openness to foreign investment. Governments seeking to capture the full benefits of private sector participation should therefore seek to reduce, as far as possible, limitations and obstacles to foreign investment in infrastructure projects.

Step 3: Choosing a Delivery Model Based on the Project Characteristics and Overall Approach

At the sectoral level, governments can contemplate the full range of delivery options for meeting infrastructure needs–from direct provision to privatisation (see Box 5.1). Once a sector strategy has been decided, the focus of planning and decision-making shifts down to the project level. As discussed above, governments will exert a greater degree of influence over sectors that are characterised by forms of market failure and a high degree of political sensitivity. Under such conditions, governments are likely to play the lead role in determining investment needs, selecting projects, and choosing the appropriate mode of delivery for each project. The determination of the project delivery mode should consider all the available options, including traditional procurement and various forms of private sector participation, among them PPPs.

Achieving value for money will depend on selecting the mode of delivery that delivers the desired outcomes at the lowest possible cost. This, in turn, depends on a number of project-specific factors described below and summarised in the checklist in Box 5.2: the desired project outcomes must reflect the objectives and preferences established by policy-makers. It therefore requires a clear understanding and prioritisation of sector objectives as discussed above.

Project size and profile

The choice of modality and contract must be adapted to the size and profile of the investment. Projects with high initial capital outlays typically require longer contracts in order to enable developers to recover costs and make attractive returns. When privately financed, such a project typically involves a large proportion of debt finance and will therefore require a suitable project finance structure.

Greenfield investments typically require high initial capital outlays during the construction phase followed by smaller investments in maintenance and repairs spread over the life of the project. Brownfield investments, by contrast, are likely to require smaller initial outlays but could require higher levels of spending in maintenance and refurbishment to compensate for the age of assets. Operating and maintenance services are more labour intensive than capital intensive and are therefore more amenable to shorter-term contracts.

When projects entail elevated initial investments followed by significant operating and maintenance needs, there are clear advantages to bundling construction, operation, and maintenance into a single contract. Because developers seek to maximise their returns, they face a strong incentive to

Box 5.1 **Modes of infrastructure delivery**

Direct provision
Direct provision of infrastructure involves the government taking responsibility for all aspects of infrastructure delivery, including financing, construction, and subsequent service delivery. This mode affords the government a maximum level of control over the infrastructure asset.

Traditional public procurement
In the traditional public procurement mode, a government body contracts with private partners to provide infrastructure-based goods and services. The government will contract separately for the design, construction, operation, and maintenance of infrastructure assets. Contracts are allocated using competitive tender processes in order to obtain the optimal bundle of quality features and price.

State-owned enterprises
Infrastructure, particularly in network industries such as water, public transport, and electricity, is often provided by SOEs that are fully or partially owned by the government. The government may relinquish infrastructure investments to an SOE if the latter is able to raise finance independently, although the actual investment decision may still be subject to government control if it has fiscal implications. This may be an efficient mechanism for the delivery of infrastructure, especially if the SOE is corporatised as an independent legal entity and subjected to commercial pressures (see, for example, Case Study 9 in Chapter 4). An efficient solution further calls for the state's roles as enterprise owner and regulator to be conducted separately.

Public-private partnerships and concessions
PPPs involve private investors financing and managing the construction of an infrastructure asset, which they then typically operate and maintain for a long period, often extending to 20 or 30 years. In return, the private partner receives a stream of payments to cover the capital expense as well as operating and maintenance costs. This payment stream may be derived from the national budget, user fees, or a combination of the two. Private firms are responsible for financing, constructing, and operating the infrastructure asset, while governments retain control over project selection, establish the framework conditions, and retain some regulatory powers.

Privatisation
Under privatisation, private firms are not only responsible for the financing and delivery of infrastructure, but they also make investment decisions relating to which infrastructure assets to build. When privatisation has been the preferred option, governments have strengthened regulatory oversight in the sector at stake; this has been notably the case with the establishment of independent regulators in the energy and water sectors when systems have been privatised.

Box 5.2 Checklist for investigating relevant delivery mode

Project size and profile
- Is there a large initial capital outlay and long payback period?
- Does project size justify the legal, technical, and financial costs of the delivery mode?
- Can quality enhancements in the design and construction phase generate savings during the operating phase of the project?
- Do these savings justify the additional transaction costs involved in bundling construction, operation, and maintenance in a single contract?

Revenue and usage
- Can user fees be charged, are they affordable for the majority of users, and are they politically acceptable?
- Are user fees sufficient to cover the majority of capital and operating costs?
- Can usage be monitored?

Quality
- Can the quantity and quality of project outputs or outcomes be specified and measured efficiently?
- Will design innovation be required to achieve improvements in efficiency and value for money?

Uncertainty and risk
- What is the level of uncertainty related to future technological conditions?
- What risks is each sector (public vs private) most capable of influencing and managing?
- Is demand relatively predictable over the lifetime of the project?
- Who is best placed to influence demand for the infrastructure-based service?
- Is the private sector willing to and capable of bearing some or all of the demand risk?
- Are there particular integrity risks in terms of corruption and undue influence that merit attention?

Competition
- Will there be sufficient qualified bidders in the case of a PPP/concession project to enable a competitive bidding process?

---

complete the project on time; the earlier an asset begin operations, the earlier revenues flow. Moreover, project developers will seek to optimise costs over the lifecycle of a project, which means they are less likely to compromise on quality during construction since they will have to bear the costs of future repairs and inefficient operation. For infrastructure projects with such a profile, PPPs offer, in theory, the optimal set of incentives for delivering efficiencies over the entire lifecycle of the project.

On the other hand, PPPs may not be suitable for smaller projects because the benefits from bundling may not be sufficient to compensate for what are typically elevated transaction costs due to the complexity of the contracting and negotiating process.

Revenue and usage

A key consideration for the choice of delivery mode is how a project will ultimately be funded. In an ideal world, both capital and operating costs would be fully covered by user fees that are affordable for all potential users. User fees have the double advantage of ensuring that project costs are paid for by the beneficiaries of the service and providing a mechanism for regulating demand. When user fees are practicable and when they cover a substantial proportion of the total project cost, then concessions might be a preferred option.

However, user fees on their own are seldom sufficient to cover project costs, and there may be externalities that justify government subsidies. For investments in sectors that have a non-excludable nature, user fees will not be practicable. Even when user fees are technically feasible, equity considerations may cap them at a level below what would be sufficient to cover costs and provide an adequate rate of return. Under such circumstances, user fees would need to be supplemented through other sources of revenue, typically availability payments or shadow tolls funded by general government taxation.

Quality

When contracting out infrastructure development, governments have the choice of defining deliverables in terms of inputs, outputs, or outcomes. For example, a government buyer contracting for the construction of a school may specify in detail the design of the building down to the type of construction materials to be used (input-based). Alternatively, a government may wish to specify the desired performance of an urban transport system in terms of passenger capacity and provide a private counterparty with discretion on how best to achieve it (output-based). Finally, a government may contract with a view to obtaining certain outcomes, such as increasing the number of students that graduate from high school, while again allowing a private counterparty to decide on the optimal combination of inputs (outcome-based). The decision on whether to base a contract on inputs, outputs, or outcomes therefore depends on whether quality can be adequately specified and monitored. The extent to which quality is contractible is thus an important factor in determining the most appropriate mode of delivery for infrastructure (Hart 2003).

When quality is difficult to specify and monitor, contracts are likely to be costly and time-consuming to develop and will be highly vulnerable to renegotiation. When inputs are easy to specify and verify but outputs and outcomes are difficult to specify and/or monitor, then traditional procurement would be the most suitable approach.

A related factor has to do with the extent that innovation is important for achieving efficiency and value for money in project outcomes. When improvements in outcomes depend on innovative solutions provided by the private sector, then a public sector manager should not specify design but rather the quality of outputs or outcomes (Burger and Hawkesworth 2011).

Uncertainty and risk

Infrastructure developers face the very significant challenge of making large investments in fixed assets with long intended lifetimes while equipped with highly limited knowledge of future conditions (see Chapter 2). Many of the most catastrophic infrastructure investments are the result of poor assumptions about future needs, often made worse by excessive optimism (Flyvbjerg 2014). Even when evaluations of future needs are subject to rigorous analysis, e.g. through applying scenario planning, and independent review, long-term foresight of societal needs and technologies is necessarily imperfect.

On the other hand, long-term infrastructure contracts require a high degree of certainty and are implicitly grounded in an epistemological view that the future is relatively predictable and that changes can be foreseen and therefore planned for. However, evidence from past PPPs, for example, suggests that long-term contracts that fully incorporate knowledge of all future conditions and are therefore robust to changing circumstances are the exception rather than the rule. Research examining PPP concessions in Latin America granted between 1985 and 2000 found that more than half of the contracts underwent significant renegotiations (Guasch, 2004).

Thus, for sectors and projects where change is likely to be rapid and dramatic, modes of delivery and associated contracts must incorporate a degree of flexibility. At the contractual level, contracts should contain trigger points for renegotiations or tariff adjustments, though even this requires a certain level of foresight in order to imagine what changes are plausible (Guasch 2004). In sectors where change is highly unpredictable, e.g. where technology is in flux, and therefore impossible to foresee with any level of confidence, preferred modes of delivery should be supple and adaptable, thereby avoiding lock-in to specific technologies or business models. This might include more relational forms of contracting or shorter-term contracts.

Compounding the risks that this uncertainty entails, large infrastructure projects are highly complex undertakings involving numerous interdependencies and multiple stakeholders. As a consequence, they are vulnerable to a plethora of potential causes of failure. Moreover, the risk profile of infrastructure evolves over time as the project progresses from design and construction to operation (see Chapter 4).

Achieving project success in a value for money sense depends on achieving an efficient allocation of risks. As a basic principle, risks should be allocated to those parties best able to mitigate or manage them. In addition, risk-bearing parties should have not only the capacity but also incentives to mitigate them. When risks are poorly allocated, both the probability of occurrence and the expected loss given occurrence increase. Thus, failures are more likely to occur, and their impact becomes greater when risks are borne by the wrong parties.

Efficient risk allocation can be achieved through an appropriate choice of delivery mode along with careful contract design that explicitly identifies and allocates responsibility for all risks. Delivery modes such as PPPs offer the potential to achieve an efficient allocation of risks between public and private parties. Moreover, the structure of PPPs, which involves bundling design, construction, and operation, provides strong incentives to the private partner to mitigate risks during each phase of the project. In addition, the financial structure of most PPPs, which involves a significant proportion of debt finance, means that lenders have a strong incentive to perform due diligence and monitor the actions of the project company.

Ultimately, the allocation of demand risk is highly contingent upon the nature and circumstances of the project and depends on a range of factors including affordability, excludability, and ability to influence.

Governance Challenges and Nine Preconditions

Regardless of which modality is used, there are a number of challenges, discussed below, that all projects face. On this basis, nine preconditions for good infrastructure governance are then suggested.

Governance challenges

The main governance issues drawn from OECD member country experience can be summarised as:

Government capacity for designing a strategic vision is crucial. A necessary condition for a successful infrastructure program is appropriate strategic planning. This requires identifying what investment should be undertaken and determining essential components, needs, and trade-offs and how they should be prioritised.

Without well-managed consultation good projects may falter. Involving stakeholders such as users, civil society organisations, and the private sector can improve legitimacy, the quality of planning efforts, and ultimately the effectiveness of the asset. Stakeholder involvement can establish a shared vision for development, improve the assessment of investment needs, reveal the importance of cross-border linkages, strengthen trust in government, and cultivate support for specific investment projects. For example, as noted in Chapter 3, the decision to build a new runway at Frankfurt Airport made effective use of public consultation with a mediation process initiated by the state government of Hesse.

Coordination across levels of government is essential. Public investment is generally a shared responsibility across levels of government, whether through shared policy competences or joint funding arrangements, requiring capacities at different levels to design and implement public investment projects (OECD 2013; see also Chapters 2 and 3). Governing complex interactions across levels of government for public investment holds important potential for improving efficiency and effectiveness and hence investment outcomes.

Uncertainty with regard to revenue flows and sources can erode confidence in a project's affordability. Long-term financial sustainability can be an important challenge in regulated infrastructure sectors that rely on user charges, in particular water, energy, and to some extent transport. Evidence shows that tariff-setting and updating are very difficult tasks in both OECD and non-OECD countries and tend to be highly political endeavours. To remedy the situation, a number of countries have chosen to make tariff regulation a key function of independent regulators and to issue tariff methodology (OECD 2015f).

A political jurisdiction and an infrastructure asset's functional area are often not the same. Investing at the relevant functional socioeconomic scale requires coordination across jurisdictions to increase efficiency through economies of scale and affordability of an asset for users and government (OECD 2014d). This is particularly true for metropolitan areas (see Chapter 3 on subnational governments) but can be complex to achieve for political reasons, and there are numerous examples of bad infrastructure decisions linked to inadequate perimeters of investment.

A lack of systematic data collection on performance makes it difficult to determine which type of procurement is most cost-effective. Countries should carefully assess which investment modality is likely to yield the most value for money. Good practice requires the use of comprehensive cost-benefit techniques and a robust assurance process, which may be challenging due to a lack of systematic data. Experience shows that numerical value for money tests must be treated with caution and that they can be subject to a degree of manipulation. Indeed, such calculations should not be perceived as pass or fail tests.

Allocating risks between public and private parties can be difficult. Many projects founder due to a misalignment between what private sector partners will accept in terms of risk and the expectations of some public sector entities. It falls to the public sector to design projects that only transfer to the private side those risks that it is better able to manage. For instance, as noted above, the private sector will usually be less suited to overcome land and right of way issues than the public side. While this risk can be offloaded to the private side, it will not be cost-efficient.

Institutional incentives may generate suboptimal investment choices. At times, projects may be chosen for reasons other than maximising cost-effectiveness. Motivations might include a wish to capitalise on an existing subsidy or a wish to finance the asset in a non-transparent manner off the government's balance sheet by using, for example, a PPP.

Unstable regulatory frameworks can prevent long-term decisions. The instability of institutions in charge of infrastructure development and management as well as frequent changes in the regulatory framework will increase the sense of risk for project developers.

Infrastructure procurement is vulnerable to corruption. The size of the projects and the multiplicity of stages and stakeholders involved make infrastructure projects prone to corruption. The OECD Foreign Bribery Report (2014c) identified that two-thirds of all foreign bribery cases occurred in four sectors highly related to infrastructure: extractive (19 per cent), construction (15 per cent), transport and storage (15 per cent), and information and communication (10 per cent). In the European Union, corruption in general is estimated to cost €120 billion per year (European Commission 2014b).

Political and business cycles strongly impact infrastructure. Usually, the level of public investment rises during the year that precedes municipal elections before declining in the first years following the election. In the case of France, for example, gross fixed capital formation rises by 5.9 per cent on average during the year that precedes an election then declines by 0.5 per cent just after the election and 1.4 per cent the year after that (Besson 2002).

Governance preconditions

Drawing on the extensive body of OECD recommendations that address the issues raised above, we can identify a number of good infrastructure governance preconditions that need to be in place regardless of the choice of delivery modality. These can be available in a multiplicity of organisational and institutional models and to a greater or lesser extent. A strong capacity with regards to one precondition can to some extent compensate for a weaker capacity in another. The preconditions are:

1. A national long-term strategic vision for the use of infrastructure should be established.
2. The choice of how to deliver an infrastructure service, i.e. delivery modality, should balance political, sectoral, economic, and strategic aspects.
3. Regulation, practices, and policies should encourage the sustainable and affordable development, management, and renewal of infrastructure.
4. The process for managing infrastructure should be user-centric, i.e. focusing on users' needs. It should rest on broad-based consultations, structured engagement, and access to information.
5. There should be robust coordination mechanisms for infrastructure policy within government and across levels of jurisdiction. The mechanisms should encourage a balance between a whole of government perspective and sectoral and regional views. See Chapters 2 and 3 regarding coordination challenges and good practices.
6. There should be rigorous processes for addressing absolute and relative value for money, e.g. cost-benefit analysis; affordability for the public purse and users; and transparency of key information on both the project and the overall asset portfolio.
7. Infrastructure governance should be based on data. Governments should put in place systems that ensure a systematic collection of relevant data and institutional responsibility for analysis, dissemination, and learning from this data.
8. Systems should be in place to ensure a focus on the performance of the asset throughout its lifespan.
9. Corruption entry points should be mapped at each stage of the public infrastructure project, and integrity and anti-corruption mechanisms should be enhanced.

Concluding Recommendations

The above discussions have illustrated why infrastructure represents a chronic challenge for the public sector and for society at large. The checklists and governance preconditions introduced in this chapter point towards some immediate actions that decision-makers need to take.

First, decision-makers should conduct a sober assessment of the national infrastructure governance system. Initially this should begin at the big picture level by focusing on essential questions such as: Is there a long-term vision in place? Are there processes in place that enforce a balanced assessment of projects? Are issues of sustainability, transparency, value for money, affordability, and renewal integrated into the decision-making process? Is there a focus on users? Does coordination across levels of government and within government work? Are there systems in place that ensure the collection, analysis, and distribution of data regarding infrastructure performance? Is there an anti-corruption and integrity policy in place, and is its impact being measured?

Second, and in parallel, a more specific analysis of how good sectoral policy is developed as well as how the choice of delivery is made, i.e. the relationship between the public and private in the delivery of the public service, should be undertaken. This would mean taking a clear-eyed look at what governments are trying to accomplish in various sectors, e.g. quality, access, price, and innovation; what characterises the market and possible market failure; and the political sensitivities involved. Such an analysis would have to include government and private sector capacities and the enabling legal and market frameworks in order to filter a possible strategy through the facts on the ground.

Finally, at the project level, a detailed analysis of whether governments have the right principles, processes, and tools in place to decide on the most appropriate delivery modality should be conducted by taking into account issues such as the potential for enhanced efficiency through bundling construction and operation in a single contract; the potential for cost recovery from the users of the asset; the degree to which quality can be quantified; the degrees of technological change, uncertainty, and risk allocation; and the potential for competition for the contract.

It should be emphasised that the focus in these assessments is on systems, principles, processes, and tools rather than on sectoral policies. The issue is not that country decision-makers do not understand the factual issues of, say, good waste management. The issue is that suboptimal governance and decision-making systems impede good decision-making, thereby undermining good infrastructure service delivery. This chapter has sought to raise these issues and provide a first step in addressing this much neglected challenge.

Appendix: Delivery modes and governance mechanisms

Delivery modes	Direct provision	Traditional public procurement	SOEs	PPPs	Regulated privatisation	Privatisation with liberalisation
Role of government	Planner, manager, producer	Planner and manager	Owner and planner	Planner and regulator	Regulator	Referee
Responsibility for project selection	Government	Government	SOE and government	Government	Private firms with government influence	Private firms
Governance mechanisms	Command and control	Public procurement law	Corporate governance	Contractual agreements	Sector regulation	Competition policy
Relevant guidelines	OECD Draft Principles on Budgetary Governance	OECD Principles for Integrity in Public Procurement	OECD Guidelines on Corporate Governance of State-owned Enterprises	OECD Principles for the Public Governance of Public-Private Partnerships	OECD Recommendation of the Council concerning Structural Separation in Regulated Industries	OECD Recommendation of the Council concerning Structural Separation in Regulated Industries

Endnotes

1   This chapter is based on the infrastructure work of the OECD, including in the areas of public-private partnerships (PPPs), fiscal policy and governance across levels of government, regulatory policy, integrity and anti-corruption, budgeting, water governance, and public sector innovation. The original paper this chapter is based on was welcomed by the Ministerial Council Meeting, 3–4 June 2015 in Paris and at the G20 Finance Ministers and Central Bank Governors Meeting, 4–5 September 2015 in Ankara, Turkey. More details can be found at http://www.oecd.org/gov.

VI. Governance Innovations
Infrastructure

HELMUT K. ANHEIER *and* SONJA KAUFMANN

As the preceding chapters of this Report have made clear, the governance of infrastructure has changed significantly in recent decades. After a long period of state-dominated infrastructure planning and delivery, the private sector's re-entry into public services in the 1980s was promoted as the way to 'improve efficiency, promote innovation, and enhance services' (Kessides 2004: 1; see also Kettl 2000). The wave of deregulation and privatisation that followed did not, however, meet the often high expectations of that era, and already by the 2000s privatisation policies were seen as 'oversimplified, oversold, and ultimately disappointing' in many countries (Kessides 2004: 52; see also Hood 1991 as an early critical voice; Ferlie et al. 1996).

By the 1990s, public-private partnerships (PPPs) had come to be seen as a 'middle ground' between public ownership on the one hand and full privatisation of public services on the other (Grimsey and Lewis 2007). Covering a wide range of business models and approaches, PPPs held the promise of better financing, provision, and maintenance through market incentives.[1] As with privatisation, the track record of PPPs is mixed (see Hodge and Greve 2007; Flinders 2005; da Cruz and Cruz forthcoming), leading to many adaptations and modifications in terms of governance, risk allocation, accountability, and responsibility as well as coordination.

New approaches to financing, delivering, and operating infrastructure have emerged within–and often as a direct result of–prevailing governance models.

Shifts in governance and search periods for new ways and means are nothing unusual in the field of infrastructure. Over time, new approaches to financing, delivering, and operating infrastructure have emerged within–and often as a direct result of–prevailing governance models.[2] In most major market economies, heavy private sector involvement in infrastructure shifted gradually to greater government involvement, a shift significantly amplified by the Great Depression. By the 1940s and 1950s, this resulted in near state monopolies in many fields of infrastructure and for two main reasons: first, to meet national security needs, e.g. during World War II and the Cold War, and second, to compensate for market imperfections in the first three decades of the twentieth century and for anticipated and actual market failures during reconstruction. By the 1970s, the state-led and state-dominated model began to be challenged by neoliberal thinking, gradually giving way to privatisation and PPPs, especially in the United Kingdom and Canada, and eventually spreading to most developed market economies and many developing countries as well.

During each of these periods, major governance transformations took place, usually as the result of innovations that changed the overall architecture as well as the thrust of the systems in place. But more often–during as well as between such periods–many smaller, incremental innovations came about and took hold, modifying and improving existing ways of infrastructure governance. Over recent decades, infrastructure governance gained in the number of voices demanding to be heard as technological and financial opportunities, and hence complexity, increased. Today, infrastructure is a prototypical case of multi-stakeholder and multi-level governance. Innovations now respond to challenges at different levels–international, national, regional, local–and involve diverse stakeholders, be they governments, public agencies, businesses, or civil society groups. In search of improvement, these stakeholders can aim at adjusting existing arrangements, or they can seek to establish new arrangements for what might be regarded by some as under-governed or even ungoverned areas.

Governance Innovations[3]

The term 'innovation' has many different meanings and is often associated with technological progress and business opportunities rather than governance. Therefore, especially in the field of infrastructure, where new technology is crucial and easily seen as the main driver, it is important to highlight the difference between governance innovation and innovation policy. Innovation policy includes proposals, laws, measures, and tools to support innovation, for example research and development policies for better technologies (Anheier and Fliegauf 2013). Governance innovations, by contrast, are 'novel rules, regulations, and approaches that, compared to the current state of affairs, seek to address a public problem in more efficacious and effective ways, to achieve better policy outcomes, and, ultimately, to enhance legitimacy' (Anheier and Korreck 2013: 83).

Put differently, governance innovations are about improvements in the ways and means by which we manage public problems. Innovations and their actual adaptation are highly context-related, meaning that some fields are more likely to spur innovations than others (Anheier and Korreck 2013). Innovations take place more frequently in fields where diverse interests and expertise overlap outside established centres of power or influence. In other words, innovations are more likely to happen at the complex margins of systems.

Innovations come about through two kinds of processes (Mahoney and

Thelen 2010). First, innovations in more or less stable systems involve gradual changes and slow improvements over time. This was the case, for example, as to how PPP procurement and contracting improved over time as parties learned from past experience. Second, innovations can be a response to sudden threats, jolts, or external shocks. In this case, they may involve more fundamental rather than gradual changes, even some turnaround. Here, cases in point are the German government's recommitment in 2011 to phase out nuclear energy and shift to renewable sources, as well as the US state of California's Global Warming Solutions Act of 2006, which mandates an approximately 30 per cent statewide reduction in greenhouse gas emissions and necessitates far-reaching changes in mobility patterns. Important in both processes are windows of opportunity, especially in regard to technological developments and political openings.

Reintroducing Governance into Infrastructure

In Chapter 1 of this Report, we laid out four key strategies for improved governance: (re)allocation, reform, trust-building, and future-proofing. As Table 6.1 shows, these responses address typical issue areas based on different combinations of political, financial, social, technological, and environmental challenges. One such issue area is the increased frequency of multi-stakeholder models and their implications for project planning and management; a second relates to decision-making and coordination; a third arises from considerations of the impact on and involvement of affected constituencies and stakeholders such as consumers and civil society groups; and a fourth issue area deals with unforeseen changes under context-specific conditions, including technological advancements.

To a certain degree, each of the four governance-based strategies requires different types of capacities on the part of the stakeholders involved. In *The Governance Report 2014*, Lodge and Wegrich (2014a) presented a framework for understanding how governments exercise their functions according to four core administrative capacities (see also Chapter 1 of this Report):

- Analytical, i.e. the capacity to provide 'intelligence' and advice in conditions of uncertainty;
- Coordination, i.e. the capacity to mediate between and bring together dispersed actors to achieve joint action;
- Regulatory, i.e. the capacity to provide oversight over heterogeneous private and public organisations; and
- Delivery, i.e. the capacity to execute and manage policy requirements at the frontline.

The four capacities are no longer limited to state actors and involve business corporations and civil society organisations of many kinds. They are also closely connected to, and can build on, each other. For example, good analytical capacities make coordination tasks easier, which in turn enhances delivery. Conversely, weak regulatory capacity cannot be compensated by better analytics, though regulatory tasks may become more manageable through better coordination.

Governance Innovations 2016: The Cases

In order to gain a broad overview of recent innovations taking place in infrastructure governance worldwide, we initiated an extensive online search and literature review for cases coming from four infrastructure sectors: water, transport, energy, and IT/communications. We also identified innovations that deal with processes in planning, delivery, or procurement that could be applied across all major infrastructure sectors. In addition, we consulted experts and considered the suggestions of a high-level focus group, convened by the OECD and the Hertie School of Governance and having met in Paris on 29 January 2015 to consider infrastructure governance challenges. Lastly, we revisited innovations presented in past editions of *The Governance Report* that related to infrastructure with the aim of re-evaluating their potential today. These included community crowdfunding of broadband access in Germany and the Transportation 2035 plan in California (Wise, Wegrich, and Lodge 2014), as well as the website FixMyStreet.com (Anheier and Korreck 2013).

After this initial search, we examined 40 cases in more detail by looking at the key governance challenges addressed and the solutions offered, especially as they relate to both the four governance-related responses (see Table 6.1) and the four administrative capacities. Lastly, we narrowed down our selection to the six cases presented below, as based on the following criteria:[4]

- Occurring within the past 15 years;
- Addressing a governance problem clearly relating to infrastructure;
- Taking a significantly new approach;
- Having been applied in at least one instance or context;
- Having the potential for scalability and replicability; and
- Showing promise of leading to better policy outcomes and higher levels of public welfare.

These cases represent innovative approaches that address issues that can occur in all kinds of infrastructure projects and programmes. Some arise in particular geographic regions, but others have been or could be applied

Table 6.1 **Potential governance-related responses to key infrastructure challenges**

Infrastructure Challenges	Governance-Related Responses
Increased frequency of PPPs and other financing and stakeholder management models that require the participation of diverse stakeholder groups; varying degrees of involvement from different levels of government, including transnational organisations (see Chapters 4 and 5).	**Allocation**, or the reconfiguration of existing governance arrangements, whether at the project, programme, or policy level. Allocation refers to how responsibilities, risks, and decision-making are assigned and shared among stakeholders, as well as how stakeholder groups coordinate tasks for the most efficient, effective, and equitable outcomes.
Differing decision-making set-ups and other coordination challenges between levels of government, including between countries, and between different stakeholder groups—public-private, as well as private-private (see Chapters 2 and 3).	**Reform** to ensure that optimised governance arrangements are embedded in practice. Reform can mean setting standards and enforcement mechanisms through policy-making and regulation, establishing best practices, or informal norm dissemination among stakeholders.
A rising awareness of both real and perceived mismatches between concentrated negative effects and widely distributed benefits of infrastructure projects, and other real and perceived impacts of infrastructure on citizen's daily lives (see Chapters 2 and 3).	**Trust-building** by engaging civil society in decision-making processes about infrastructure, possibly throughout the life cycle of an asset. Trust-building can involve organised interest groups and individual citizens and may improve resource allocation, ensure best possible decisions, and ideally boost legitimacy and transparency of those decisions.
Unforeseen needs, for example due to demographic changes; technological advancements requiring specialised infrastructure; and events, including those arising from climate change, that change the requirements for infrastructure assets (see Chapters 4 and 5).	**Future-proofing**, or ensuring that existing and future infrastructure policy and assets are resilient and adaptable to unforeseen needs, developments, and events. A proactive stance on the part of governance actors and a willingness to engage in learning and collaboration between regions, stakeholder groups, and sectors are crucial.

more widely, too. Table 6.2 provides an overview of the cases, the challenges they address, the governance responses they employ directly or indirectly, the capacities called for, and key elements of the different innovative approaches, though not all are covered in the analyses.

Table 6.2 **Overview of selected cases (in order of appearance)**

Case	Main Challenges	Main Governance Responses	Main Governance Capacities Required	Innovative Approaches
Samsø	• Major 'policy' change directly involving citizens • Local decision-making processes • Little external funding or support and limited local knowledge, but instalment of new technology necessary	Trust-building Future-proofing Allocation	Coordination Analytical Delivery	• Use an explicit bottom-up approach involving citizens in multiple roles and organisational forms • Initiate multilevel, networked governance restructuring and seek diverse sources of funding
Mobile infrastructure sharing	• Opening of market leading to stakeholder diversification and loss of state monopoly while facilitating entry into new markets • High risk and expense entailed in roll-out of new technology • Potential loss of competition due to sharing	Reform Allocation	Delivery Regulatory	• Share location, hardware, and software to minimise costs and risks and to broaden coverage • Establish clear regulations laying out acceptable uses of sharing and preventing monopolies
Southern African Power Pool	• Insecurity in energy supply due to lack of production • Limited cross-border energy exchange, no coordinated efforts to expand grid • Cost-inefficiency of new projects due to small consumer base	Future-proofing Allocation	Coordination Analytical Delivery	• Create multi-level governance system for coordination, planning, and harmonisation of rules • Broaden consumer base to increase cost-efficiency • Adapt elements from other types of power pools in consideration of local needs and constraints

Case	Main Challenges	Main Governance Responses	Main Governance Capacities Required	Innovative Approaches
The Bus Rapid Transit Standard	• Need for efficient and far-reaching urban transportation to serve growing populations • No clear definition of what makes such a system efficient	Reform Trust-building	Analytical	• Set standards and define best practice through non-governmental stakeholder(s) in order to allow benchmarking • Create a planning framework to enable cost-efficient planning and achieving best cost-benefit ratio
Water Use Master Plans	• Local disputes over water sources hindering access to water • Involvement of all segments of population • Possibility of a lack of local ownership due to top-down planning	Allocation Trust-building	Analytical Coordination	• Take stock of available resources and develop a plan for priority projects • Use a participatory governance approach, especially involving marginalised groups in the analytical and planning process in village committees
RAKLI Procurement Clinics	• Uncertain conditions and changing environment for procurement of projects • Lack of involvement of stakeholders in the initial phase of procurement planning, leading to inefficiency and waste of resources • Lack of transparency of procurement process	Allocation Trust-building	Analytical Coordination	• Use a dialogue-based approach to procurement, limiting uncertainty and risk and increasing efficiency and transparency • Engage a wide range of stakeholders, allowing for better solutions to complex project procurement challenges

Samsø–The Renewable Energy Island

The increasing use and production of renewable energy (RE) is a challenge in many OECD countries, as this transition requires several interdependent and potentially complex infrastructure adjustments, from building wind turbines and installing solar panels to expanding grids. Those efforts often involve a second challenge: a 'not in my backyard' (NIMBY) mentality among citizens who are opposed to the installation of RE sources such as wind turbines and high-voltage power lines in their region. The Danish island of Samsø responded to both challenges at the end of the 1990s, when the island committed to convert its energy supply to 100 per cent renewable in the span of a decade. Two governance responses were crucial for gaining the necessary support of the island's then-4,400 citizens: trust-building and the (re)allocation of responsibilities by enlisting islanders in multiple project roles and organisational forms.

Governance challenge: A competition initiated by the country's Ministry of Environment and Energy in 1997 and funded by the Danish Energy Authority invited Danish islands to propose plans to convert to 100 per cent RE within ten years. After approaching the mayor of Samsø, a mainland-based engineer submitted a preliminary plan based on several existing measures: cutting consumption and increasing efficiency; building and expanding a district heating supply system; installing on- and offshore wind power plants; and converting transportation to electrical power (Saatamoinen 2009: 8).

In October 1997, Samsø was awarded the title of Denmark's Renewable Energy Island. However, with no existing local environmental or energy organisations, the island lacked the expertise and analytical capacity to implement such a project on its own. As the competition had been intended to emphasise the feasibility of an RE transition based on community engagement and independent of government funding, financial and project management support from the Danish government was limited to individual sub-projects (Danish Energy Authority 2003: 18). As a result, citizen support, key stakeholder participation, competencies in renewable energy and project management, and an appropriate governance arrangement had to be generated from the ground up.

Governance innovation: With an explicit bottom-up approach, Samsø's successful transition relied on trust-building and reallocation of traditional energy project roles in order to enlist citizens–households, businesses, and civil society organisations–as not only supporters and planners but also active project co-implementers.

The project was initiated when the municipality established two local offices: the Samsø Energy and Environment Office (Jørgensen 2007: 43), tasked with counselling local residents on RE and representing their interests as a citizens' association, and the Samsø Energy Company, which focused on implementing wind turbine and district heating projects. The two offices enabled the project to operate within a multi-level governance partnership with the Danish Energy Agency, Århus Regional Authority, and Samsø Municipality–the latter operating several project-related agencies. At the national level, the government agency Region Midtjylland funded the creation of a research, industry, and RE network between facilitating organisations (Jørgensen 2007: 42), and additional funding from the EU supported certain project activities for the first few years.

Citizen trust in the project and the will to cooperate were strengthened by forming networks between existing stakeholder associations. For example, the on- and offshore wind turbine project was carried out by the Samsø Energy Company with a board composed of the Samsø Island Municipality, Samsø Agricultural Association, Samsø Business Forum, and Samsø Energy and Environment Office. The formation of informal citizen groups was crucial for building trust among consumers. The Samsø Energy and Environment Office and Samsø Energy Company organised information campaigns and citizen group meetings from the start of the project. Social pressure from within the island's small, fairly homogenous community played a role in widening project participation. NIMBY-related conflicts, for example, were avoided when onshore windmill location proposals were generated by landowners and communities themselves.

Campaigns and initiatives directed at households and communities were supported by the EU's ALTERNER program and the Danish Energy Authority. Direct grant schemes provided financial incentives for residents to convert their heating and energy systems. Although existing residences were not required to convert to district heating systems at the beginning of the project, Samsø's model was designed to differ significantly from the rest of Denmark, making it very inexpensive to register a household for district heating prior to plant construction. As a result, citizens were particularly involved in door-to-door campaigning for the construction of new district heating plants that would cover their regions.

Citizens remained involved throughout the decade-long project life cycle. After the planning phase, they were invited to make investments and act as technology operators. As a result, ownership of Samsø's energy system was reallocated according to a new model: 50 per cent ownership by the municipality, which reinvests proceeds in future energy projects; 30 per cent by local households, mostly small farmers who pool resources; and 20 per cent sold on a cooperative basis to small shareholders (Energy Academy 2011). Local businesses were also brought into the RE transition, which strengthened positive social dynamics between citizen stakeholders: notably, craftsmen received training in RE technology from the Danish Technological Institute to install and service components, and citizens using local partners and authorised household systems were eligible to receive grants to cover installation costs (Jørgensen 2007: 13).

With the Samsø experiment, the Danish government intended to prove that switching to renewable energy was possible on a small scale. Samsø was indeed able to transition to 100 per cent self-produced RE in only eight years, two years ahead of schedule. The project's networked governance structure opened up a similarly diverse set of funding options. With limited public subsidies of around €4 million, the bulk of the project's €53.3 million costs was contributed by local authorities, citizens, and companies (Saatamoinen 2009).

The key to success in Samsø's transition to renewable energy was citizen involvement (see Donnay et al. 2011; Saatamoinen 2009; Nevin 2010). A network of voluntary working groups and stakeholder associations enabled citizens to cooperatively influence the direction of individual steps during project implementation. Though some factors that contributed to the experiment's success might limit its replicability elsewhere, others, in particular the role of stakeholders in and the inclusive approach to planning, decision-making, and financing, can be taken up in both community-based and broader initiatives.

Mobile infrastructure sharing

Mobile telecommunications are increasingly important in both emerging and advanced economies. The number of mobile telephone and internet connections has increased tremendously: The International Telecommunications Union (ITU) estimated that there would be more than 7 billion mobile telephone subscriptions by the end of 2015, up from 5.2 billion in 2010 (ITU 2015). This increasing demand requires widened geographical coverage as well as greater capacity for handling the rising number of users.

In order to share the risks of rolling out new technology or entering new markets, mobile telecom operators are more frequently resorting to what is known as mobile infrastructure sharing: the joint use of non-electronic mobile technology locations such as a cellular antenna or of transmission and network technology, for example frequency. This innovative governance reallocation–the rearranging of existing ownership models in the telecom sector based on cooperation among competitors–can create benefits, namely lower barriers to market entry, for companies that are then passed on to consumers. However, cooperation may also have a negative effect on competition in certain scenarios. Therefore, part of this governance innovation is also the spread of regulatory framework reform, requiring regulatory capacity from the governmental side in order to institutionalise fair standards and enforcement mechanisms regarding sharing.

Governance challenge: Technological advancements and telecom market developments create opportunities as well as challenges for private and public actors. Adopting new technology and continuously upgrading infrastructure has traditionally required massive fixed investments–a high risk factor for mobile telecom operators (Hasbani et al. 2007: 4). Regulators, on the other hand, may focus on sharing as a way to incentivise technological progress and optimise investments in telecom sector development. However, when sharing creates an added risk of decreased market competition–for example when sharing infrastructure borders on collusion, or when third parties are discriminated against in favour of parties to a sharing agreement (see Hasbani et al. 2007: 4 f.; Meddour, Rasheed, and Gourhant 2011: 1577)– regulators must also protect consumer interests by enforcing competition.

Governance innovation: Deregulation of the telecommunications market in Europe during the 1990s led to a proliferation of new network operators. At the same time, because the prices paid for 3G licenses could not be offset by revenues as expected, mobile telecom operators had to look for ways to reduce expenses (Beckman and Smith 2005: 1; Hasbani et al. 2007: 8). One way was to share physical and transmission infrastructure, which also became a popular approach for existing operators to adopt new technological standards or for existing or new companies to enter a market.

There are two major types of infrastructure sharing: passive and active. Passive sharing, more commonly used, refers to the 'sharing of space or physical supporting infrastructure which does not require active operational co-ordination between network operators' (GSMA 2012: 12), for example sharing physical sites for the installation of transmission equipment. Active sharing goes beyond this to encompass the sharing of transmission and network technology, for example frequency and spectrum or the radio access network. Some definitions include national and international roaming agreements as well (GSMA 2012).

The benefits of mobile infrastructure sharing are shared by companies and consumers alike. Markets with already good coverage and a sufficient number of operators can make use of active sharing to lower barriers to market entry by reducing investment requirements, shift operators' focus onto better customer service and more innovation, and even reduce the environmental and health impacts of technology (Hasbani et al. 2007: 4 f.). In other markets, site or antenna sharing and national roaming can be particularly useful for increasing coverage in underserved areas and may also help diversify markets and introduce new operators (Hasbani et al. 2007).

Mobile infrastructure sharing emerged as an innovative reallocation of roles and responsibilities from within the private sector. However, it is only truly innovative when regulatory frameworks are reformed to maximise benefits for all stakeholders by establishing, monitoring, and enforcing optimal sharing standards, as well as ensuring their wider dissemination and adoption across a market. The exact nature of regulations varies among countries.

Even in the EU, where basic competition and telecommunication regulation such as the EU Radio Spectrum Policy is the same for every member state, countries deal with sharing differently, depending on their national regulatory framework and design of the telecommunication market. While passive sharing has become commonplace, some countries have more supportive regulations for active sharing than others. For example, Sweden has been at the forefront of encouraging the sharing of radio transmission technology (BEREC and RSPG 2011: 21). Several organisations have tried to define a best practice framework for regulating sharing arrangements. The ITU highlighted elements such as a dispute resolution mechanism, transparency in the availability of and conditions for shared infrastructure, and incentives to increase coverage in rural areas through sharing as part of a good regulatory framework (ITU 2008).

Sharing infrastructure has been a promising way to facilitate faster rollout of new technology in the mobile telecommunications market. With the rising importance of broadband internet connections, infrastructure sharing has been reapplied to achieve wide and affordable broadband access. In a recent EU public consultation process in preparation for a new directive on reducing the cost of rolling out high-speed broadband, stakeholders such as operators, national regulatory agencies, and public authorities cited several best practices for the use of infrastructure sharing (European Commission 2012: 2). Highlighted in particular were French and Portuguese regulations that require dominating companies to share conduits with competitors, as well as Germany's countrywide mapping of infrastructure potentially available for sharing.

Southern African Power Pool

Pooling resources across regional or national borders has become a common tool in many sectors to stave off supply shortages and make the most of scarce resources. In the energy sector, power pools have moved beyond their initial role of guaranteeing steady energy supply. Modern pools in Scandinavia and the United States have transformed into competitive marketplaces in which energy is traded as a commodity with the goal of reducing electricity prices (Barker, Tenenbaum, and Woolf 1997). However, in emerging economies, a power pool in the sense of 'an arrangement between . . . interconnected electric systems that plan and operate their power supply and transmission' (PA Consulting Group 2008: 1) in a coordinated manner can help to establish the infrastructure, e.g. grids, necessary to move toward a more market-oriented type of pooling.

Several power pools have emerged on the African continent under the leadership of their respective regional organisations: the Southern African Power Pool (SAPP), the West African Power Pool, the East African Power Pool, and the Central African Power Pool. Founded in 1995 as part of the Southern African Development Community (SADC), SAPP is the oldest and most advanced pool in Africa (Kambanda 2013). It aims to increase the reliability of energy supply and reduce production costs. Introducing a new, supranational stakeholder, namely the pool operator, into the existing governance system leads to a reallocation of responsibility and requires a high level of coordination capacity on the pool operator's side.

Governance challenge: Securing a steady and sufficient energy supply is a prerequisite for economic development in any country. Limitations in resources for energy production or an inadequate grid can lead to energy supply crises. Energy trading between utilities, both within and across borders, can be an instrument to increase energy security in the short run. However, due to short-term contracts and therefore changing terms of contracts, energy trading does not necessarily allow for strategic long-term planning. A key governance challenge therefore is how to achieve a balanced mix of energy sources and long-term strategic planning that involves coordination among various levels of government and regulatory authorities as well as utility and grid operators.

Governance innovation: The Southern African Power Pool is a case of recombination and refunctionality (see Anheier and Korreck 2013: 88 f.) of key elements from different types of existing power pools, while at the same time introducing a new element of coordination and integration at the level of a multi-national regional organisation. The general set-up and purpose of SAPP corresponds to the idea of what is now called an 'old style' pool: it primarily focuses on energy reliability, minimising operating costs, and controlling decision-making (Barker, Tenenbaum, and Woolf 1997: 19). Such pools, so-called 'tight' pools, coordinate strategic planning between utilities, producers, and grid owners. Where they have been set up in the US, they are governed by independent system operators (ISOs): non-discriminatory, independent bodies tasked with overseeing market coordination, transmission facilities, and grid reliability (IRC 2015; FERC 1996: 280).

The second element adopted by SAPP comes from a different type of pool, with the Nord Pool[5]–the first international power exchange market, initially between Norway, Finland, Sweden, and Denmark–as its prototype. The focus here is on competitive market behaviour and cost reduction rather than energy security and coordinated planning. The Day-Ahead Market (DAM), which opened trading in 2009 and replaced the Short Term Energy Market, was aimed at moving SAPP from a purely coordinative pool to a competitive one.

SAPP's multi-level governance system brings a new element to the governance structure of power pools by introducing a supranational component. The institutional embedding of SAPP reallocates responsibilities, for example grid expansion, and benefits, such as diversity in generation sources, but also risks–here especially undersupply–to the regional level.

Existing bilateral trading arrangements at the country level have been reorganised into a multi-level governance system through the introduction of the SAPP governing bodies as new stakeholders.

SAPP is governed through a multi-level system involving governmental, especially SADC bodies and national governments, and non-governmental stakeholders, such as grid operators and utility companies. The SADC Infrastructure and Services Directorate functions as an umbrella body for the governance of the pool. Decisions on day-to-day management remain with the utility companies in the member states, and decisions on financing are still made by the national governments (ECA 2009: 38). Currently, 16 utility companies–some private, some public–participate in the pool. The Executive Committee, which includes one utility company chief executive per country, acts as a governing board and formulates the pool's general objectives (SAPP 2016). At the level below the Executive Committee, the Management Committee, composed of utility representatives, oversees actual operations with the aid of four sub-committees.

In 2000, the SAPP Coordination Centre was established in order to facilitate coordination between pool members, oversee the implementation and running of the energy market, and handle administrative duties such as budget preparation and dispute settlement (ECA 2009: 37 f.). It basically functions as the ISO, though with less authority than those in the US, as described above. Initially more focused on technical issues, the Centre has taken up the role of coordinator for projects relevant to the region (The World Bank 2014b: 6 f.). This also includes finding capital from public and private sources for those projects. The Pool Plan, last revised in 2009, sets forth the strategic objectives of the pool and emphasises the importance of a coordinated expansion plan and the need for deeper regional integration (ECA 2009: 4). In an effort to achieve this, the Executive Committee compiled a list of regional priority projects that was eventually approved by national governments in 2013 (ICA 2011: 57; The World Bank 2014b: 6).

Investment in power generating capacity has increased due to SAPP's efforts. A total of 4203 MW in net capacity were added between 2007 and 2012, with a total installed capacity of 58,387 MW and sufficient capacity expected in 2017 (Oseni and Pollitt 2014: 11 f.; SAPP 2014). The DAM as well as the recently introduced Intraday Market move the pool towards competition, though bilateral trading through contracts still accounts for 90–95 per cent of energy traded due to limited transmission capacity (Oseni and Pollitt 2014: 11). Meeting the rising energy demand continues to be a challenge for the pool, with the main concern being the installation of new power generation plants and transmission lines (SAPP 2014: 5).

Critiques of SAPP have encouraged enhanced involvement of national governments and regional authorities so as to help reach agreements and to ensure actual implementation of policies (Castalia Strategic Advisors 2010: 26; 26 f.). Further, to accelerate efforts to increase reliability in supply and expand transmission and production capacities, project management for significant projects is now the responsibility of the SAPP Coordination Centre. However, transforming SAPP into a modern, competitive pool will also require a separation of electricity production and the grid on the national level in order to reallocate more authority, for example the management of transmission lines, to the regional governance level. Thus far national governments have been hesitant to take such necessary steps (USAID 2013). Lessons learned as SAPP develops further can help shape the governance of similar regional power pools in Africa and elsewhere.

The Bus Rapid Transit Standard

Developing a mass transit system capable of meeting the mobility needs of growing urban populations while trying to minimise environmental and social impacts is a demanding task for any local or regional government. This is not only true for rising megacities in emerging economies but also for metropolises with underdeveloped public transport systems.

When it comes to developing transit systems, planning authorities have a variety of options, including light rail, subways, commuter rail, and bus service. In a cost-benefit analysis, bus service seems to be attractive at first given the lower investment requirements compared to rail-based systems. Going beyond conventional bus services, bus rapid transit (BRT) systems combine two basic components: first, infrastructure measures such as designated busways and specially designed stations for speeding up both bus traffic and passenger loading and offloading; and second, high-quality and comfortable buses that run reliably and at high frequency (Hidalgo and Gutiérrez 2013; Nikitas and Karlsson 2015). The first BRT system was introduced in Curitiba, Brazil in 1974 and has been adapted for many other systems, for example those in Bogotá, Mexico City, Jakarta, Istanbul, and Beijing (Nikitas and Karlsson 2015: 15).

In 2012, the non-governmental organisation Institute for Transportation and Development Policy (ITDP) introduced 'The BRT Standard', establishing basic criteria for bus lines to qualify as actual BRT corridors. Through a scorecard exercise, the Institute also benchmarks corridors and highlights best practice cases by awarding bronze, silver, or gold status. At the same time, the Standard can serve as a guide for planners and decision-makers to develop a BRT system that takes into account local needs and challenges while delivering an effective solution for mass transit.

Governance challenge: Due to their lower investment costs when compared to rail-based transit systems, BRT has become an attractive alternative for revenue-starved municipalities. However, not every bus system can or should be called a BRT system. Thus far there has been no universal understanding of what actually constitutes BRT. Planners and decision-makers often do not know which elements are crucial to achieve a bus-based system that provides the same capacity, comfort, and environmental benefits as more popular rail-based solutions. Substandard design of BRT corridors can render the whole system inefficient, wasting money and resources and ultimately reducing the public's support for them. This happened in Delhi, India, where a BRT corridor was scrapped in 2015 when faulty design–including difficult access to stations and major intersections along the route–led to slow service and criticism from citizen groups (Hidalgo 2015). The lack of a clear definition has led to mislabelling of a number of marginally improved but still conventional bus systems as BRT despite not actually achieving the benefits associated with BRT. Political decision-makers can also cut corners, leaving out initially planned, essential elements during construction in order to, for example, reduce costs.

Governance innovation: Tackling the need for a common yardstick for BRT as an efficient mode of transport, the ITDP, with funding from the Rockefeller Foundation, started developing the BRT Standard in 2010, based on the organisation's many years of experience in supporting BRT in emerging economies. Though the initial target audience was the United States, it soon became obvious that given the surge of new bus systems designated as BRT, a common definition was needed on a worldwide level (ITDP 2012b: 4). A number of institutions, such as the Barr Foundation, the Deutsche Gesellschaft für Internationale Zusammenarbeit (GIZ, Germany), and the United Nations Environment Programme, have endorsed the Standard, supporting its promotion and application (ITDP 2016a).

While different actors have tried to classify relevant elements and evaluate existing BRT systems to help better design current and future projects–for example in academic research (see Galicia et al. 2009; Muñoz and Hidalgo 2013) or, as in the US, on the part of national government (FTA 2004, 2009)–those attempts were not as practically oriented or were limited geographically. The key innovation in this case is a non-governmental organisation–the ITDP–stepping in to establish and introduce a worldwide standard in transport policy that provides policy-makers and the general public with guidance and greater clarity with regard to expectations, much like other forms of labelling and certification do in other industries. Introducing such a standard establishes a new norm that actors can strive for, thereby ensuring that governance arrangements have adequate guidance during planning and implementation. In addition, establishing an objective label can help build trust among citizens, both by managing expectations and by giving citizens a framework with which to assess new projects.

The BRT Standard introduced by the ITDP can be applied toward at least two purposes. First, it can be used to evaluate existing systems and recognise best practices; second, it can serve as a guiding framework for planners and decision-makers to assess planned projects (ITDP 2012b: 9). In the ITDP's evaluation of existing systems, points are awarded to individual corridors in six categories with a total score of up to 100 points. The BRT Basics distinguish BRT from standard bus service: dedicated right of way, busway alignment, off-board fare collection, intersection treatment, and platform-level boarding. For a corridor to be considered a BRT system, it has to score at least 20 out of 38 possible points in the Basics category. Gold standard is awarded to BRT corridors scoring 85 points or higher, silver standard to 70–84 points, and bronze to 55–69 points. In the 2014 evaluation of such systems in cities worldwide, 15 corridors received the gold standard, 28 silver, 41 bronze, and six were qualified as basic, while eight did not qualify as BRT systems at all (ITDP 2016b). The scoring criteria were developed and are updated by a technical committee selected by the ITDP. Currently, it consists of 11 BRT experts from academia, international organisations, and civil society who contribute their technical advice and experience in the field. The technical committee also certifies corridors.

A label for quality BRT service can motivate city authorities to make bold decisions when designing a system. For example, the China branch of the ITDP, together with the Guangzhou Municipal Engineering Design Research Institute, planned and executed a BRT corridor in Yichang, financed by the Asian Development Bank. The corridor was planned according to the gold standard and service began in July 2015 (ITDP 2015; Worldbrt.net 2015).

However, the 'gold standard' may not be the appropriate target leading to the most cost-efficient solution in all settings (ITDP 2012b: 8). By defining clear requirements for meeting different levels, the BRT Standard allows decision-makers to tailor transport systems to their needs and available resources and still achieve satisfying results. For example, in the case of Montgomery County, Maryland in the United States, due to low ridership potential the ITDP recommended making more modest improvements to existing bus systems while implementing gold standard measures on one particularly promising corridor (ITDP 2012a). Planners, decision-makers, and interest groups need to apply analytical capacity to assess which BRT Standard elements can improve public transport with the best possible use of resources.

Water Use Master Plans

Access to clean water and available sanitation are prerequisites for basic well-being, and functioning irrigation systems play a crucial role in the development of efficient agriculture. Even when national efforts successfully expand and improve water infrastructure, such achievements can be set back by local disputes over access and by a lack of capacity to operate and maintain basic facilities. Such was the case in Nepal. Though the implementation of national policies–and significant international aid–increased the availability of improved water by 2011 to some 85 per cent of the population (The World Bank 2014a), many of the installed systems still require repair or simply do not function properly. Disputes over water sources and distribution hinder access, especially for marginalised groups and the poor (Bhatta and Bhatta 2011: 2).

In response to this challenge, HELVETAS Swiss Intercooperation has been implementing and adapting the Water Use Master Plan (WUMP) process since 2001 as part of its Water Resources Management Programme. At the heart of the innovation is the application of a participatory governance approach to local water and sanitation infrastructure, with clear allocation of responsibilities based on trust-building efforts and the creation of ownership among the local population.

Governance challenge: Access to clean water for household consumption and dependable supplies for irrigation can easily cause conflicts. Despite the decentralisation of responsibility for the management of water-related infrastructure to the local level in Nepal, policy decisions are still frequently made at the national level, often without consideration of local factors such as community needs and resources and thus resulting in improper or wasteful water usage. When water-related infrastructure is planned and constructed in a top-down fashion, facilities such as public water taps can turn into very small 'white elephants' that remain un- or underused for lack of repair or lack of a sense of ownership (Rautanen, van Koppen, and Wagle 2014: 161). Compounding the situation, local source disputes between neighbours can intensify, and parts of the community, especially marginalised and poorer households, can be denied access when coordinated, inclusive planning is lacking (ICIMOD and Helvetas 2013: 2).

Governance innovation: Aimed at achieving the effective, efficient, and equitable use of water by reorganising water governance roles and responsibilities at the local level, the WUMP process brings together all community members, local government authorities, service providers, and potential funders to participate in the planning and implementation of water-related infrastructure projects. The WUMP is intended to strengthen the responsibility and capacity for planning at the local level through the smallest government entity, the Village Development Committee (VDC). The WUMP process includes three phases and entails 17 steps, each of which needs to be properly executed and completed before moving on to the next (see Figure 6.1). A pre-planning phase focuses on social mobilisation both to raise awareness of the water programme and to ensure inclusive and equitable participation. The district-level government signs a memorandum of understanding with VDCs that are selected based on criteria such as poverty status, percentage of excluded groups, and situation of water resource facilities (Government

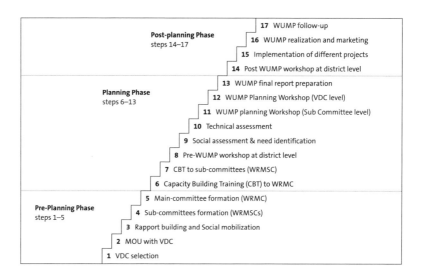

Figure 6.1 **Step-wise WUMP Process**
© HELVETAS Swiss Intercooperation

of Nepal 2008: 4). Within the selected communities, Water Resource Management Subcommittees are first formed, taking care that their membership represents all segments of the local population. Representatives of the Subcommittees and other stakeholders then join together with staff from the VDC to form a Water Resource Management Committee[6], which coordinates the WUMP's planning and implementation.

In the second, planning phase, the WUMP is developed from the ground up. In the first step, this phase mobilises analytical capacity to inventory existing and potential water sources as well as actual demand and basic socioeconomic data using technical and social assessments. An external WUMP consultant provides capacity-building training for Committee members, who in turn train the Subcommittees. A profile based on this inventory is then discussed, first among the Subcommittees and then at the level of the Water Resource Management Committee, which formulates a list of priority projects to improve water supply and sanitation (Bhatta and Bhatta 2011: 3 f.). Through trust-building within and between local stakeholder groups via an inclusive decision-making process and by considering social aspects such as gender equality and poverty, the WUMP process addresses the issue of legitimacy and ownership for water infrastructure development. The final phase of the WUMP process involves actual implementation of the projects prioritised within the plan. The post-planning phase also includes an evaluation process and updating of the WUMP using the same participatory planning approach (Bhatta and Bhatta 2011: 5).

Under Helvetas' ongoing Water Resources Management Programme, 92

VDCs developed WUMPs between 2001 and 2012, and the schemes implemented according to the WUMPs benefitted some 125,000 people in Nepal (Helvetas 2016). WUMPs were also found to have ensured the equal participation of disadvantaged groups in decision-making, established more equitable access to water, created a knowledge base, and resolved disputes regarding access and control of water sources (Bhatta and Bhatta 2011: 7). In a joint programme of the Nepalese and Finnish governments that adopted the WUMP approach, the share of households in 47 participating VDCs reporting the best level of water service rose from 6 per cent in 2007/8 to 27 per cent in 2010/11, while the share of households with the lowest level of water service declined from 38 per cent to 21 per cent (Rautanen, van Koppen, and Wagle 2014: 165). However, an evaluation of that project also uncovered several shortcomings that led to adjustments to the process. For example, water resources were originally underreported in several cases. As a result, data collected are now reviewed by local project staff to ensure a comprehensive inventory (Rautanen, van Koppen, and Wagle 2014: 167).

While the approach has been taken up in Nepal by other projects working in the water sector, it has also been expanded to incorporate new concepts. For example, since 2012, Helvetas has partnered with the Dutch RAIN Foundation, whose flagship Smart 3R Solutions concept–referring to the recharge, retention, and reuse approach–aims at sustainable water supply management. This concept has been integrated into existing project communities in Nepal and is now called the WUMP+3R approach (RAIN 2014). Helvetas, RAIN, and several other project partners have initiated an expansion of WUMP+3R into new communities in Nepal as well as Pakistan. In addition, Helvetas introduced WUMP+3R in Ethiopia in 2015, hoping to reapply the local participatory governance approach to water management in that country as well.

RAKLI procurement clinics

The procurement and contract design phase is critical for any infrastructure project. As discussed in Chapter 4, the logistical complexity of larger infrastructure projects in particular poses significant governance risks. At the same time, the procurement phase can be heavily influenced already during project planning, when determining ownership structures and developing a sound implementation plan.

The Finnish Association of Building Owners and Construction Clients (RAKLI), a non-profit organisation of private and public stakeholders in the construction and real estate industries, has introduced a reform based on a structured process in the form of procurement or purchasing clinics. By facilitating dialogue between procurers and potential suppliers before contracts are actually tendered, the clinics also enhance trust-building among the actors involved. The key innovation optimises public-private infrastructure governance arrangements through inclusion, i.e. by bringing together all relevant groups in a series of workshops to find the best and most cost-efficient approach to procurement.

Governance challenge: Infrastructure procurement poses a particular set of governance as well as practical challenges due to the public nature of infrastructure and to the often large investments and financial commitments at stake. For one, infrastructure projects can be very complex, involving multiple steps that need to be executed either in a particular order or sometimes simultaneously, and often by different providers. Some projects require new technologies or untested solutions. At the same time, public procurement regulations that are intended to ensure transparency and a level playing field for potential bidders often allow for limited communication between procurers and providers only once the formal tendering process is opened and under way. What is more, tenders can be drafted in a way that is too specific, limiting the pool of potential bidders, or too vague, making it difficult for bidders to calculate and submit accurate quotes.

Governance innovation: RAKLI's clinic framework reforms the way procurement is planned. It establishes a new method that enables the public procurer, potential bidders, and interested parties to share knowledge, thereby improving the purchasing process and overall outcome and minimising risks. The establishment of a 'market dialogue' before the actual procurement phase allows potential bidders to gain better knowledge of the work required and also to offer the procurer ideas and feedback to improve the tendering process, especially the technical, financial, and contractual terms. To achieve this goal, the method requires analytical capacity from all actors when it comes to defining the objectives, identifying challenges, and coming up with solutions during the workshop series.

In 2007, RAKLI facilitated the first procurement clinic for linking the Helsinki-Vantaa Airport to the city's commuter railway system via a new connection that was to involve the merging of two tracks, the construction of several tunnels, and the building of new stations. The Finnish Railway Administration hoped to find ways of managing the project's complex planning process and ultimately find an optimal solution given limited public resources for planning and execution. The clinic came up with different options for the planning process for the city to decide on (Kuronen and Vaara 2013: 268; Horn, Schuldes, and Mendle 2015: 7).

To start a clinic process, procurers, for example city administrations or government agencies, can submit requests. In order to be considered, a case should potentially contribute to sustainable urban development and good public procurement (Horn, Schuldes, and Mendle 2015: 5). Once RAKLI selects a case, the RAKLI facilitator and the procurer identify relevant stakeholders for inclusion and define the objectives of the clinic, e.g. developing strategies for projects in the early planning phase or, in cases where concrete tenders are the next scheduled outcome, generating input about procurement processes, specifications, and contract notices (Mendle and Horn 2015: 11). This phase has been diagnosed as the most important part of the clinic: only when a clinic's objectives and key questions are clearly spelt out can the dialogue be fruitful and generate relevant and helpful knowledge (Kuronen and Vaara 2013: 268).

An initial seminar aims to attract a wide variety of stakeholders from the public, private, and academic sectors. In this step, the case, its challenges, and the objectives of the clinic are introduced to the audience. At the end of the seminar, interested stakeholders register for the workshop phase (Horn, Schuldes, and Mendle 2015: 5). During the two to five sessions open only to those who registered, participants engage in open dialogues about the project and discuss possible procurement options (for a more detailed description of the workshop process see SCI-Network 2011). In cases where the clinic is to be followed by a tendering process, the workshop can also develop the terms of reference and necessary documents (Horn, Schuldes, and Mendle 2015: 5). The final phase of the clinic is the output seminar, open to the general public. The seminar presents the outcomes of the workshops and through an evaluation process allows the participants to comment on the outcome or put forth any further ideas. Finally, a report of the process is published online (Horn, Schuldes, and Mendle 2015: 6).

Overall, the process takes between three and six months. The RAKLI facilitator acts as a neutral mediator, enabling and guiding the dialogue between the participants. The clinics, with costs ranging from €10,000 to 50,000, are partly funded by Tekes, the Finnish Funding Agency for Innovation. The remaining costs are split between the client, i.e. the procurer, and the main interested parties.

As of December 2015, 22 clinics had been facilitated by RAKLI, many related to infrastructure projects such as roads and railways but others related to housing and green urban development. RAKLI's clinic method is also being applied to a broader set of goals. Instead of preparing the actual procurement process, some clinics look at analysing challenges of planning and infrastructure delivery in general and are now rather referred to as concept clinics (Horn, Schuldes, and Mendle 2015: 4). For example, in 2009 the city of Varkaus approached RAKLI to hold a clinic on outsourcing its municipal engineering services. In the end, the dialogue brought forward a new operating model that led to a tendering procedure and new knowledge that could be used in similar situations in other cities (Vilén and Palko 2010: 5; SCI-Network 2011). Other non-procurement focused clinics have dealt with the potential of solar energy generation in Helsinki and the possible installation of district heating in Espoo.

Concluding Comments

In some ways, infrastructure governance has become a more crowded field: governments, public administration and specialised agencies, businesses, and civil society groups all seek to stake out their claims and further their interests. Just as previous eras of infrastructure governance involved shifts in allocations of roles and responsibilities, risks and benefits, and incentives and sanctions among stakeholders, today's diversity of models and approaches is in response not only to current uncertainties but also to prior innovations by governments and public administrations or as initiated by the private sector and civil society.

If anything, the crowded field of infrastructure governance requires a better spread of governance capacities across stakeholders. As we have seen in the six cases presented above, uneven playing fields and varying capacities were common deficiencies that produced a need for innovation in order to avoid planning or delivery failures. Importantly, coordination capacity among and across stakeholders, including adequate communication and inclusion strategies, becomes critical in that regard. Thus, coordination capacity emerges as a proactive, even pre-emptive tool for infrastructure management and decision-making–not only in the case of complex projects with uncertain framework conditions but more generally as well.

Coordination capacity emerges as a proactive, even pre-emptive tool for infrastructure management and decision-making.

Will the field remain crowded? In 2016, when public administrations in many countries are still coming to terms with the aftermath of the 2008–9 financial crisis, weakened state capacities and eroding political legitimacy make it seem unlikely that the state will return to the quasi-monopolist role that was characteristic of the post-World War II era. It is equally unlikely that privatisation schemes as witnessed during the 1980s and 1990s will make a domineering comeback. A more likely scenario is that PPPs of various sorts will remain a fixture of infrastructure policy, with continuing reform attempts to improve allocation and future-proofing. For this to happen, not only are more voices of civil society needed as a counterbalance, but new approaches are also required to shield against NIMBYism and other deficiencies.

In any case, the numerous and varied innovations taking place in the field of infrastructure governance may be pointing us to some future pattern that has not yet become clear and is yet to reach fuller fruition. We can, however, already detect some contours. By themselves and jointly, regulatory and delivery capacity may no longer be enough, if they ever sufficed. By contrast, analytical and especially coordination capacity are likely to gain in importance: The governance arrangements of the future may require adequate ways and means to manage not only the state-market interface but the state-civil society and the market-civil society interfaces as well.

Endnotes

1. While often conflated in both academic and professional discussions, privatisation and PPPs are not actually one and the same. Privatisation refers to the material sale of assets, after which a company or its shares are owned by the private sector. PPPs refer to a range of models: for example, the private sector may own and operate assets while assuming a significant level of risk under certain PPP contractual arrangements, but only for the duration specified in the contract (see da Cruz and Cruz forthcoming for an explanation of different PPP arrangements and classifications).

2. For example, in the United States and without regulatory agencies in place, the federal government used public funds to attract private sector developers to transcontinental railroad expansion beginning as early as 1850 (White 2012). The US Congress supported railroad corporations with loan guarantees to relieve owners from having to use their own capital for expansion projects. Despite the fact that the loans effectively cost the government US$43 million, loan guarantees—pioneering when first introduced more than 150 years ago—are now considered key government strategies for encouraging and providing infrastructure.

3. In addition to the innovations presented in this chapter and on the Governance Report website, many other innovations and best practices are identified throughout this Report, especially in Chapters 2 to 5.

4. Additional innovations and best practices can be found on the Governance Report website at www.governancereport.org.

5. Nord Pool consulted on the design and implementation of SAPP's first competitive market (The Southern Times 2009).

6. In many locations, the functions of these Committees have been taken up by VDC WASH Coordination Committees, which were formed as per Nepal's National Hygiene and Sanitation Master Plan of 2011. WASH refers to water, sanitation, and hygiene programmes.

VII. Governance Indicators
Infrastructure

Matthias Haber

In the recent past, consultancies, academics, international organisations, and government agencies have produced multiple reports on the state of the world's infrastructure and its need for improvement and more investment (see Chapter 1 for a sampling). There is little doubt that infrastructure matters, yet the evidence that these reports base their findings on is surprisingly weak. Previous works have focused foremost on the financing and quality of infrastructure while ignoring the actual governance of infrastructure. Despite the many insights generated in the last decade, we still know relatively little about what role administrations and internal decision-making processes play in the success or failure of large infrastructure projects. This lack of knowledge about the capacities of governments to manage their infrastructure has led to contradictory conclusions about the effect of infrastructure spending on infrastructure outcomes and has produced confounding messages for policy makers.

> *Lack of knowledge about the capacities of governments to manage their infrastructure has produced confounding messages for policy-makers.*

The indicator suite developed for *The Governance Report 2016* treats governments' capacities to manage infrastructure as a distinct component of infrastructure governance that translates infrastructure inputs, i.e. funding and planning, into outcomes. Our indicators are based on a combination of macroeconomic variables of infrastructure outcomes and expert evaluations of countries' performances regarding the planning and management of infrastructure. We constructed the latter from a novel survey jointly created by the Hertie School of Governance and the OECD (see below). Our framework allows us to capture broad differences in governments' abilities to provide high quality infrastructure, though these abilities are difficult to detect when looking only at macroeconomic data.

Although we provide an aggregate, comparable measure of countries' infrastructure performances, we also keep in line with previous editions of *The Governance Report* (Hertie School of Governance 2013, 2014, 2015) by offering a number of disaggregated indicators. This allows us to explore potentially interesting relationships and address questions that cannot be answered by a single measure such as where a government needs to focus its attention and where it should take action in order to improve the state of infrastructure in its country.

In the next section we introduce the framework, the methodology, and the data used to measure infrastructure performance. We then present the results of our analyses and compare countries' ranks. The final section of this chapter explores the implications of our analyses for policy-makers.

Three Dimensions of Infrastructure Governance

In contrast to previous studies, we pay heightened attention to the decision-making and administrative processes involved in infrastructure policy and offer a holistic assessment of countries' abilities to plan, manage, and carry out infrastructure projects. Specifically, we measure governments' readiness to respond to the diverse and complex issues involved in infrastructure decision-making by looking at what we believe are three key dimensions of infrastructure governance: infrastructure planning, infrastructure management, and infrastructure outcomes.

At its core, our framework captures all four of the administrative capacities that we believe to be at the heart of contemporary discussions about governance and have featured in previous editions of *The Governance Report* (see Lodge and Wegrich 2014). Infrastructure planning, our first key dimension of infrastructure governance, requires expansive analytical capacity on the part of governments and concerns the organisation of knowledge and type of advice that informs governmental policy-making. It involves project and policy analytics related to making decisions about planning and funding infrastructure projects. Our second dimension, infrastructure management, captures governments' coordination and regulatory capacities. While regulation is about control and oversight over project and decision-making processes, coordination capacity is the ability to coordinate between multiple actors and organisations with diverse interests and goals. Finally, our third dimension, infrastructure outcomes, captures governments' delivery capacity in terms of the ways in which they execute policies and provide quality services.

We measure performance on each of these three dimensions using a novel set of indicators and variables. This allows us to present scores of countries' aggregate planning, management, and outcomes performances as well as identify nuanced differences all the way down to the individual variable level. Table 7.1 lists a partial selection of the indicators and variables that constitute the three dimensions. An even broader range of variables that may be used to test relationships are available in our online dashboard (http://www.governancereport.org/home/governance-indicators/).

To create the aforementioned indicators we collected original data from the Global Expert Survey on Public Infrastructure, jointly created by the

Table 7.1 **Selection of indicators on infrastructure governance**

Dimension	Indicator	Variable	Data Source
Planning	Infrastructure Funding	Funding development	Hertie School—OECD
		Funding gaps	Hertie School—OECD
		Private actor funding	Hertie School—OECD
	Planning and monitoring	Existence of a national plan	Hertie School—OECD
		Delivery modalities	Hertie School—OECD
	Actor involvement	Private actors	Hertie School—OECD
		Other actors	Hertie School—OECD
Management	Coordination challenges	Coordination at the central and regional levels	Hertie School—OECD
		Coordination across infrastructure sectors	Hertie School—OECD
	Corruption	Single bidder contracts	Corruption Risk index (Fazekas, Toth, and King 2013)
	Practices and instruments	Use of IT-based planning tools	Hertie School—OECD
		Public databases to track information	Hertie School—OECD
Outcomes	Access to infrastructure	Access to ICT	Global Innovation Index
		Access to utilities	World Development Indicators
	Infrastructure quality	Overall quality	Global Competitiveness Report
		Reliability	Enterprise Survey
		Logistics performance	World Development Indicators
		Road safety	OECD Statistics

Hertie School of Governance and the OECD in 2015. The goal of the survey was to provide an assessment of international trends, challenges, and potential solutions in the planning, funding, implementation, and monitoring of public infrastructure projects as seen from the perspective of infrastructure experts worldwide. The survey participants were experts in the key infrastructure areas of transportation, energy, water, waste and sanitation, IT/communications, building, and defence, and working in national governments, academia and research institutions, media, and the private business sector. These infrastructure experts were identified through systematic desk research using various online and offline sources and based on criteria such as position in a relevant public infrastructure-related organisation, publications on public infrastructure-related topics, and participation in national and international public infrastructure events.

Invitations to participate in the survey were sent to 1,485 experts in all 34 OECD member states plus ten additional non-OECD countries of particular size and significance within their respective regions: Romania and Russia in Europe; Brazil and Venezuela in Latin America; China, India, and Indonesia in Asia; and Egypt, Nigeria and South Africa in Africa. On average, we identified and contacted 30 experts per country and up to 50 experts in large economies such as Brazil, Canada, China, France, Germany, United States, and United Kingdom. Our sampling strategy followed approaches in previous large-scale international surveys (e.g. Curry, van de Walle, and Gadellaa 2014; Dahlström et al. 2015) and was designed to ensure an adequate response rate to create a sufficiently large number of observations for statistical analyses.

We asked the experts to respond to a set of 23 questions based on their country experience with developments in four key areas of public infrastructure governance: planning, funding, implementation, and monitoring. The questionnaire replicates items from the 2015 OECD–Committee of the Regions consultation on the governance of infrastructure investment across levels of government (see Chapter 3 for more details), the OECD regional survey on the effectiveness of public investment at the subnational level in times of fiscal constraints (OECD 2012), and the OECD framework for the governance of infrastructure (OECD 2015g). The design and order of the questions reflected our goals to minimise bias and maximise response rates.

The survey was conducted online and in English. We sent out email invitations to the group of experts in May 2015 followed by two additional email reminders to non-respondents. We also encouraged respondents to forward the survey link to other key public infrastructure experts with whom they were acquainted. To improve country coverage, we sent out additional invitations after the launch of the survey to countries with low response rates: Belgium, Canada, Denmark, France, Finland, Hungary, Japan, Mexico, Portugal, Mexico, Slovakia, South Korea, and Turkey. The survey was active for six weeks until July 2015.

Of the nearly 1,500 experts we invited to participate in the survey, 301 responded, resulting in a response rate of about 20 per cent. We excluded the responses of experts who answered fewer than half of the questions and removed countries with less than three expert evaluations. As shown in Figure 7.1, our final sample consists of 251 expert responses from 29 OECD and seven non-OECD countries. We used the mean expert response to each question to create our variables for the aforementioned indicators.

We complemented our survey data with infrastructure-related and macroeconomic data from World Bank sources such as the World Development Indicators (The World Bank), Doing Business reports (The World Bank), and Enterprise Surveys (The World Bank), OECD Statistics, the World Economic Forum's Global Competitiveness Report (WEF 2015), the Global Innovations Index (2015), and survey data from Gallup.

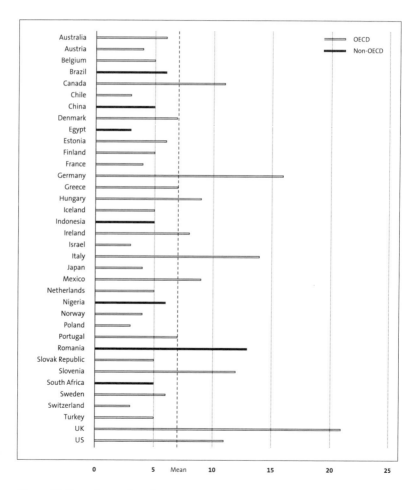

Figure 7.1 **Experts per Country**

Measuring What We Cannot Observe

To compare countries' performances according to our three dimensions of infrastructure governance, we aggregated our individual variables using a sophisticated statistical approach. We considered infrastructure governance and its three dimensions to be latent concepts that cannot be measured directly. Each of our variables, therefore, is a realisation of some underlying level of governance relating to one of the three dimensions, and this information can be used to estimate countries' underlying levels of infrastructure governance.

More specifically, we generated our estimates of countries' levels of infrastructure governance from a Bayesian factor analysis (BFA) model. Bayesian statistics seeks to answer one simple question: given the data that we observe about a country, what should we believe is its underlying level of infrastructure governance? One of the main advantages of Bayesian statistics is that it defines probability in a very intuitive way that follows how people actually reason, namely an indication of the plausibility of a situation. Using Bayesian statistics, one is able to provide a direct answer about the plausibility of a possible outcome. This contrasts with other approaches that assume that probabilities represent long-run frequencies with which events are bound to occur. Non-Bayesian approaches would not be able to give direct answers regarding the plausibility of outcomes but would instead make statements about a random sample from a fictitious population.

To have a better idea of how BFA works, imagine that we want to estimate a country's underlying level of infrastructure management capacity. We cannot observe the concept of infrastructure management capacity directly, but we do have a number of variables that we believe are related to it, such as challenges with coordinating different actors and monitoring the decision-making process. Although all of these variables are to some extent realisations of the underlying governance dimension, we assume that some have a stronger association with the latent dimension than others. The measure of this association is called the discrimination parameter.[1]

Before estimating a BFA model, we must first form prior beliefs, or assign weights, in terms of the extent to which our observed variables are linked to the dimension of infrastructure governance. Scholars often manually assign specific weights to the variables in order to capture their level of importance. In our BFA, we included highly 'uninformative' prior beliefs for all variables and let the data and the statistical model determine the ultimate weights. This ensures that the model does not prize any one variable over the others, and it also makes the analysis more reliable.[2] Given this setup, we can estimate the unobservable level of infrastructure governance using information gleaned from the variables collected for our set of countries.

We were able to perform several tasks in one step by using a BFA approach, which provides a principled approach to aggregation, avoids the use of pre-defined weights, and finally, scales different sources so that they can be meaningfully combined. In addition, the Bayesian approach, rooted in the probability of our estimates, allowed us to make probabilistic statements about the quantities we had estimated. For example, we were able to calculate the probability that a given country is or is not in the top five countries in the world for a dimension of infrastructure governance, or the probability that a country has a higher level of governance compared to another country. As a result, all of our dimensions can be, and in fact are, accompanied by measures of uncertainty. We also avoided the potential arbitrariness in weight selection when using weighted averages to attempt to construct an index, as the data informed us of the most appropriate weights of variables included in the form of the discrimination parameters.[3] Finally, our approach is completely transparent as well as replicable, given adequate knowledge of the model setup and access to the data.

To prepare the data for our BFA, we standardised all of our variables by subtracting the mean and dividing by the standard deviation. Finally, to simplify the presentation of our results, we rescaled all scores to fit between 0 and 100, with countries with stronger performances receiving higher scores.

Exploring Patterns and Relationships

In the following section, using the results from our BFA, we first compare the countries' rankings on each of our three dimensions of infrastructure governance. Then, we show the relationships between these three dimensions as well as highlight countries which are 'overachievers' and 'underachievers', i.e. whose performance on a governance dimension is greater or worse than expected, according to the relationships between these scores. Afterwards, we present how these dimension scores correlate with countries' levels of economic development as represented by their GDP per capita. Finally, we examine how spending and selected aspects of infrastructure management are associated with various outcomes.

Country performance across three dimensions

Figure 7.2 ranks the 36 countries according to how well they perform on each of the three dimensions of infrastructure planning, infrastructure management, and infrastructure outcomes. The black dots show the countries' scores while the black horizontal lines represent the statistical uncertainty around the scores. The vertical line illustrates the mean scores for all countries. The five top-performing countries in terms of infrastructure

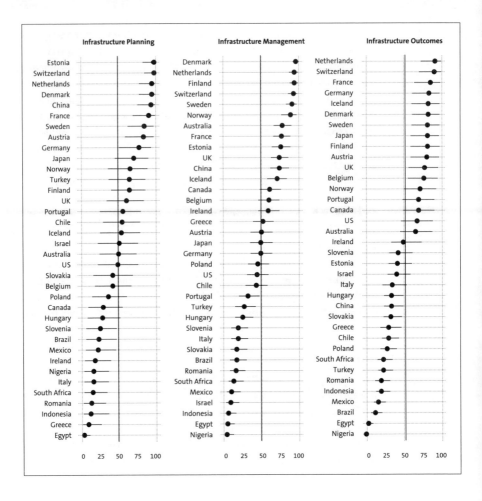

Figure 7.2 **Country performance in infrastructure planning, management, and outcomes**

planning are Estonia, Switzerland, the Netherlands, Denmark, and China, scoring close to if not more than 90 points. China's performance is particularly remarkable, as all other non-OECD countries perform well below the average. France, Sweden, Austria, Germany, and Japan also perform quite strongly with scores between 70 and 90, while Israel, Australia, and the United States rank squarely in the middle. With the exception of China, non-OECD countries ranked in the bottom third of countries, together with countries such as Greece, Italy, and Ireland that were strongly affected by the financial and economic crisis that began in 2008–9. Brazil's below-average performance echoes the discussion in Chapter 2 on infrastructure governance and government decision-making, which suggests that the country's ability to directly invest in public infrastructure was somewhat limited by the privatisation of dozens of state-owned companies in the early 2000s.

Similar patterns emerge when we look at the infrastructure management dimension in the second panel in Figure 7.2. Denmark, the Netherlands, and Switzerland still rank among the top five, but the scores for Estonia and China drop to around 75 out of a possible 100 points. Similarly, Germany's and Turkey's infrastructure management performances are significantly lower than their performances on the planning dimension. In contrast, countries such as Ireland and Greece that scored near the bottom in terms of infrastructure planning show rather average management performances. Australia, ranked in the middle on the planning dimension, is among the top performers in terms of infrastructure management. This is not surprising, as Australia is a country with strong platforms for coordination of infrastructure decisions, e.g. Infrastructure Australia, as pointed out in Chapter 2 on government decision-making in infrastructure and in Chapter 3 on subnational infrastructure governance. Egypt, Indonesia, and Nigeria again show some of the strongest deficiencies in infrastructure management.

Regarding the third dimension, infrastructure outcomes, the Netherlands, Switzerland, France, Germany, and Iceland rank the highest. The Netherlands and Switzerland then are the only two countries that score among the top five on all three dimensions of infrastructure governance. Another top performer in terms of infrastructure outcomes, Germany, scores around 85, which stands in rather stark contrast to the country's performance on the first and especially second dimensions. Similarly, Iceland's performance is much better than the country's near average scores on the other two dimensions. In contrast, China, a top performer in terms of infrastructure planning, places much lower in the ranking on outcomes. The scores of two other BRICS states, South Africa and Brazil, are below 25 and place them among the bottom ten performers.

Figure 7.3 illustrates our aggregate infrastructure governance index, which ranks the countries by averaging the scores that they received on each of the three dimensions. Switzerland, the Netherlands, Denmark, Sweden, and France are the top five performers overall, scoring high on each of the indices. The big economies Japan and the United States rank among the middle third of the set of countries, and the worst performers overall are Romania, Mexico, Indonesia, Nigeria, and Egypt. There are also some interesting cases that emerge with large variations among the different dimensions. For example, while Iceland's performance scores increase when moving from planning to outcomes, China's and Estonia's decline significantly. Finland, Ireland, and Greece perform relatively poorly on planning and outcomes in comparison with higher management scores. The reverse is true for Austria, Germany, Japan, and Portugal, which have a relatively poor infrastructure management performance compared to their strong showing with regards to planning and outcomes.

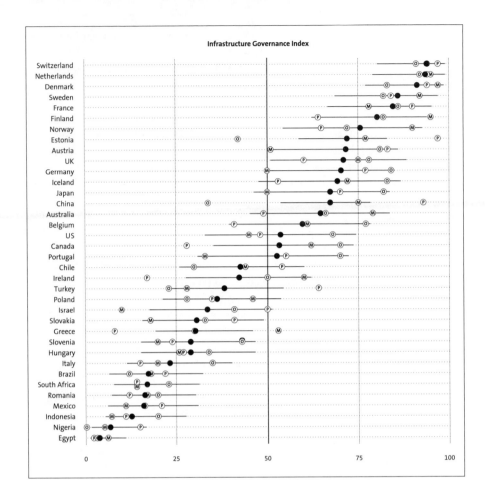

Figure 7.3 **Infrastructure Governance Index**
Note: P=Planning; M=Management; O=Outcomes

The results of our analysis show that countries' infrastructure performances can vary widely depending on whether we look at infrastructure planning, management, or outcomes. A country can execute good infrastructure planning without equally good infrastructure outcomes, as the examples of Estonia and China highlight. These differences demonstrate the importance of separating the evaluation of infrastructure governance into distinct dimensions and the need to pay close attention to the processes that happen in between planning and outcomes, i.e. what we call infrastructure management. Our framework allows us to paint a broad but at the same time much more nuanced picture of infrastructure governance than any single, aggregated measure could.

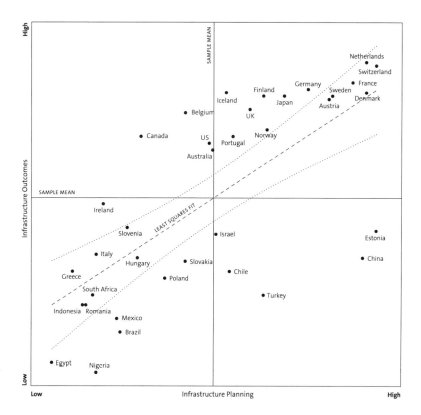

Figure 7.4 **Infrastructure planning and infrastructure outcomes**

Good outcomes require planning and management

The next set of figures, Figures 7.4 to 7.6, shows the degree of association behind the three dimensions and provides further insights into the countries' performances. The graphs plot the scores of each country on two infrastructure governance dimensions including a least squares linear fit as a measure of association. The solid black lines represent the average (mean) scores across all countries for each dimension. In all three figures, countries in the top right quadrant are those that perform well on the two dimensions being compared, while countries in the lower left quadrant perform poorly.

All three figures–indicating infrastructure planning in relation to infrastructure outcomes (Figure 7.4), infrastructure planning in relation to infrastructure management (Figure 7.5), and infrastructure management in relation to infrastructure outcomes (Figure 7.6)–show strong positive associations between pairs of infrastructure governance dimensions. Countries that perform well on one dimension also tend to perform well on the other dimensions, albeit with some variation. For example, in Figure 7.4, which

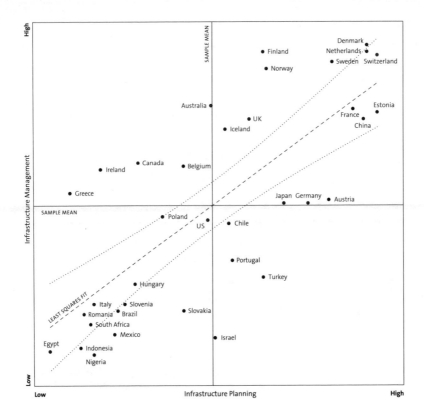

Figure 7.5 **Infrastructure planning and infrastructure management**

shows the relationship between infrastructure planning and outcomes, a number of countries perform relatively strongly in terms of planning but relatively poorly in terms of outcomes. For instance, China and Estonia–both found in the lower right quadrant–are ranked at or near the top in terms of infrastructure planning but receive below average scores for outcomes. The opposite is true for Belgium and Canada, situated in the upper left quadrant: Both countries show very strong infrastructure outcomes performance but receive relatively weak scores on planning.

Though most countries score as well (or poorly) on infrastructure planning as they do on management, this is not always the case. As shown in Figure 7.5, Austria, Japan, and Germany appear to have very good planning systems in place, but only average management processes. And while Canada and Ireland score well below average on planning, they seem to manage infrastructure better than average.

When looking then at the relationship between infrastructure management and outcomes (see Figure 7.6), we find Austria, Japan, and Germany again with average management, but with outcomes ranking well above

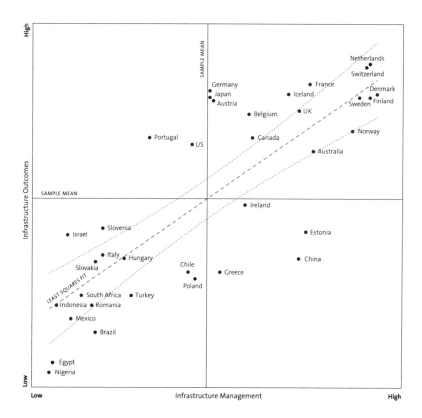

Figure 7.6 **Infrastructure management and infrastructure outcomes**

average. Portugal too performs much better on outcomes than management. China and Estonia are outliers, as they were in Figure 7.4, showing relatively high performance in management but below-average outcomes.

Figure 7.7 extends the above discussion and illustrates whether a country is 'over-' or 'underachieving' on the management and outcomes dimensions. In other words, does a country perform better or worse than expected, given what we would anticipate based on its scores on planning and management?[4] A number of countries are overachievers, i.e. they perform much better on one dimension than their scores on another dimension would suggest they might. Iceland and Belgium, for example, are overperforming in all three scenarios, whereas other countries such as Nigeria and Turkey are chronic underachievers. Furthermore, some countries, such as Finland, perform very well in terms of infrastructure management and outcomes, in spite of planning performance that is closer to the average.

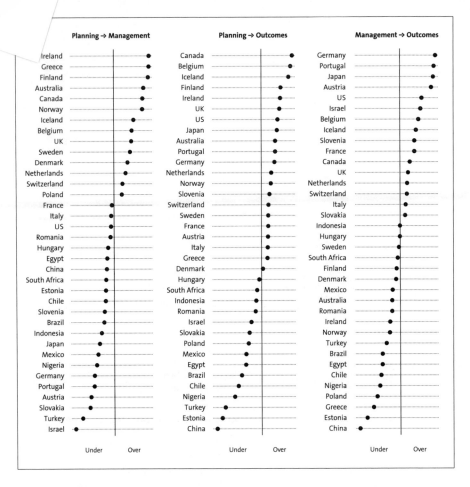

Figure 7.7 **Estimation of over- and underachievement based on expected performance**

The level of economic development matters

To further explore the state of infrastructure governance in our set of countries, we adjusted their performance on all three dimensions by levels of economic development (see Stanig 2014: 138). The idea behind our approach is that less economically developed countries might struggle more to achieve high infrastructure governance scores than more developed countries. For such countries, receiving a high score on any dimension is far more impressive than for economically developed counterparts. Our approach removes any effects of economic development from the main dimension scores, thus allowing us to see whether the associations between indices are solely a product of differing development levels.

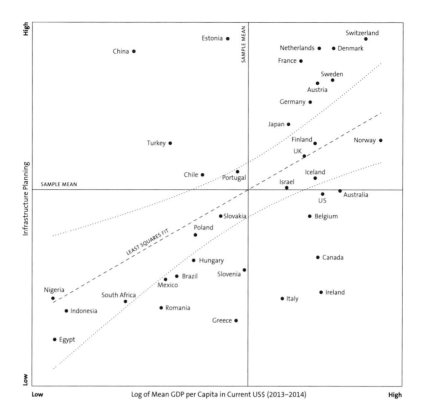

Figure 7.8 **Level of economic development and infrastructure planning**

Figures 7.8 to 7.10 illustrate this concept by displaying the relationship between the three dimensions and the countries' levels of development as measured by GDP per capita. As seen across the three figures, there is a general positive association, in that higher levels of economic development are related to higher scores on each of the dimensions. However, this is not an iron law, with some countries appearing to over- or underachieve relative to their GDP per capita. In particular, there is a considerable amount of variation with regard to the infrastructure planning dimension (Figure 7.8). While some countries are seen to be doing well in terms of planning despite relatively low levels of economic development, for instance China, Estonia, and Turkey (upper left quadrant), others are considerable underachievers, for instance Italy, Ireland, and Canada (lower right quandrant).

A similar pattern, albeit with less overall variation, can be seen with regard to infrastructure management (Figure 7.9) and outcomes (Figure 7.10). Again, China and Estonia perform much better on the infrastructure management dimension than their level of economic development would suggest. In contrast, Italy and Israel (in the lower right quadrant of Figures

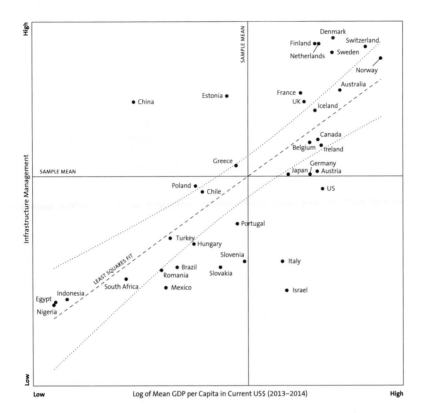

Figure 7.9 **Level of economic development and infrastructure management**

7.9 and 7.10) have not been able to translate their economic potential into good scores on infrastructure management or outcomes. Portugal is the only country that clearly performs better on outcomes than its level of economic development would suggest. All other countries' performance on this dimension is generally as expected.

Using these insights, we again constructed a measure of over- and underarchievement in Figure 7.11. This time, however, we adjusted for the countries' levels of economic development, which allows us to test whether countries' over- or underperformance is simply a function of their economic development. For example, we see that China, a previous underperformer on management and outcomes, is now listed as a top performer on those two dimensions in light of its economic development. Indonesia, Egypt, and Nigeria, all at the bottom of the overall ranking, fare better when taking into account their level of economic development, all now at or somewhat above where they would have been expected to be on the three dimensions. In contrast, whereas the United States was previously around or just above average in terms of all three dimensions, its performance is below average given its

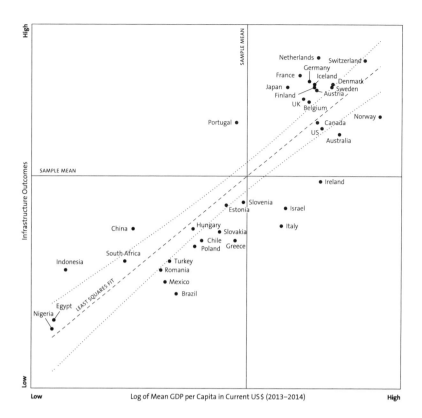

Figure 7.10 **Level of economic development and infrastructure outcomes**

level of economic development. Notably, Switzerland and the Netherlands, the two countries topping the overall ranking, prove to achieve well above what would be expected, while Brazil and Mexico perform much less well than predicted. Thus, corresponding with the findings shown in Figures 7.8 to 7.10, though there seems to be some relation between level of economic development and performance on the three dimensions of infrastructure governance, particularly outcomes, many countries go above and beyond, while others fail to meet their potential.

The determinants of outcomes

In the final set of figures presented in this chapter, we examine how financial spending on infrastructure and different management modalities affect infrastructure outcomes such as quality and productivity. Looking first at spending, Figure 7.12 shows the association between the countries' total investment in inland infrastructure as a percentage of their GDP (OECD 2016d) and their

Figure 7.11 **Estimation of over- and underachievement based on level of economic development**

performance on the infrastructure outcomes dimension of our indicators set. Inland infrastructure investment covers spending on new transport construction as well as improvements of existing networks and includes road, rail, inland waterways, maritime ports, and airports. Quite surprisingly, we found that a negative relationship exists between the two variables, suggesting that increased spending on infrastructure does not automatically lead to better infrastructure outcomes. For some countries, this effect is particularly obvious. Romania, for example, invests more than 2.2 per cent of its GDP in public infrastructure, but its performance on the index is among the weakest. By contrast, Iceland, the Netherlands, and Germany achieve relatively high outcome scores despite investing a relatively small fraction of their GDP in their infrastructure.

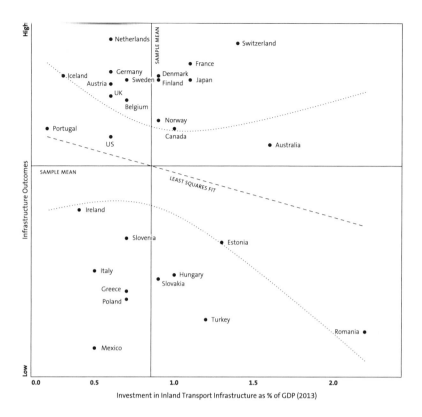

Figure 7.12 **Total investment in inland infrastructure as a percentage of GDP and infrastructure outcomes performance**

Figure 7.13 shows that the negative association between spending and infrastructure outcomes holds even when looking at changes in infrastructure spending over a five-year period, as reported by respondents to the Hertie School–OECD expert survey on infrastructure. As before, several countries do not seem able to translate their investment into good outcomes. For instance, though China is reported to have increased spending, it ranks well below average on outcomes. This echoes the findings reported in Chapter 1 that China outspends its needs and focuses many of its investments on infrastructure abroad, rather than on its own territory. In other countries where an investment increase over the past five years was noted but outcomes remain relatively low, either the spending has not yet borne fruit or its application might have gone awry. In contrast, a number of countries in the periphery of Europe, such as Portugal and Ireland, are considered to have average or better infrastructure although investment has declined over the past five years, most likely as part of cost-cutting measures.

Our analysis uncovered similar relationships between spending and

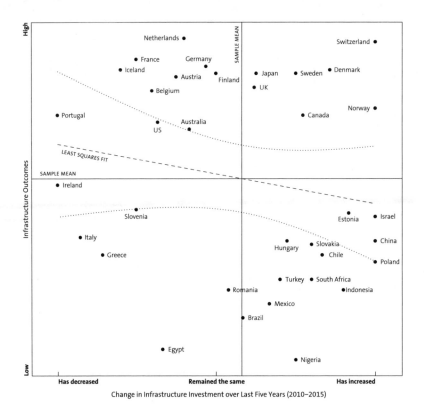

Figure 7.13 **Change in infrastructure spending over the last 5 years and infrastructure outcomes performance**

other measures of infrastructure outcomes. Figure 7.14, for example, shows the relationship between changes in infrastructure investments over five years as reported by experts responding to the Hertie School–OECD survey and a country's quality of infrastructure as measured by the World Economic Forum's *Global Competitiveness Report* (WEF 2015). That report ranks countries based on the quality of their roads, railroads, ports, and air transport infrastructure and on the reliability and stability of their energy and telecommunication networks. The horizontal slope in Figure 7.14 indicates that increased spending has not necessarily led to improved infrastructure quality. A number of countries increased their investment over the last five years but only a handful such as Chile manage to significantly improve the overall quality of their infrastructure. Many countries experienced no, or only small, improvements despite increased investments. Poland, one of the low performers on our aggregate infrastructure index, ranks lowest on this measure of infrastructure quality although investment is reported to have increased. In contrast, a number of countries such as Austria, France, and especially Egypt

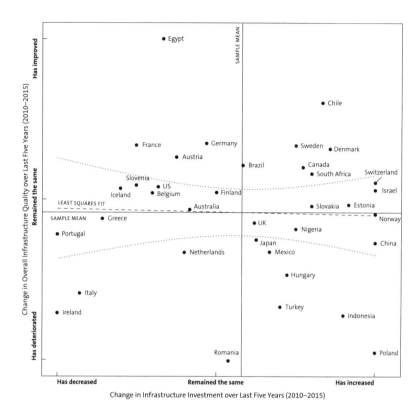

Figure 7.14 **Change in infrastructure spending and overall infrastructure quality over the last 5 years**

managed to significantly improve the quality of their infrastructure despite declining levels of investment.

Gains in productivity could also be considered an outcome of infrastructure investment. Thus, similar to the associations presented in the previous three figures, we can also explore the relationship between infrastructure investment and productivity growth. In contrast to the previous findings, however, Figure 7.15 illustrates a positive correlation between infrastructure investment and change in multifactor productivity over a ten-year period (OECD 2016c) although the uncertainty bands allow for a negative relationship as well. The data show quite a large amount of variation, and the association between the two variables seems to be strongly driven by South Korea, which invested only a slightly above average proportion of its GDP in infrastructure but saw a major return in increased productivity. In the United States and to a lesser degree Germany, below average investment still seems to translate into above average productivity gains, whereas Italy's near average investment was matched with a decline in productivity over the ten-year period. Australia, on the other hand,

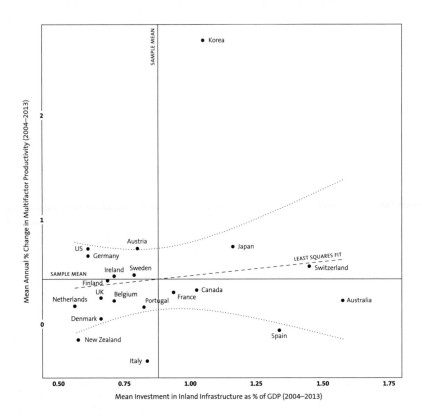

Figure 7.15 **Infrastructure investment as a percentage of GDP and productivity growth (2004—2013)**

shows only a moderate increase in multifactor productivity in spite of relatively substantial investments in infrastructure over the years. This finding is further supported by a Standard & Poor's (2015) report, mentioned in Chapter 1, which found that Australia has a smaller multiplier effect of infrastructure spending.

Finally, Figure 7.16 examines the relationship between one aspect of our second dimension, infrastructure management, and our third dimension, infrastructure outcomes. Specifically, we use data from the Hertie School–OECD survey to test how transparency of decision-making processes, including those processes related to planning and procurement, might affect countries' performances on the outcomes dimension. As Figure 7.16 shows, countries can improve their infrastructure outcomes when transparency is a key element of their decision-making processes. The effect is particularly apparent in the Netherlands, Switzerland, Denmark, Finland, and Sweden. This suggests that these countries' strong performances on the outcomes dimension may be driven at least in part by the fact that their governance systems are very transparent, notably all ranking among the top ten countries in Trans-

Figure 7.16 **Transparency as relevant planning criterion of infrastructure management and infrastructure outcomes**

parency International's Corruption Perceptions Index (Transparency International 2016). Other countries such as Egypt, Nigeria, and Mexico, where transparency is not considered a relevant criterion in planning, perform significantly worse.

Conclusion

Providing high quality infrastructure demands more than financial investment. As has been shown throughout this Report, it is a multi-stage endeavour that involves complex decision-making processes at multiple levels and coordination among diverse groups of actors. For that reason, this chapter introduced an indicator suite that goes well beyond existing measures by addressing three key dimensions of infrastructure governance. By simultaneously assessing governments' abilities to effectively plan, manage, and carry out infrastructure projects, we address the fundamental capacities that are at the very heart of contemporary discussions about governance.

The analyses presented here–there could be many others–have revealed a number of insights that may be of particular use to infrastructure decision-makers, especially those in national as well as subnational governments. Generally, we have shown that countries that perform well on one dimension also tend to perform well on the other dimensions and furthermore that OECD member states tend to perform significantly better than the non-OECD countries we cover. Nevertheless, we also find that only few countries, such as Switzerland and the Netherlands, manage to perform equally strongly across all three dimensions of infrastructure governance. For example, Estonia and China are top performers in terms of infrastructure planning but score below average when it comes to actual infrastructure outcomes. We see much less variation at the bottom half of the three indices, where less developed economies such as Nigeria and Indonesia and countries strongly impacted by the economic crisis of 2008–9 such as Greece, Italy, and Ireland perform average at best or relatively poorly on all dimensions.

Notably, the picture slightly changes when we take into account levels of economic development. Although higher levels of economic development generally tend to translate into higher scores on all dimensions, a number of previously low-scoring countries such as Nigeria and Egypt score near the middle of the ranking when adjusted for GDP per capita. In the case of China in particular, we see that the country moves to the top of the planning and management dimensions and scores near the top on the outcomes dimension.

We also examined how spending on and investment in infrastructure and different management modalities affect infrastructure outcomes. Surprisingly, we found a negative relationship between a country's infrastructure investment and its performance on the infrastructure outcomes dimension. China is again a good example. Despite apparent increases in investment over the past five years, it continues to rank below average on infrastructure outcomes. In contrast, countries such as Portugal and Ireland have relatively good infrastructure despite declining infrastructure investment. In effect, increased spending and investment do not necessarily improve infrastructure quality, at least not in the medium term. On the other hand, when it comes to the relationship between investment and productivity growth, there appears to be a positive correlation, with South Korea, the United States, and Germany as prime examples. Finally, we tested the relationship between one aspect of infrastructure management, using data from the Hertie School–OECD expert survey, and outcomes. As the analysis showed, we can expect, for example, that increased transparency of decision-making processes will improve infrastructure outcomes.

Ultimately, what the analyses here indicate is that broad, highly aggregated infrastructure governance indicators are not necessarily the best tool for informing policy-makers how they might improve infrastructure governance. As we have shown, behind a single country score or ranking are often significant variations: some states might perform well on infrastructure planning but less well in terms of management and outcomes. In this sense, more nuanced disaggregated indicators such as those developed for this Report seem to provide better indications of which dimension of the process needs to be addressed in order for a country to improve its infrastructure governance.

Endnotes

1. More formally, given K indicators, denote y_{ik} the observation of indicator $k \in \{1,2,\mathbf{K},K\}$ for country i, and let θ_i be the the unobservable underlying level of governance for country i. The model is then,

   $$y_{ik} = \alpha_k + \beta_k \theta_i + \varepsilon_{ik}$$

   where β_k is the discrimination parameter mentioned previously, α_k is an indicator specific intercept term, and ε_{ik} is the error term. This error term is assumed to be distributed according to a normal distribution with mean 0 and standard deviation σ_k, capturing the previous intuition that some variables may be more 'noisy' than others.

2. More formally, we impose the following prior distributions upon the parameters of interest in the model:

   $\alpha_k \sim$ Normal$(0,\sigma_a)$, $\beta_k \sim$ Normal$(0,5)$, $\theta_i \sim$ Normal$(0,1)$, $\sigma_a \sim$ Uniform $(0,5)$, $\sigma_k \sim$ Uniform $(0,5)$.

   Note that our prior on the level of association between the observed variables and the underlying governance score is sufficiently wide so that the results are data-driven. In addition, the distributional assumption on θ_i results in a model that is practically identified locally (Jackman 2009). This means that our parameters are identified up to a 180 degree rotation of the latent scale (Jackman 2009). Rather than impose a sign restriction on one of the variables used, which would ensure global identification, we instead simply rotate the latent scale so that it follows a natural interpretation of higher values, meaning better performance on this index.

3. This arbitrariness also applies to non-weighted averages, as these are simply weighted averages where every variable receives the weight of one.

4. This is calculated using regression residuals. For example, suppose we are interested in calculating which countries are overachieving and which are underachieving in infrastructure management given their performances in infrastructure planning. To do so we estimate a least squares regression, with management scores as the dependent variable and planning scores as the independent variables. The residuals from this regression then tell us whether a given country's management score is different than expected given its planning score. Positive residuals indicate overachieving, and negative residuals indicate underachieving.

VIII. Improving Infrastructure Governance
Implications and Recommendations

HELMUT K. ANHEIER *and* ROLF ALTER

This Report began by pointing to the perplexing picture that infrastructure policies present from a macroeconomic perspective. Never has there been more investment in infrastructure, yet in many countries actual spending falls behind estimated future needs that are often based on widely differing estimates. Substantial plans are realised irrespective of changing needs and framework conditions, while others remain on the drawing board even though needs remain high and conditions unchanged. There is a pattern of underinvestment in some countries, overinvestment in others, frequent delays and cost overruns, and a puzzling relationship between infrastructure investment, productivity, and quality. Indeed, the *ultima ratio* of such investments, i.e. the allegedly tight connection with productivity growth and improved infrastructure quality, seems less clear-cut empirically than conventional textbook economics assumes.

Any assessment of the ability to provide high-level infrastructure needs to take into account the resources that countries have at their disposal.

The governance indicators in Chapter 7 have shown that any assessment of the ability to provide high-level infrastructure needs to take into account the financial and institutional resources that countries have at their disposal. At first, this seems like a commonplace, and not surprisingly, on average OECD countries outperform non-OECD countries on the three dimensions of infrastructure governance, i.e. planning, management, and outcomes. Clearly, OECD countries have more financial capabilities and institutions in place to provide for higher quality infrastructure. Yet when taking a closer look, the indicators reveal that countries vary significantly in the ways and the extent to which they

---

The opinions expressed and arguments employed herein are solely those of the authors and do not necessarily reflect the official views of the OECD or of its member countries.

manage to translate resources into good outcomes. Some larger, developed economies such as the United States, Canada, and Italy perform relatively poorly despite their potential. Others such as Indonesia, China, and even Nigeria perform better in terms of outcomes than expected given their level of economic development (Figure 7.11).

The results presented in Chapter 7 also suggest that increased infrastructure spending over the last decade has had little impact on infrastructure quality and has improved productivity only slightly (Figure 7.15). This is surprising, as the debate on the poor state of the world's infrastructure, which intensified in the aftermath of the recent financial and economic crisis, saw low quality infrastructure as both a reason for stagnant or declining productivity and an opportunity for recovery. Indeed, countries heavily impacted by the economic crisis such as Greece, Ireland, and Italy also perform worse than their peers in the aggregate scores for infrastructure governance (Figure 7.3).[1]

Against these and other findings (see Chapter 1), the main thrust of this Report was to help correct the long-standing negligence of policy analysts and academics alike when it comes to the governance of infrastructure: what does it take to make infrastructure investment perform well in the public interest? Governance, this Report argues, is key to the success not only of individual projects but also of overall country performance of infrastructure investments in meeting needs, contributing to productivity growth, and realising quality improvements. Governance readiness–defined as the conditions in which active problem-solving can be achieved and which requires analytical, regulatory, coordination, and delivery capacities (Lodge and Wegrich 2014a)–means going beyond the mobilisation of financial resources as the frequently assumed primary bottleneck behind lagging infrastructure investments. In fact, good governance might well reduce the bottleneck of infrastructure finance as it helps achieve the expected private and social returns on investment.

Several authors in this Report saw infrastructure policies caught in some kind of systemic uncertainty, seemingly locked in a complex, contested triangle of needs, capacities, and technology. The response, they contend, cannot simply be more finances, more public funds, more regulation, more civil society participation, or more public-private partnerships. While these may all be components of good infrastructure governance and policies, they are insufficient by themselves.[2] Instead, as the chapters in this Report suggest, the proper response is about how infrastructure policy is more generally decided upon and implemented.[3] Indeed, the governance capacities in place make a difference in terms of policy performance as well as the success or failure of individual infrastructure projects.

Yet the very multidimensionality and indeed complexity of infrastructure, as Wegrich and Hammerschmid point out in Chapter 2, make needs assessments difficult and performance hard to measure over time, leading to ambiguity of outcomes and ambivalence among stakeholders and the population at large.[4] How much countries, regions or cities are to invest in infrastructure, and how, seems less fixed, more relative, and dependent on current as well as future macroeconomic conditions. At the local level in particular, the macroeconomic needs easily get lost in the dispersion of power across levels of government and in the influence of professions and lobby groups over conflicting subfields of infrastructure (e.g. rail versus road transport instead of mobility). Vice versa, context conditions may be ill-suited to the effective realisation of large-scale projects and infrastructure maintenance generally.

Main Conclusions and Recommendations

What, then, can we conclude and recommend based on the preceding analyses in terms of the four governance capacities–analytical, regulatory, coordination, and delivery–and the four key issues identified, i.e. allocation, reform, trust and participation, and future-proofing? Contributions to this Report have already reached conclusions, suggested best practices, and put forth rich sets of recommendations in the context of their respective chapters. Here we go beyond them and propose, based on what we regard as overarching implications, a select number of concrete steps with the potential to enhance performance in the field of infrastructure.

Acknowledge tensions

The first implication and indeed recommendation is to acknowledge the tensions that are endemic to the field of infrastructure but seem too easily disregarded as they usually affect debates about the macroeconomic conditions of infrastructure. These tensions rest between politics, i.e. priority-setting and decision-making based on political values and normative considerations; policies, i.e. their programmatic implementation into concrete action and financial allocations; and the technological and logistical requirements at the project level. Gas pipelines between the European Union (EU) and Russia are an obvious example, as are the German *Energiewende*–the decision to phase out nuclear energy and shift to renewable energy sources–and Japan's response to the Fukushima disaster, which was to not change the country's energy policy in any fundamental way.

Too often and rather naively, infrastructure is considered as policies without politics and technocratic implementation without broader political considerations, thereby creating the illusion of technocratic decision-making. Cases in point are the demise of the nuclear power industry in many countries and the Stuttgart 21 planning fiasco in Germany.[5] They illustrate how entire policies and projects can become discredited even though regulatory and planning requirements and processes have been observed. Legitimation through proper processes–the long-established principle of public administration–no longer seems to apply.

Vice versa, some infrastructure politics are without proper regard for the administrative, economic, and technical feasibility of specific projects. In such cases, political clouds overshadow the 'sober assessment' that Hawkesworth and Garin in Chapter 5 associate with sound infrastructure policies and planning. As a result, needed infrastructure may never be built or may be significantly delayed–sometimes for decades–such as the light rail systems in Los Angeles; infrastructure may end up being built even when there is no real need, like some airports in Spain[6]; or blatant cost overruns and delays, even apparent dilettantism, may occur, as the governance failures of Berlin's BER airport illustrate (see Case Study 1 in Chapter 4).

The issue of projects without proper regard for politics and politics without proper regard for project requirements is characteristic of similar tensions in public-private partnerships: between what March and Olsen (1996) call the logic of appropriateness, i.e. the public sector principle of following a set process to achieve legitimacy, and the logic of consequence, i.e. the private sector principle of gaining legitimacy by results. By themselves, both principles are insufficient due to the complexity and long-term nature of infrastructure; brought together, they can produce political or managerial-technical conflicts, even gridlock. And they feed back to the caution on the part of private investors to engage in infrastructure financing (Arezki et al. 2016).

Thus, any attempt to improve decision-making about infrastructure needs to take into account the inherent complexity and risks of the field and needs to accept that political logics rather than mere needs assessments or financial or technical aspects alone can suffice as main drivers. The Hertie School-OECD expert survey conducted for this Report clearly indicates that political priorities are the key criteria for decision-making about infrastructure. Yet these priorities may not necessarily reflect actual governance capacities, and vice versa. The systemic uncertainty of infrastructure governance may well be rooted, at least in part, in denying the crucial relationship between politics and capacities, or between the different logics, as March and Olsen (1996) point out. Disregarding that relationship and the uncertainty thus created may well be behind the perplexing picture of infrastructure investments, productivity growth, and quality.

Thus, there is a dual need: on the one hand, to complement the currently dominant economic-technocratic perspective of infrastructure governance and planning with a politically sound macroeconomic perspective, and on the other hand, to assess political expectations in the context of actual governance capacities by demanding analytically and empirically firmer footing and a sounder evidence base.

Put differently, when this Report advocates bringing governance into infrastructure policies, it highlights the need to acknowledge rather than deny their inherent political nature: for example, China[7] and Japan overinvest for political reasons, in the case of China to encourage massive urban development and in Japan to shore up a sluggish domestic economy via expected multiplier effects of infrastructure investments (see The Economist 2013). Other countries underinvest in infrastructure–also for political reasons–usually based on budgetary decisions that attach greater emphasis to current expenditures such as serving entitlement programs than to infrastructure investments.[8]

But underinvestment can also stem from the political or administrative inability to create more efficient and effective planning, future-proofing, and procurement and delivery systems for infrastructure projects. This is the case in Germany, where many finance-strapped local governments lack adequate administrative capacity to assess and manage infrastructure projects and acquire financing for them (Expertenkommission 2015), or in countries like Brazil, where, as described in Chapter 2, the Growth Acceleration Program (PAC and PAC II) has suffered from significant planning and coordination problems. Corruption plays a role, of course, but such inability can also extend to the handling of influential NIMBY ('not in my backyard') constituencies, where public authorities let infrastructure projects go astray for fear of alienating needed political support bases. Likewise, infrastructure policies and projects are sometimes linked to pork barrel politics and backroom deals rather than rational planning efforts. This is a tendency often observed in polities divided along ethnic, religious, or cultural lines, including significant differences in economic development.

Develop coordination capacity

The second implication relates to the relative underdevelopment of governance capacities, especially coordination, compared to the over-institutionalisation of others, namely regulation. In other words, whereas the field of infrastructure seems dense in terms of rules and regulations for procurement, technical specifications and administrative requirements, and oversight more generally, it seems less populated with institutions that properly address the governance challenge of coordination.

Not only are coordination failures behind some of the more spectacular cases, e.g. contested, politicised projects such as Berlin's BER airport and Boston's Big Dig, but also there is a more general pattern that seems to emerge: the Hertie School-OECD expert survey (see Chapter 2) demonstrates how significantly experts rank coordination problems. Similarly, the OECD-CoR survey of infrastructure governance reported on in Chapter 3 reveals the importance of coordination between national and subnational levels and different agencies. Kostka in Chapter 4 in terms of project life cycles and Hawkesworth and Garin in presenting the decision tree for choosing delivery models in Chapter 5 also emphasise the issue of coordination. Furthermore, in analysing governance innovations, Anheier and Kaufmann report coordination problems at the heart of many innovations reviewed in Chapter 6.

Coordination capacity is about mediating and managing different actors, stakeholders, and tasks in order to succeed in the kind of collective action required for complex infrastructure projects. It would, however, be too strong to conclude that infrastructure governance suffers from institutional voids (Hajer 2003), a syndrome of under-institutionalisation leading to systemic governance failures. Nonetheless, we argue that coordination deficiencies stand out so significantly that they seem to be a key determining factor of overall performance. Arising from institutional weaknesses, they not only relate to the relationship between different levels and units of government (see Chapter 3) but also extend to coordination with business and civil society as well. Similarly, the cases reviewed by Anheier and Kaufmann in Chapter 6 reveal the challenges of coordination that can then lead to governance innovations, e.g. RAKLI's procurement clinics in Finland, the Water Use Master Plan in Nepal, or regional power pools such as the Southern African Power Pool.

What is more, given the complexity of many infrastructure projects, a lack of coordination between different stakeholders creates as well as reinforces information asymmetries, opening up opportunities for market inefficiencies and various forms of contract failures, including corruption. Underlying are the tensions between the logics of appropriateness and consequence: each involves different sectors, agencies, professions, and other stakeholders, a situation prone to communication problems and mismatched expectations. Again, the Finnish case of RAKLI illustrates how the very complexity of infrastructure projects makes it difficult to create level playing fields for all stakeholders, in this case potential bidders in procurement processes. It also creates friction with civil society and vocal constituencies by inviting NIMBYism and opposition generally, leading to an erosion of trust, a major challenge facing renewable energy policy that was resolved in Samsø, Denmark (see Chapter 6).

Improve the evidence base

The third implication refers to analytical capacity and is indeed closely related to the coordination challenge. Efficient and effective coordination is more likely to happen if actors have the capacity to provide sufficient data and have adequate knowledge and expertise for project planning, risk assessment, and implementation, especially under conditions of political, financial, or technical uncertainty. Such intelligence is by no means limited to these domains of uncertainty, let alone restricted to legal and regulatory issues; rather it includes certain process sensitivity, even leadership, in understanding the expectations and constraints of the various stakeholders involved. It requires longer-term, systemic views as well as attention to detail, especially when information is contested among the parties involved.

Unfortunately, analytical capacity that is both encompassing and strategic, politically savvy and astute, and technically and economically sound seems all too rare, as the various chapters in this Report have pointed out. There is a paucity of systematic data collection by governments at all levels to strengthen the evidence base with an emphasis on processes and outcomes and going beyond the limited set of macroeconomic indicators. Too few countries have dedicated institutions capable of providing such intelligence on an ongoing basis. In most countries, analytical capacities are divided by disciplines, e.g. economics, legal, administrative, and technical, and levels, e.g. national, regional, and local, and scattered across ministries as well as public agencies.

Thus, one of the most important functions of governments, i.e. providing and maintaining infrastructure for current and future well-being, has no identifiable home in the political-administrative systems of many countries. Infrastructure policy seems less hardwired and connected. What is more, few countries and regions conduct systematic evaluations of large-scale projects in order to build up repertoires of best practices to guide future infrastructure policies and planning. As a result, infrastructure policy becomes far more a series of one-off projects than a more steady state approach allowing for cross-learning and build-up of expertise.

The Need for Dedicated Infrastructure Institutions

In view of the main recommendations below, it is important to recall the underlying causes of deficiencies in coordination and analytic capacity. In Chapter 2, Hammerschmid and Wegrich suggest four such causes: first, the complexity and ambiguity of the field resulting from a clash between the long-term macroeconomic perspective, the conflicting demands of infrastructure subfields, and the conflicting interests and constituents on the ground; second, the horizontal and vertical dispersion of power (Jensen, Koop, and Tatham 2014) in multi-level, multi-stakeholder governance systems; third, the demise of hierarchical coordination capacity and weaker political centres; and fourth, underdeveloped analytical capacity for planning, managing, and handling infrastructure in such governance systems.

But where does such a diagnosis leave us? Are we to lament the influence of politics on infrastructure policies or the absence of political thinking in technocratic planning approaches? Rather, we propose to bring political influence out into the open and to confront it with economic, administrative, and technical expertise, and vice versa. Are we simply to complain about a lack of coordination capacity and hope that more and tighter regulation and contract regimes with stronger incentives and clearer sanctions may do the trick? Rather, we propose to address the relative under-institutionalisation of coordination capacities head-on and to compensate it through institution building. And are we content to complain about the seeming lack of analytical capacity in the field and stop at that? Rather, we propose, as in the case of coordination, to create institutions to remedy such weaknesses.

In essence, we propose infrastructure institutions that not only reflect the diversity of political views among stakeholders and affected constituencies but also rest on technical, economic, and administrative-managerial expertise and comparative data. Such institutions should combine elements of deliberation and inclusion with expert knowledge in terms of macroeconomic framework conditions and finance, administrative-managerial capacities, and technical options and feasibilities. Importantly, they would bring the complex relationship between politics, policies, and projects out in the open; or, in the words of March and Olsen (1996), they would let the logics of appropriateness and consequence confront each other.

Such institutions can be more permanent organisations set up at different levels of government–including at the regional and municipal level–depending on the constitutional and administrative structure of countries. They can address infrastructure generally or specific fields like transport, electricity, water, or information technology. They can also be bespoke, time-limited entities dedicated to specific and typically complex projects such as constructing or expanding major airports, setting up power grids, laying long-distance pipelines, or coordinating the digitalisation of large public agencies. And indeed, a more permanent institution can set up and work with more temporary task forces or units.

The institution can take the form of permanent boards, standing committees, commissions, or review panels. Irrespective of their organisational form and the tools they use–for example, reports, hearings, best practice models, and the like–they would conduct needs assessments, review the state of relevant governance capacities, especially coordination, and advise governments and agencies at national and subnational levels. If deemed necessary, they could also provide capacity-building. They would track past and current investment decisions, estimate and assess future needs, monitor maintenance costs and expenditures, and generally build an evidence base in the form of an information system on infrastructure.

Such boards, committees, commissions, or panels could conduct the sober assessment of the national infrastructure governance system that Hawkesworth and Garin demand in Chapter 5. They can begin with the big picture level by focusing on essential questions and issues that are behind policy-making, planning, and implementation. They can, at the sector or project level, carry out specific analyses of what good governance would mean, what the coordination requirements are and how they might be fulfilled, how the choice of delivery is made, and what the public-private balance should be. Such analyses can lead to possible strategies through the facts on the ground, i.e. at the project level, and review aspects of risk allocation, participation, and stakeholder management as well as future-proofing.

Whatever their actual structure and charge, infrastructure institutions should share several design features. The first is the arm's-length principle: they must neither be part of official decision-making nor under the control of the government in power. They must, in other words, be set up and function as a politically and administratively independent institution, irrespective of their public or private status. The arm's-length principle ensures such independence and would allow infrastructure institutions to serve their deliberative functions of debating and reviewing policy alternatives as well as to explore and assess financial and technical options for long-term investment, way beyond electoral cycles.

Independence is one basic source of the legitimacy of such institutions. A second source relates to both input and output legitimacy, and indeed, potential impact: analytical capacity in the form of expertise that is trusted and accepted by the majority of stakeholders; a reputation for giving impartial, well-founded guidance across a wide range of infrastructure projects; and with a premium on coordination capacity in the complex and ambiguous world of infrastructure governance. In other words, analytical capacity gives the institution the voice needed to discharge its coordination tasks legitimately and with authority in the context of political decisions made or being contested.

For this reason, the institution should have no direct decision-making capacity as to which infrastructure projects are to move forward or get funded, when, or by how much. That would be the decision of the respective level of government or the public-private partnership systems in place. The institution can however make recommendations on, lobby for, and contest particular policies and projects, which the political level must acknowledge and take into account when making decisions. The institution can also issue assessments of current and past decisions, evaluate performance, and generally act as a critical but constructive voice of, for, or against particular policies and projects, hence building analytical capacities.

Finally, the institution should address coordination between national, regional, and local levels, which Allain-Dupré, Hulbert, and Vincent in Chapter 3 identified as one of the main challenges of infrastructure governance across EU member states. Many smaller constituencies, be they municipalities or regions, are easily overwhelmed by the complexity of infrastructure projects, and more so when they face funding bottlenecks or lack managerial capacity to attract sound financing in the first place, especially from the private sector (Expertenkommission 2015). This relates not only to technical aspects but also, and often particularly, to legal and financial issues. Contracts with private corporations are increasingly complex as is the financing infrastructure, exposing smaller public authorities and agencies to information asymmetries given their likely limited governance capacities. These potential failures can be avoided through institutions that can serve as trusted coordinators, thereby relieving weaker agencies.

Of course, by itself, the arm's-length principle is no guarantee against capture by special interests, given the often large sums of funds involved and the potential of building up market-distorting asset specificity. Therefore, a parliamentary or congressional appointment and oversight function is needed to safeguard the appropriate inclusion of stakeholders and the overall political balance. The same would apply to the balance between national, regional, and local concerns to ensure vertical and horizontal coordination, especially in view of avoiding political and administrative fragmentation (see James and van Thiel 2011). Here, too, countries or regions would have to find the institutions best suited to the situation given existing models of governance to optimise impact and impartiality in terms of input and output legitimacy.

The proposal to establish infrastructure institutions as such is not new, and several countries such as Australia, the United Kingdom, Canada, and New Zealand have set up their own versions.[9] However, the various governance institutions to enhance coordination and analytical capacity vary significantly: from dedicated agencies to one-time commissions, from being a separate, independent entity to being located within existing departments, and from having a broader or narrower remit in terms of infrastructure fields and activities. Importantly, they differ from the proposal made here in several regards. First, they do not fully apply the arm's-length principle, even though Infrastructure Australia (see Chapter 2) goes some way towards its full implementation. Second, they are not inclusive enough in terms of covering the various stakeholders and political views. And third, they are not geared towards addressing the coordination and analytical capacity problems as centrally and systematically, albeit with the new UK Commission attempting just that, nor across different levels of government and administration, although the New Zealand and Ontario cases come close.[10]

These examples show that the need for coordinating institutions is being recognised.[11] At the same time, as Wegrich and Hammerschmid caution in Chapter 2, one should not expect such institutions to be effective on their own unless they are actually given adequate consideration in the political process and can add transparency and evidence to decision-making. Political forces may well find their ways to influence and co-opt the institution and its activities, or they may choose to ignore it. The proposal here is not one of naive institutionalism (Roberts 2010), which assumes that simply setting up a new agency would improve matters. To the contrary, the proposal implies that the institution must prove itself through impact performance over time.

At a minimum and consequently, the performance criteria for the governance institution should be threefold: first, principally, if the arm's-length principle has been observed and independence and inclusiveness in terms of giving and affecting voice have been achieved; second, procedurally, if deliberations and proposals by the institution have enhanced the quality of political decision-making such as by requiring political actors to justify decisions about infrastructure policies with independently vetted evidence or by requiring project managers to be mindful of the wider social, environmental, and economic impact, including future-proofing; and third, outcome-oriented, if infrastructure needs have been met and with the quality intended.

Hammerschmid and Wegrich also caution us about generalisations in proclaiming best practices for all. Countries, their governance, and their administrative cultures matter, and they vary considerably in structure, expectations, and performance. Each display different patterns of strengths and weaknesses, and such differences filter through to infrastructure policies and sectors. In this sense, the proposal to establish infrastructure institutions should be taken as a generic suggestion to be fitted to the needs as well as governance arrangements of each country, region, or project.

If such were the case, with coordinating governance institutions properly designed and adapted, they harbour the potential to instil infrastructure policies with the three sets of factors that Kostka in Chapter 4 identified with successful project delivery:

- Comprehensive, front-end policy and planning reviews across all four phases of the infrastructure project life cycle–planning, contracting, construction, and operation–to both determine strategy and incorporate effective risk management in the context of macroeconomic perspectives and frameworks;
- Flexible governance regime with sufficient capacity for vertical and horizontal coordination to mitigate market risks, allow for efficient stakeholder consultation, and reduce social and environmental risks; and
- Incorporation of risk management techniques including performance measurement, contractor monitoring, and supervision of the planners themselves across project phases to create feedback loops to the policy level, especially in view of macroeconomic considerations and future-proofing.

And indeed, if increased investments have not automatically led to better infrastructure outcomes in the past, the reason may well have been the lack of attention to inadequate analytical and coordination capacities. The same lack of attention may also explain to some extent the prudence of long-term private investors to engage in infrastructure financing. The proposal made here points to a way forward for how such deficiencies could be corrected. Yet for any arm's-length body to work as intended, most if not all stakeholders need to support that role. This will be a difficult political undertaking at the beginning, made easier only if the institution develops a strong reputation early on and builds on it over time. Such a process may take longer and may be more difficult in some contexts than in others, to be sure. In any case, as a governance innovation, the proposal of an arm's-length institution to coordinate infrastructure, grounded in sound analytical capacity, will take time to develop and will hopefully improve with experience gained. Yet given the state of infrastructure governance, such innovation may well be worth the effort.

Endnotes

1. On the governance performance of European Union (EU) member states over time, especially in the aftermath of the 2008–9 financial crisis and the 2011–12 eurozone crisis, see the The Governance Report 2015, especially Chapter 5.

2. In the case of Germany, the findings from the Expert Commission on Increasing Investment in Germany are a good example of the complexity of the interaction of financial and governance aspects in infrastructure planning and delivery. This includes questions of taxation and public sector borrowing—and its limitations in the form of a debt brake—, the role of private funding and PPPs, the absorption capacities of local governments, as well as the importance of fiscal accountability at all levels of government. For more information, see Expertenkommission (2015).

3. In the EU context, integrating the institutional capacity for governance especially in border regions has become a focus area of the European Structural Fund; see European Commission (2016).

4. Two examples suggested by members of the high-level focus group convened by the OECD and the Hertie School of Governance in preparation of this Report both illustrate and reemphasise this key point:

    Howard Chernick, Professor of Economics at Hunter College and the Graduate Center of the City University of New York, reports that in the United States, mass transit grants from the federal government to local transit agencies favour fixed rail projects for bringing commuters from suburbs into cities. The politics of the Congressional grant system encourage such spending, as capital grants are more easily capped than grants for operating funds. What is more, for political reasons as well, mayors are more likely to support capital projects than seek funds for operating budgets, especially for already outdated infrastructure facilities. Yet the capital grants for fixed rail systems have not been as successful as hoped in their goal of getting commuters out of their cars. Furthermore, the most pressing need of urban commuters, and one with the highest equity score, is for expanded inner-city bus service for improving job access for low-income workers and for serving the poor and the elderly. Even here, there is some evidence that grants for new buses may encourage suboptimal early retirement of older buses and may not lead to general capacity expansion or increased frequency.

Klaus Grewe, manager of very large infrastructure projects, including the London Olympics, reports a case of how a 'not in my backyard' mentality, or NIMBYism for short, combined with broader citizen distrust to create a virtual stalemate when the citizens of Hamburg, Germany, rejected a popular referendum to bid for the Olympic Games 2024. In the context of past local failures, e.g. the Elbe Philharmonic Hall's cost overruns and significant delays (see Case Study 3 in Chapter 4), and recent highly publicised scandals, e.g. those involving the International Athletic Federation and FIFA, a lack of trust in the local government to handle such a major sports event may at first seem understandable. Yet those behind the bid made every effort to involve the public from the very beginning, published detailed budget information and risk assessment, and focused more on the benefits remaining after the games than on the Olympics itself. Every public opinion survey before the referendum showed a robust majority of over 60 per cent in favour of hosting the Olympics. In Grewe's view, proponents of the Olympic failed mainly because a high number of well-educated, voting citizens feared change.

5   In the 1980s, the nuclear industry was caught off guard by the emerging environmental movement, as were politicians and administrators by local, middle-class protesters in the case of Stuttgart 21 some 30 years later.

6   Even though the runway expansion of Cordoba airport was deemed unnecessary by an official master plan in 2001, the Spanish government nonetheless decided in 2008 to move forward, and without needs assessments and cost-benefit analyses. The volume of air travel, however, did not increase, also due to two larger airports (Malaga and Seville) nearby (European Court of Auditors 2014). Other examples of overbuilding are the terminal enlargement in Fuerteventura, one of the Canary Islands; Madrid's Ciudad Real Central Airport; or Valencia's Castellón–Costa Azahar Airport (Mistry and Steward 2014).

7   The Jiaozhou Bay Bridge in Qingdao opened in 2011 and was hailed as the world's longest sea bridge. At the same time, a tunnel had already been built along the shortest distance between the two bay sides, in addition to an already existing high-speed highway around the bay (Holland 2012; Zhou 2013).

8   The Trans-Hudson Express ARC Tunnel was cancelled by New Jersey Governor Chris Christie citing potential cost overruns and the risk of overburdening New Jersey. The US Government Accounting Office reviewed the case but could not substantiate the Governor's claims (US GAO 2012). Critics, however, alleged that Christie aimed to appear as an enforcer of fiscal discipline while preparing for the 2016 presidential election campaign. By cancelling the tunnel project, the Governor avoided having to raise the state tax on gasoline—an earlier, gubernatorial campaign promise, which would have been needed in order to fund the tunnel project; see: Zernike 2012).

9   For example: Australia: Infrastructure Australia (2008) (see Infrastructure Australia 2016; Given 2010); USA: National Infrastructure Advisory Council (2001) (see US DHS 2015; Chen et al. 2013); UK: National Infrastructure Commission (2015) (see HM Government 2016); Singapore: Urban Redevelopment Authority (URA) (1974) (see URA 2016, Soh and Yuen 2006); Canada: Infrastructure Ontario (2008) (see Infrastructure Ontario 2016; Siemiatycki 2015); New Zealand: National Infrastructure Unit (2009) (National Infrastructure Unit 2016; Liu and Wilkinson 2011).

10 As noted in Chapter 3, in Canada, the federal government is represented in the various provinces via regional development agencies and councils whose interests lie not only in representing the national government's priorities in the provinces but also in conveying provincial preferences to the Federal level. This results in tripartite agreements, i.e. formal contractual arrangements among federal, provincial, and local authorities that support the implementation of infrastructure policies.

11 A longer list of such institutions can be found on the Governance Report website at www.governancereport.org.

References

Aaltonen, K., and Kujala, J. (2010). 'A Project Lifecycle Perspective on Stakeholder Influence Strategies in Global Projects', *Scandinavian Journal of Management*, 26(4): 381–97.

Albalate, D., Bel, G., and Fageda, X. (2012). 'Beyond the Efficiency-Equity Dilemma: Centralization as a Determinant of Government Investment in Infrastructure', *Papers in Regional Science*, 91(3): 599–615.

Allain-Dupré, D., Hulbert, C., and Vincent, M. (forthcoming). Effective Infrastructure Investment at the Sub-national Level. The Governance Levers. OECD Regional Development Working Papers. Paris: OECD.

ASCE (American Society of Civil Engineers) (2013). Failure to Act. The Impact of Current Infrastructure Investment on America's Economic Future. Washington, DC: ASCE.

Ammermann, H. (2015). Squaring the Circle. Improving European Infrastructure Financing. Munich: Roland Berger Strategy Consultants.

Amora, D. (2014) [website]. *Só habitação bateu metas provisória na segunda fase do PAC*. Retrieved from http://www1.folha.uol.com.br/mercado/2014/07/1481684-so-habitacao-bateu-metas-previstas-na-segunda-fase-do-pac.shtml (accessed 28 January 2016).

Anheier, H. K. (2013). 'Governance: What Are the Issues?', in Hertie School of Governance (ed), *The Governance Report 2013*. Oxford: Oxford University Press, 11–31.

Anheier, H. K., and Fliegauf, M. T. (2013). 'The Contribution of Innovation Research to Understanding Governance Innovation: A Review', in H. K. Anheier (ed), *Governance Challenges and Innovations: Financial and Fiscal Governance*. Oxford: Oxford University Press, 137–69.

Anheier, H. K., and Korreck, S. (2013). 'Governance Innovations', in Hertie School of Governance (ed), *The Governance Report 2013*. Oxford: Oxford University Press, 83–116.

Ansar, A., Flyvbjerg, B., Budzier, A., and Lunn, D. (2014). 'Should We Build More Large Dams? The Actual Costs of Hydropower Megaproject Development', *Energy Policy*, 69: 43–56.

Arezki, R., Bolton, P., Peters, S., Samama, F., and Stiglitz, J. (2016). From Global Savings Glut to Financing Infrastructure: The Advent of Investment Platforms. IMF Working Paper 16/18. Washington, DC: International Monetary Fund.

Asian Development Bank (2011) [website]. *Viet Nam: Phu My 2.2 Power Project: Validation Report*. Retrieved from http://www.adb.org/documents/viet-nam-phu-my-22-power-project (accessed 14 September 2015).

Australian Government (2014). Australian Government Response: Productivity Commission Inquiry Report Into Public Infrastructure. Canberra: Commonwealth of Australia.

Autodesk (2012) [website]. *Rising to New Heights With BIM*. Retrieved from http://www.autodesk.com/case-studies/shanghai-tower-construction-development (accessed 1 October 2015).

Bach, T., and Wegrich, K. (forthcoming). 'Regulatory Reform, Accountability and Blame in Public Service Delivery: The Public Transport Crisis in Berlin', in T. Christensen, and P. Lægreid (eds), *The Ashgate Research Companion to Accountability and Welfare State Reforms in Europe*. Farnham: Ashgate.

Barker, J., Tenenbaum, B., and Woolf, F. (1997). Governance and Regulation of Power Pools and System Operators. An International Comparison. World Bank Technical Paper 382. Washington, DC: The World Bank.

Becker, S. (2016) [website]. *Bundesautobahngesellschaft: Verkehrsminister wehren sich gegen 'Mamutbehörde'*. Retrieved from http://www.spiegel.de/auto/aktuell/bundesautobahngesellschaft-widerstand-der-verkehrsminister-a-1074198.html (accessed 19 February 2016).

Beckers, F., Chiara, N., Flesch, A., Maly, J., Silva, E., and Stegemann, U. (2013). A Risk-management Approach to a Successful Infrastructure Project. Initiation, Financing, and Execution. McKinsey Working Papers on Risk 52. McKinsey & Company.

Beckman, C., and Smith, G. (2005). 'Shared Networks: Making Wireless Communication Affordable', *IEEE Wireless Communications,* April: 78–85.

Bel, G. (2011). 'Infrastructure and Nation Building: The Regulation and Financing of Network Transportation Infrastructures in Spain (1720–2010)', *Business History*, 53(5): 688–705.

Bel, G., Estache, A., and Foucart, R. (2013). 'Transport Infrastructure Failures in Spain: Mismanagement and Incompetence, or Political Capture?', in T. Søreide, and A. Williams (eds), *Corruption, Grabbing and Development: Real World Challenges*. Cheltenham: Edward Elgar, 129–39.

Bellier, M., and Zhou, Y. M. (2003). Private Participation in Infrastructure in China. Issues and Recommendations for the Road, Water, and Power Sectors. World Bank Working Paper 2. Washington, DC: The World Bank.

BEREC (Body of European Regulators for Electronic Communications), and RSPG (Radio Spectrum Policy Group) (2011). Joint BEREC/RSPG Report on Infrastructure and Spectrum Sharing in Mobile/Wireless Networks. Riga, Brussels: BEREC, RSPG.

Besson, D. (2002). L'investissement des administrations publiques locales. INSEE Premiere No. 867. Paris: Institut national de la statistique et des études économiques.

Bhatta, M. R., and Bhatta, M. R. (2011). Experiences of Water Use Master Plan in Nepal. Kathmandu: Helvetas Swiss Intercooperation Nepal.

Bielschowsky, R. (2002). Investimento e reformas no Brasil. Indústria e infraestrutura nos anos 1990. Brasília: United Nations Economic Commission for Latin America and the Caribbean.

Broyer, S., and Gareis, J. (2013). How Large is the Infrastructure Multiplier in the Euro Area? Flash Economics 227. Paris: Natixis.

Bryde, D., Broquetas, M., and Volm, J. M. (2013). 'The Project Benefits of Building

Information Modelling (BIM)', *International Journal of Project Management*, 31(7): 971–80.

Budzier, A., and Flyvbjerg, B. (2013). Making Sense of the Impact and Importance of Outliers in Project Management Through the Use of Power Laws. Proceedings of IRNOP, Volume 11. Oslo: International Research Network on Organizing by Projects.

Burger, P., and Hawkesworth, I. (2011). 'How to Attain Value for Money: Comparing PPP and Traditional Infrastructure Public Procurement', *OECD Journal on Budgeting*, 11(1): 91–146.

Caldas, M. F., and Vale, M. L. (2014). O Programa de Aceleração do Crescimento e as Obras de Infraestrutura Urbana. Avanços e Desafios. São Bernardo do Campo.

Calderón, C., and Servén, L. (2010). Infrastructure in Latin America. Policy Research Working Paper 5317. Washington, DC: The World Bank.

Câmara dos Deputados (2004) [website]. *Lei Nº 11.079, de 30 de Dezembro de 2004*. Retrieved from http://www2.camara.leg.br/legin/fed/lei/2004/lei-11079-30-dezembro-2004-535279-norma-pl.html (accessed 16 February 2016).

Casa Civil (2010) [website]. *Planejamento, Investimento, Desenvolvimento. PAC2: O Brasil vai continuar crescendo*. Retrieved from http://www.casacivil.gov.br/uploads/pac2_web_1_28.pdf (accessed 28 January 2016).

Castalia Strategic Advisors (2010). Manual for RERA Guidelines for Regulating Cross-border Power Trading in the SADC Region: A User's Guide. Report to the Regional Electricity Regulators' Association of Southern Africa. Washington, DC: Castalia Strategic Advisors.

CDU, CSU, and SPD (2013). Deutschlands Zukunft gestalten. Retrieved from https://www.bundesregierung.de/Content/DE/StatischeSeiten/Breg/koalitionsvertrag-inhaltsverzeichnis.html (accessed 22 February 2016).

Charron, N., Dijkstra, L., and Lapuente, V. (2015). 'Mapping the Regional Divide in Europe: A Measure for Assessing Quality of Government in 206 European Regions', *Social Indicators Research*, 122(2): 315–46.

Chen, J., Chen, T. H. Y., Vertinsky, I., Yumagulova, L., and Park, C. (2013). 'Public-Private Partnerships for the Development of Disaster Resilient Communities', *Journal of Contingencies and Crisis Management*, 21(3): 130–43.

Coelho, M., Ratnoo, V., and Dellepiane, S. (2014). The Political Economy of Infrastructure in the UK. London: Institute for Government.

Cohen, I., Freiling, T., and Robinson, E. (2012). The Economic Impact and Financing of Infrastructure Spending. Washington, DC: Associated Equipment Distributors.

Contas Abertas (2016) [website]. *PAC 2*. Retrieved from http://www.contasabertas.com.br/website/noticia/pac2 (accessed 16 February 2016).

Cour des comptes (2015). Les finances publiques locales: Rapport sur la situation financière et la gestion des collectivités territoriales et de leurs établissements publics. Paris: Cour des comptes.

Curry, D., van de Walle, S., and Gadellaa, S. (2014). Public Administration as an Academic Discipline: Trends and Changes in the COCOPS Academic Survey of European Public Administration Scholars. COCOPS.

da Cruz, N. F., and Cruz, C. O. (forthcoming). 'Public-Private Partnership: A Framework for Private Sector Involvement in Public Infrastructure Projects', in G. Hammerschmid, G. Kostka, and K. Wegrich (eds), *The Governance of Infrastructure*. Oxford: Oxford University Press.

Dahlström, C., Teorell, J., Dahlberg, S., Hartmann, F., Lindberg, A., and Nistotskaya, M. (2015). The QoG Expert Survey Dataset II. Gothenburg: The Quality of Government Institute, University of Gothenburg.

Danish Energy Authority (2003). Renewable Energy. Danish Solutions. Copenhagen: Danish Energy Authority.

del Río, P., and Linares, P. (2014). 'Back to the Future? Rethinking Auctions for Renewable Electricity Support', *Renewable and Sustainable Energy Reviews*, 35: 42–56.

Deutsche Welle (2015) [website]. *Japan, China Spar Over Asian Infrastructure*. Retrieved from http://www.dw.com/en/japan-china-spar-over-asian-infrastructure/a-18466966 (accessed 27 January 2016).

Dobbs, R., Pohl, H., Lin, D.-Y., Mischke, J., Garemo, N., Hexter, J., Matzinger, S., Palter, R., and Nanavatty, R. (2013). Infrastructure Productivity. How to Save $1 Trillion a Year. Seoul, San Francisco, London: McKinsey Global Institute.

Donnay, A., Chaptzipoulidis, I., Gibeaud, A., Graf, J., and Le Fol, Y. (2011). Altering Energy Future. A Case Study From Samsø Island, Denmark. Aalborg: Department of Development and Planning, Aalborg University.

ECA (Economic Consulting Associates) (2009). The Potential of Regional Power Sector Integration. South African Power Pool (SAPP) Transmission and Trading Case Study. London: ECA.

Eisenhardt, K. M. (1989). 'Agency Theory: An Assessment and Review', *Academy of Management Review*, 14(1): 57–74.

Energy Academy (2011) [website]. *RE-Island*. Retrieved from http://energiakademiet.dk/en/vedvarende-energi-o/ (accessed 18 January 2016).

European Commission (2016) [website]. *Guidance on European Structural and Investment Funds 2014–2020*. Retrieved from http://ec.europa.eu/regional_policy/en/information/legislation/guidance/ (accessed 15 February 2016).

European Commission (2014a). An Investment Plan for Europe. COM(2014) 903 final. Brussels: European Commission.

European Commission (2014b). Report From the Commission to the Council and the European Parliament. EU Anti-Corruption Report. COM(2014) 38 final. Brussels: European Commission.

European Commission (2012) [website]. *Results of the Public Consultation on How to Reduce the Cost of Roll Out of High Speed Broadband*. Retrieved from https://ec.europa.eu/digital-agenda/en/news/results-public-consul

tation-how-reduce-cost-roll-out-high-speed-broadband (accessed 26 November 2015).

European Court of Auditors (2014). EU-funded Airport Infrastructures: Poor Value for Money. Luxembourg: Publications Office of the European Union.

Expertenkommission (2015). Stärkung von Investitionen in Deutschland. Bericht der Expertenkommission im Auftrag des Bundesministers für Wirtschaft und Energie, Sigmar Gabriel. Berlin: Bundesministerium für Wirtschaft und Energie.

Fazekas, M., Toth, I., and King, L. (2013). Anatomy of Grand Corruption. A Composite Corruption Risk Index Based on Objective Data. Working Paper Series in Economics and Social Sciences CRC-WP/2013:02. Budapest: Corruption Research Center Budapest.

FERC (Federal Energy Regulatory Commission) (1996). Order No. 888. Washington, DC: FERC.

Ferlie, E., Ashburner, L., Fitzgerald, L., and Pettigrew, A. (1996). *The New Public Management in Action*. Oxford: Oxford University Press.

Fiaschi, D., Lavezzi, A. M., and Parenti, A. (2011). Productivity Dynamics Across European Regions. The Impact of Structural and Cohesion Funds. Discussion Paper 84. Pisa: Dipartimento di Scienze Economiche, Università di Pisa.

Fiedler, J., and Wendler, A. (2016). 'Berlin Brandenburg Airport', in G. Kostka, and J. Fiedler (eds), *Large Infrastructure Projects in Germany: Between Ambition and Realities*. London: Palgrave Macmillan.

Fiedler, J., and Schuster, S. (2016). 'The Elbphilharmonie Hamburg', in G. Kostka, and J. Fiedler (eds), *Large Infrastructure Projects in Germany: Between Ambition and Realities*. London: Palgrave Macmillan.

Finch, S. (2015). Ex-post Evaluation at the UK Department for Transport: Presentation to CGEDD, 24th June 2015. Retrieved from http://www.cgedd.developpement-durable.gouv.fr/IMG/pdf/09_UK_Department_for_Transport_ex-post_evaluation_d1_cle77691a.pdf (accessed 4 January 2016).

Flinders, M. (2005). 'The Politics of Public-Private Partnerships', *The British Journal of Politics and International Relations*, 7(2): 215–39.

Flyvbjerg, B. (2014). 'What You Should Know About Megaprojects and Why: An Overview', *Project Management Journal*, 45(2): 6–19.

Flyvbjerg, B. (2013). 'Quality Control and Due Diligence in Project Management: Getting Decisions Right by Taking the Outside View', *International Journal of Project Management*, 31(5): 760–74.

Flyvbjerg, B. (2009). 'Survival of the Unfittest: Why the Worst Infrastructure Gets Built and What We Can Do About It', *Oxford Review of Economic Policy*, 25(3): 344–67.

Flyvbjerg, B., and Sunstein, C. R. (2015). 'The Principle of the Malevolent Hiding Hand; or, the Planning Fallacy Writ Large', *Social Research*, Forthcoming. Retrieved from http://papers.ssrn.com/sol3/papers.cfm?abstract_id=2654423 (accessed 15 January 2016).

Flyvbjerg, B., Bruzelius, N., and Rothengatter, W. (2003). *Megaprojects and Risk: An Anatomy of Ambition*. Cambridge: Cambridge University Press.

Flyvbjerg, B., Garbuio, M., and Lovallo, D. (2009). 'Delusion and Deception in Large Infrastructure Projects: Two Models for Explaining and Preventing Executive Disaster', *California Management Review*, 5(2): 170–93.

Flyvbjerg, B., Holm, M. S., and Buhl, S. L. (2004). 'What Causes Cost Overrun in Transport Infrastructure Projects?', *Transport Reviews*, 24(1): 3–18.

Fratzscher, M. (2016) [website]. *Ungleichheit, Reformstau, marode Infrastruktur: Die Illusion vom deutschen Wirtschaftsboom*. Retrieved from http://www.spiegel.de/wirtschaft/soziales/wirtschaft-in-deutschland-die-illusion-vom-wirtschaftsboom-a-1068970.html (accessed 28 January 2016).

Frischtak, C. R. (2008). 'O Investimento em Infraestrutura no Brasil: Histórico recente e perspectivas', *Pesquisa e Planejamento Econômico*, 38(2): 307–48.

FTA (Federal Transit Administration) (2009). Characteristics of Bus Rapid Transit for Decision-Making. Washington, DC: FTA.

FTA (Federal Transit Administration) (2004). Characteristics of Bus Rapid Transit for Decision-Making. Washington, DC: FTA.

Funk, A. (2016) [website]. *Woran Dobrindts Straßenpläne kranken*. Retrieved from http://www.tagesspiegel.de/politik/bundesautobahngesellschaft-woran-dobrindts-strassenplaene-kranken/12927986.html (accessed 19 February 2016).

Galicia, L. D., Cheu, R. L., Machemehl, R. B., and Liu, H. (2009). 'Bus Rapid Transit Features and Deployment Phases for U.S. Cities', *Journal of Public Transportation*, 12(2): 23–38.

Garcia-Escribano, M., Goes, C., and Karpowicz, I. (2015). Filling the Gap. Infrastructure Investment in Brazil. IMF Working Paper WP/15/180. Washington, DC: International Monetary Fund.

Garemo, N., and Mischk, J. (2013) [website]. *Infrastructure: The Governance Failures*. Retrieved from http://www.voxeu.org/article/infrastructure-governance-failures (accessed 28 January 2016).

Garlichs, D. (1980). 'Grenzen zentralstaatlicher Planung in der Bundesrepublik', in H. Wollmann (ed), *Politik im Dickicht der Bürokratie: Beiträge zur Implementationsforschung*. Opladen: Westdeutscher Verlag, 71–102.

Given, J. (2010). 'Take Your Partners: Public Private Interplay in Australian and New Zealand Plans for Next Generation Broadband', *Telecommunications Policy*, 34(9): 540–9.

GIZ (Deutsche Gesellschaft für Internationale Zusammenarbeit) (2015). *Renewable Energy Auctions*. Retrieved from http://www.giz.de/expertise/downloads/giz2015-en-energy-newsletter-no-43.pdf (accessed 14 September 2015).

Government of Nepal (2008). Rural Village Water Resources Management Project (RVWRMP) Nepal (Nepal-Finland Cooperation). Implementation Guidelines. Kathmandu: Ministry of Local Development.

Grimsey, D., and Lewis, M. (2007). *Public Private Partnerships: The Worldwide Revolution in Infrastructure Provision and Project Finance.* Cheltenham: Edward Elgar.

GSMA (2012) [website]. *Mobile Infrastructure Sharing.* Retrieved from http://mph.gsma.com/publicpolicy/infrastructure-sharinga (accessed 26 November 2015).

Guasch, J. L. (2004). Granting and Renegotiating Infrastructure Concessions. Doing It Right. WBI Development Studies. Washington, DC: World Bank Institute.

Hajer, M. (2003). 'Policy Without Polity? Policy Analysis and the Institutional Void', *Policy Sciences*, 36: 175–95.

Hamburg Port Authority (2013) [website]. *St. Pauli-Elbtunnel: HPA legt Sanierungsplan vor.* Retrieved from http://www.hamburg-port-authority.de/de/presse/pressearchiv/Seiten/Pressemitteilung-04-02-2013.aspx (accessed 14 September 2015).

Hamburger Abendblatt (2014). 'Sanierung des Alten Elbtunnels soll noch teurer werden', 6 March 2014. Retrieved from http://www.abendblatt.de/hamburg/article125523570/Sanierung-des-Alten-Elbtunnels-soll-noch-teurer-werden.html (accessed 14 September 2015).

Hart, O. (2003). 'Incomplete Contracts and Public Ownership: Remarks, and an Application to Public-Private Partnerships', *The Economic Journal*, 113(486): C69-C76.

Hasbani, G., El-Darwiche, B., Abou Chanab, L., and Mourad, M. (2007). Telecom Infrastructure Sharing. Regulatory Enablers and Economic Benefits. Beirut: Booz & Company.

Hauptverband der Deutschen Bauindustrie e.V. (2013) [website]. *Fleischer: Weniger Kosten und weniger Staus durch Bonus-Malus-Regelungen im Straßenbau.* Retrieved from http://www.bauindustrie.de/presse/presseinformationen/presseinfo-0113/ (accessed 8 December 2015).

Heilbrunn, J. R. (2004). Anti-Corruption Commissions. Panacea or Real Medicine to Fight Corruption? Washington, DC: World Bank Institute.

Helvetas (2016) [website]. *Water Resources Management Programme.* Retrieved from https://nepal.helvetas.org/en/programmes___projects/warm.cfm (accessed 21 February 2016).

Hertie School of Governance (ed) (2015). *The Governance Report 2015.* Oxford: Oxford University Press.

Hertie School of Governance (ed) (2014). *The Governance Report 2014.* Oxford: Oxford University Press.

Hertie School of Governance (ed) (2013). *The Governance Report 2013.* Oxford: Oxford University Press.

Heuser, T., and Reh, W. (2015). 'Die Bundesverkehrswegeplanung: Anforderungen an die zukünftige Verkehrsinfrastrukturpolitik des Bundes', in W. Canzler, A. Knie, and O. Schwedes (eds), *Handbuch Verkehrspolitik*. 2nd ed. Wiesbaden: Springer, 237–64.

Hidalgo, D. (2015) [website]. *Learning From Delhi's BRT Failure, and Looking to the City's Future*. Retrieved from http://thecityfix.com/blog/learning-from-delhis-brt-failure-looking-citys-future-dario-hidalgo/ (accessed 18 January 2016).

Hidalgo, D., and Gutiérrez, L. (2013). 'BRT and BHLS Around the World: Explosive Growth, Large Positive Impacts and Many Issues Outstanding', *Research in Transportation Economics*, 39(1): 8–13.

HM Government (2016) [website]. *National Infrastructure Commission*. Retrieved from https://www.gov.uk/government/organisations/national-infrastructure-commission (accessed 15 February 2016).

HM Government (2015) [website]. *Major Projects Authority*. Retrieved from https://www.gov.uk/government/groups/major-projects-authority (accessed 14 September 2015).

Hodge, G. A. (2010). 'Reviewing Public-Private Partnerships: Some Thoughts on Evaluation', in G. A. Hodge, C. Greve, and A. E. Boardman (eds), *International Handbook on Public-Private Partnerships*. Cheltenham: Edward Elgar, 81–111.

Hodge, G. A., and Greve, C. (2007). 'Public-Private Partnerships: An International Performance Review', *Public Administration Review*, 67(3): 545–58.

Holland, T. (2012). 'Stimulus or Not, It's the Quality of New Investment That Matters', *South China Morning Post*, 11 September 2012. Retrieved from http://www.scmp.com/business/article/1033662/stimulus-or-not-its-quality-new-investment-matters (accessed 15 February 2016).

Hood, C. (1991). 'A Public Management for All Seasons?', *Public Administration*, 69(1): 3–19.

Horn, O., Schuldes, F., and Mendle, R. S. (2015). 'Finland: RAKLI Procurement Clinics', in ICLEI – Local Governments for Sustainability / World Business Council for Sustainable Development (ed), *Innovative City-business Collaboration: Urban Infrastructure Initiative-Framework for City-business Collaboration*. Bonn, Geneva: ICLEI, WBCSD.

Hulbert, C. (2012). Public Investment Across Levels of Government: The Case of Galicia, Spain. OECD 28th Territorial Development Policy Committee, 4–5 December 2012. Paris: OECD.

Hupe, P., and Hill, M. (2014). 'Delivery Capacity', in M. Lodge, and K. Wegrich (eds), *The Problem-solving Capacity of the Modern State: Governance Challenges and Administrative Capacities*. Oxford: Oxford University Press, 25–40.

ICA (2014) [website]. *La Yesca Hydroelectric Project*. Retrieved from https://www.ica.com.mx/la-yesca-hydroelectric-project (accessed 14 September 2015).

ICA (The Infrastructure Consortium for Africa) (2011). Regional Power Pool Status in African Power Pools. Report. Tunis: ICA.

ICIMOD, and Helvetas (2013). Natural Resource Management Approaches and Technologies in Nepal. Approach – Water Use Master Plan. Kathmandu: ICIMOD, Helvetas.

IMF (International Monetary Fund) (2015). Making Public Investment More Efficient. Washington, DC: IMF.

Infrastructure Australia (2016) [website]. *About*. Retrieved from http://infrastructureaustralia.gov.au/about/ (accessed 15 February 2016).

Infrastructure Australia (2013) [website]. *Infrastructure Priority List*. Retrieved from http://infrastructureaustralia.gov.au/projects/infrastructure-priority-list.aspx (accessed 16 February 2016).

Infrastructure Ontario (2016) [website]. *About Infrastructure Ontario*. Retrieved from http://www.infrastructureontario.ca/templates/AboutUsWithCarousel.aspx (accessed 15 February 2016).

IRC (ISO/RTO Council) (2015) [website]. *Learn the Lingo: Industry Glossary*. Retrieved from http://www.isorto.org/Reports/IndustryLingo (accessed 27 January 2016).

ITDP (Institute for Transportation and Development Policy) (2016a) [website]. *About the BRT Standard*. Retrieved from https://www.itdp.org/library/standards-and-guides/the-bus-rapid-transit-standard/about-the-brt-standard/ (accessed 13 January 2016).

ITDP (Institute for Transportation and Development Policy) (2016b) [website]. *BRT Standard Scores*. Retrieved from https://www.itdp.org/brt-standard-scores/ (accessed 13 January 2016).

ITDP (Institute for Transportation and Development Policy) (2015) [website]. *New 'Gold-Standard' BRT in Yichang, China Leads the Way for Mid-Sized Chinese Cities*. Retrieved from https://www.itdp.org/new-gold-standard-brt-in-yichang-china-leads-the-way-for-mid-sized-chinese-cities/ (accessed 13 January 2016).

ITDP (Institute for Transportation and Development Policy) (2012a) [website]. *MCDOT Demand and Service Planning Report*. Retrieved from https://www.itdp.org/mcdot-demand-and-service-planning-report/ (accessed 18 January 2016).

ITDP (Institute for Transportation and Development Policy) (2012b). The BRT Standard. Version 1.0. New York: ITDP.

ITU (International Telecommunication Union) (2015) [website]. *ICT Facts and Figures – The World in 2015*. Retrieved from http://www.itu.int/en/ITU-D/Statistics/Pages/facts/default.aspx (accessed 3 February 2016).

ITU (International Telecommunication Union) (2008) [website]. *Best Practice Guidelines on Innovative Infrastructure Sharing Guidelines to Promote Affordable Access for All*. Retrieved from http://www.itu.int/ITU-D/treg/Events/Seminars/GSR/GSR08/consultation.html (accessed 21 February 2016).

Jackman, S. (2009). *Bayesian Analysis for the Social Sciences*. Chichester: Wiley.

Jacobs, A. M. (2011). *Governing for the Long Term: Democracy and the Politics of Investment*. Cambridge: Cambridge University Press.

James, O., and van Thiel, S. (2011). 'Structural Devolution to Agencies', in T. Christensen, and P. Lægreid (eds), *The Ashgate Research Companion to New Public Management*. Surrey: Ashgate, 209–22.

Jensen, M. D., Koop, C., and Tatham, M. (2014). 'Coping With Power Dispersion? Autonomy, Co-ordination and Control in Multilevel Systems', *Journal of European Public Policy*, 21(9): 1237–54.

Jordana, J. (forthcoming). 'Accountability and Legitimacy in Infrastructure Governance', in G. Hammerschmid, G. Kostka, and K. Wegrich (eds), *The Governance of Infrastructure*. Oxford: Oxford University Press.

Jordana, J. (2014). 'Governance Dilemmas of the Contemporary State: The Politics of Infrastructure Policy', in M. Lodge, and K. Wegrich (eds), *The Problem-solving Capacity of the Modern State: Governance Challenges and Administrative Capacities*. Oxford: Oxford University Press, 163–82.

Jørgensen, P. J. (2007). *Samsø – A Renewable Energy Island: 10 Years of Development and Evaluation*. Samsø: Samsø Energy Academy.

Kahneman, D., and Tversky, A. (1979). 'Prospect Theory: An Analysis of Decision Under Risk', *Econometrica*, 47(2): 263–92.

Kambanda, C. (2013) [website]. *Power Trade in Africa and the Role of Power Pools*. Retrieved from http://www.afdb.org/en/blogs/integrating-africa/post/power-trade-in-africa-and-the-role-of-power-pools-12101/ (accessed 27 January 2016).

Kessides, I. N. (2004). Reforming Infrastructure. Privatization, Regulation, and Competition. Washington, DC: The World Bank.

Kettl, D. F. (2000). 'The Transformation of Governance: Globalization, Devolution, and the Role of Government', *Public Administration Review*, 60(6): 488–97.

Kostka, G., and Anzinger, N. (2016a). 'Large Infrastructure Projects in Germany: A Cross-sectoral Analysis', in G. Kostka, and J. Fiedler (eds), *Large Infrastructure Projects in Germany: Between Ambition and Realities*. London: Palgrave Macmillan.

Kostka, G., and Anzinger, N. (2016b). 'Offshore Wind Power Expansion in Germany: Scale, Patterns and Causes of Time Delays and Cost Overruns', in G. Kostka, and J. Fiedler (eds), *Large Infrastructure Projects in Germany: Between Ambition and Realities*. London: Palgrave Macmillan.

Kostka, G. and Fiedler, J. (eds) (2016). *Large Infrastructure Projects in Germany: Between Ambition and Realities*. London: Palgrave Macmillan.

Kuronen, M., and Vaara, P. (2013). 'Procurement Clinics in Public Procurement and Urban Development', *Municipal Engineer*, 166(ME4): 265–70.

Liu, T., and Wilkinson, S. (2011). 'Adopting Innovative Procurement Techniques: Obstacles and Drivers for Adopting Public Private Partnerships in New

Zealand', *Construction Innovation: Information, Process, Management*, 11(4): 452–69.

Lodge, M. (2014). 'Regulatory Capacity', in M. Lodge, and K. Wegrich (eds), *The Problem-solving Capacity of the Modern State: Governance Challenges and Administrative Capacities*. Oxford: Oxford University Press, 63–85.

Lodge, M., and Wegrich, K. (2014a). 'Administrative Capacities', in Hertie School of Governance (ed), *The Governance Report 2014*. Oxford: Oxford University Press, 27–49.

Lodge, M., and Wegrich, K. (2014b). 'Setting the Scene: Challenges to the State, Governance Readiness, and Administrative Capacities', in Hertie School of Governance (ed), *The Governance Report 2014*. Oxford: Oxford University Press, 15–26.

Lopez, G. (2013) [website]. *Mexico's ICA Receives $147 Mln for La Yesca Hydroelectric Project*. Retrieved from http://www.reuters.com/article/2013/12/23/mexico-ica-idUSL2N0K20Q620131223 (accessed 14 September 2015).

Mahoney, J., and Thelen, K. (2010). 'A Theory of Gradual Institutional Change', in J. Mahoney, and K. Thelen (eds), *Explaining Institutional Change: Ambiguity, Agency, and Power*. Cambridge: Cambridge University Press, 1–37.

March, J. G., and Olsen, J. P. (1996). 'Institutional Perspectives on Political Institutions', *Governance*, 9(3): 247–64.

Matsukawa, T., and Habeck, O. (2007). Review of Risk Mitigation Instruments for Infrastructure Financing and Recent Trends and Developments. Trends and Policy Options 4. Washington, DC: The World Bank.

Maurer, L. T. A., and Barroso, L. A. (2011). Electricity Auctions. An Overview of Efficient Practices. Washington, DC: The World Bank.

Maynou, L., Saez, M., Kyriacou, A., and Bacaria, J. (2015). 'The Impact of Structural and Cohesion Funds on Eurozone Convergence, 1990–2010', *Regional Studies:* 1–13.

McGraw-Hill Construction (2010). Green BIM: How Building Information Modeling is Contributing to Green Design and Construction. Retrieved from http://analyticsstore.construction.com/smartmarket-reports/smartmarket-report-green-bim-2010-how-building-information-modeling-is-contributing-to-green-design-and-construction.html (accessed 8 December 2015).

Meddour, D.-E., Rasheed, T., and Gourhant, Y. (2011). 'On the Role of Infrastructure Sharing for Mobile Network Operators in Emerging Markets', *Computer Networks*, 55(7): 1576–91.

Mello, L. de, and Sutherland, D. (2014). Financing Infrastructure. International Center for Public Policy Working Paper 14-09. Atlanta: Andrew Young School of Policy Studies, Georgia State University.

Melo, M. A., and Pereira, C. (2015). The Political Economy of Public Investments in Brazil. Unpublished Manuscript.

Mendle, R. S., and Horn, O. (2015). Innovative City-business Collaboration. Emerging Good Practice to Enhance Sustainable Urban Development.

Bonn, Geneva: ICLEI – Local Governments for Sustainability, World Business Council for Sustainable Development.

Miller, R., and Hobbs, B. (2005). 'Governance Regimes for Large Complex Projects', *Project Management Journal*, 36(3): 42–50.

Ministério do Planejamento, Orçamento e Gestão (2007). *Programa de Aceleração do Crescimento, 2007–2010: Romper barreiras e superar limites*. Retrieved from http://www.planejamento.gov.br/apresentacoes/2007/070316_pac_apresentacao_senado.pdf (accessed 28 January 2016).

Mistry, H., and Steward, D. (2014) [website]. *The Infrastructure Challenge*. Retrieved from https://www.iata.org/pressroom/facts_figures/Documents/The-Infrastructure-Challenge-presentation-gmd-2014.pdf (accessed 15 February 2016).

Mungiu-Pippidi, A. (2016a). *The Quest for Good Governance: How Societies Develop Control of Corruption*. Cambridge: Cambridge University Press.

Mungiu-Pippidi, A. (2016b). 'The Quest for Good Governance: Learning From Virtuous Circles', *Journal of Democracy*, 27(1): 95–109.

Muñoz, J. C., and Hidalgo, D. (2013). 'Workshop 2: Bus Rapid Transit as Part of Enhanced Service Provision', *Research in Transportation Economics*, 39(1): 104–7.

National Infrastructure Unit (2016) [website]. *Welcome to the National Infrastructure Unit*. Retrieved from http://www.infrastructure.govt.nz/ (accessed 15 February 2016).

Nevin, J. A. (2010). 'The Power of Cooperation', *The Behavior Analyst*, 33(2): 189–91.

Nikitas, A., and Karlsson, M. (2015). 'A Worldwide State-of-the-Art Analysis for Bus Rapid Transit: Looking for the Success Formula', *Journal of Public Transportation*, 18(1): 1–33.

OECD (Organisation for Economic Co-operation and Development) (2016a) [website]. *OECD National Accounts Statistics*. Retrieved from http://www.oecd-ilibrary.org/economics/data/oecd-national-accounts-statistics_na-data-en (accessed 27 January 2016).

OECD (Organisation for Economic Co-operation and Development) (2016b) [website]. *OECD.Stat*. Retrieved from http://stats.oecd.org/ (accessed 27 January 2016).

OECD (Organisation for Economic Co-operation and Development) (2016c) [website]. *Productivity: Multifactor Productivity (indicator)*. Retrieved from https://data.oecd.org/lprdty/multifactor-productivity.htm (accessed 15 February 2016).

OECD (Organisation for Economic Co-operation and Development) (2016d) [website]. *Transport: Infrastructure Investment (indicator)*. Retrieved from https://data.oecd.org/transport/infrastructure-investment.htm (accessed 15 February 2016).

OECD (Organisation for Economic Co-operation and Development) (2015a) [website]. *Effective Public Investment Toolkit*. Retrieved from http://www.oecd.org/effective-public-investment-toolkit/ (accessed 8 February 2016).

OECD (Organisation for Economic Co-operation and Development) (2015b). *OECD Regulatory Policy Outlook 2015*. Paris: OECD Publishing.

OECD (Organisation for Economic Co-operation and Development) (2015c). Recommendation of the Council on Budgetary Governance. Paris: OECD.

OECD (Organisation for Economic Co-operation and Development) (2015d). Results of the OECD-CoR Consultation of Sub-national Governments. Infrastructure Planning and Investment Across Levels of Government: Current Challenges and Possible Solutions. Paris: OECD.

OECD (Organisation for Economic Co-operation and Development) (2015e). Subnational Governments in OECD Countries. Key Data, 2015 Edition. Paris: OECD.

OECD (Organisation for Economic Co-operation and Development) (2015f). The Governance of Water Regulators. OECD Studies on Water. Paris: OECD.

OECD (Organisation for Economic Co-operation and Development) (2015g). Towards a Framework for the Governance and Delivery of Infrastructure. 36th Annual Meeting of OECD Senior Budget Officials. Paris: OECD.

OECD (Organisation for Economic Co-operation and Development) (2014a). Effective Public Investment Across Levels of Government. Country Profile Germany. Paris: OECD.

OECD (Organisation for Economic Co-operation and Development) (2014b). Effective Public Investment Across Levels of Government. Country Profile Switzerland. Paris: OECD.

OECD (Organisation for Economic Co-operation and Development) (2014c). *OECD Foreign Bribery Report: An Analysis of the Crime of Bribery of Foreign Public Officials*. Paris: OECD Publishing.

OECD (Organisation for Economic Co-operation and Development) (2014d). Recommendation of the Council on Effective Public Investment Across Levels of Government. Paris: OECD.

OECD (Organisation for Economic Co-operation and Development) (2013). Investing Together. Working Effectively Across Levels of Government. Paris: OECD.

OECD (Organisation for Economic Co-operation and Development) (2012). OECD Questionnaire. Multi-level Governance of Public Investment. Retrieved from http://www.oecd.org/gov/regional-policy/OECD-Questionnaire-Multi-level-Governance-Public-Investment.pdf (accessed 16 February 2016).

OECD (Organisation for Economic Co-operation and Development) (2011). Making the Most of Public Investment in a Tight Fiscal Environment. Multi-level Governance Lessons From the Crisis. Paris: OECD.

OECD (Organisation for Economic Co-operation and Development) (2008). *Public-Private Partnerships: In Pursuit of Risk Sharing and Value for Money*. Paris: OECD Publishing.

Olsen, B. E. (2010). 'Wind Energy and Local Acceptance: How to Get Beyond the Nimby Effect', *European Energy and Environmental Law Review*, 19: 239–51.

Oseni, M. O., and Pollitt, M. G. (2014). Institutional Arrangements for the Promotion of Regional Integration of Electricity Markets. International Experience. Policy Research Working Paper 6947. Washington, DC: World Bank Development Research Group.

PA Consulting Group (2008). Sub-Saharan Africa's Power Pools. A Development Framework. Arlington: United States Agency for International Development.

Pereira, A. M., and Andraz, J. M. (2013). On the Economic Effects of Public Infrastructure Investment. A Survey of the International Evidence. Working Paper 108. Williamsburg: College of William and Mary, Department of Economics.

Pereira, C., and Melo, M. A. (forthcoming). 'The Governance of Infrastructure in Multiparty Presidentialism', in G. Hammerschmid, G. Kostka, and K. Wegrich (eds), *The Governance of Infrastructure*. Oxford: Oxford University Press.

PwC (PricewaterhouseCoopers) (2014). Capital Project and Infrastructure Spending. Outlook to 2025. PwC.

PwC (PricewaterhouseCoopers), and Ecorys (2013). Identifying and Reducing Corruption in Public Procurement in the EU. Development of a Methodology to Estimate the Direct Costs of Corruption and Other Elements for an EU-Evaluation Mechanism in the Area of Anti-corruption. PwC, Ecorys.

RAIN (2014). Annual Report 2014. Amsterdam: RAIN.

Rajaram, A., Minh Le, T., Kaiser, K., Kim, J.-H., and Frank, J. (2014). *The Power of Public Investment Management: Transforming Resources Into Assets for Growth*. Washington, DC: The World Bank.

Rautanen, S.-L., van Koppen, B., and Wagle, N. (2014). 'Community-Driven Multiple Use Water Services: Lessons Learned by the Rural Village Water Resources Management Project in Nepal', *Water Alternatives*, 7(1): 160–77.

Roberts, A. (2010). *The Logic of Discipline: Global Capitalism and the Architecture of Government*. New York, Oxford: Oxford University Press.

Rodríguez-Pose, A. (2010). Do Institutions Matter for Regional Development? Working Paper Series in Economics and Social Sciences 02/2010. Madrid: IMDEA Social Sciences.

Saastamoinen, M. (2009). Samsø – Renewable Energy Island Programme. Helsinki: National Consumer Research Centre.

SAPP (Southern African Power Pool) (2016) [website]. *Executive Committee*. Retrieved from http://www.sapp.co.zw/exco.html (accessed 27 January 2016).

SAPP (Southern African Power Pool) (2014). Annual Report 2014. Harare: SAPP.

Scharpf, F. W. (2009). *Föderalismusreform: Kein Ausweg aus der Politikverflechtungsfalle?* Frankfurt am Main: Campus.

Scharpf, F. W. (1997). *Games Real Actors Play: Actor-Centered Institutionalism in Policy Research*. Boulder: Westview Press.

Scharpf, F. W. (1988). 'The Joint-Decision Trap: Lessons From German Federalism and European Integration', *Public Administration*, 66(3): 239–78.

Schwab, K. (2014). The Global Competitiveness Report 2014-2015. Geneva: WEF (World Economic Forum).

SCI-Network (2011). Case Study. RAKLI Procurement Clinic. SCI-Network.

Senatsverwaltung für Stadtentwicklung und Umwelt (2012) [website]. *Feierliche Eröffnung der A 115 – AVUS*. Retrieved from http://www.stadtentwicklung.berlin.de/aktuell/pressebox/archiv_volltext.shtml?arch_1211/nachricht4849.html (accessed 14 September 2015).

Siemiatycki, M. (2015). 'Public-Private Partnerships in Canada: Reflections on Twenty Years of Practice', *Canadian Public Administration*, 58(3): 343–62.

Simon, H. A. (1955). 'A Behavioral Model of Rational Choice', *The Quarterly Journal of Economics*, 69(1): 99–118.

Soh, E. Y., and Yuen, B. (2006). 'Government-aided Participation in Planning Singapore', *Cities*, 23(1): 30–43.

Spiegel Online (2014) [website]. *Teure Elbtunnel-Sanierung: Hamburg droht nächste Kostenexplosion*. Retrieved from http://www.spiegel.de/wirtschaft/soziales/hamburg-elbtunnel-sanierung-kostet-fast-100-millionen-euro-a-957529.html (accessed 1 October 2015).

Standard & Poor's (2015). Global Infrastructure Investment. Timing Is Everything (and Now Is the Time). New York: Standard & Poor's Financial Services.

Standard & Poor's (2014). U.S. Infrastructure Investment. A Chance to Reap More Than We Sow. New York: Standard & Poor's Financial Services.

Stanig, P. (2014). 'Governance Indicators', in Hertie School of Governance (ed), *The Governance Report 2014*. Oxford: Oxford University Press, 111–49.

Stiglitz, J. (1987). 'Principal and Agent', in J. Eatwell, M. Milgate, P. Newman, and R. H. I. Palgrave (eds), *The New Palgrave: A Dictionary of Economics. Volume 3: K-P*. London: Macmillan.

Sutherland, D., Araujo, S., Égert, B., and Kozluk, T. (2009). Infrastructure Investment. Links to Growth and the Role of Public Policies. OECD Economics Department Working Papers No. 686. Paris: OECD.

Taleb, N. N. (2007). 'Black Swans and the Domain of Statistics', *The American Statistician*, 61(3): 198–200.

Teo, L. (2015) [website]. *India's Infrastructure Investments: Huge Opportunities but No Takers*. Retrieved from https://blogs.cfainstitute.org/investor/2015/01/26/indias-infrastructure-investments-huge-opportunities-but-no-takers/ (accessed 1 October 2015).

Thaler, R. H., and Sunstein, C. R. (2008). *Nudge: Improving Decisions About Health, Wealth, and Happiness*. New Haven: Yale University Press.

The Economist (2015). 'Building Works', *The Economist,* 29 August 2015. Retrieved from http://www.economist.com/news/finance-and-economics/21662593-historic-opportunity-improve-infrastructure-cheap-danger (accessed 1 October 2015).

The Economist (2013). 'Keynes, Trains and Automobiles: Can a Fiscal and Monetary Splurge Reboot Japan's Recessionary Economy?', *The Economist,* 12 January 2013. Retrieved from http://www.economist.com/news/finance-and-economics/21569435-can-fiscal-and-monetary-splurge-reboot-japans-recessionary-economy-keynes (accessed 15 February 2016).

The Global Innovation Index (2015) [website]. *ICT Access.* Retrieved from https://www.globalinnovationindex.org/content/page/data-analysis/ (accessed 15 February 2016).

The Southern Times (2009) [website]. *Regional Power Trading System to be Implemented in November.* Retrieved from http://southernafrican.news/2009/10/23/regional-power-trading-system-to-be-implemented-in-november/ (accessed 27 January 2016).

The World Bank (2016) [website]. *Indicators.* Retrieved from http://data.worldbank.org/indicator (accessed 27 January 2016).

The World Bank (2014a). International Development Association Project Appraisal Document on a Proposed Credit in the Amount of SDR 32.4 Million (US$50 Million Equivalent) and Proposed Grant in the Amount of SDR 14.3 Million (US$22 Million Equivalent) to Nepal for a Rural Water Supply and Sanitation Improvement Project. Washington, DC: The World Bank.

The World Bank (2014b). International Development Association Project Appraisal Document on a Proposed Grant in the Amount of SDR13.2 Million (US$ 20 Million Equivalent) to the Southern African Power Pool for a Southern African Power Pool (SAPP) Program for Accelerating Transformational Energy Projects. Report No: 86076-AFR. Washington, DC: The World Bank.

The World Bank [website]. *Enterprise Surveys: Infrastructure.* Retrieved from http://www.enterprisesurveys.org/data/exploretopics/infrastructure (accessed 15 February 2016).

The World Bank [website]. *World Development Indicators.* Retrieved from http://wdi.worldbank.org/ (accessed 19 February 2016).

The World Bank [website]. *Doing Business: Historical Data Sets and Trends Data.* Retrieved from http://www.doingbusiness.org/data (accessed 21 February 2016).

Transparency International (2016) [website]. *Corruption Perceptions Index 2015.* Retrieved from http://www.transparency.org/cpi2015 (accessed 15 February 2016).

Trebilcock, M., and Rosenstock, M. (2013). Infrastructure PPPs in the Developing World. Lessons From Recent Experience. Toronto: University of Toronto, Faculty of Law.

US DHS (United States Department of Homeland Security) (2015) [website].

National Infrastructure Advisory Council. Retrieved from http://www.dhs.gov/national-infrastructure-advisory-council (accessed 15 February 2016).

US GAO (United States Government Accountability Office) (2012) [website]. *Commuter Rail: Potential Impacts and Cost Estimates for the Cancelled Hudson River Tunnel Project*. Retrieved from http://gao.gov/products/P00324 (accessed 15 February 2016).

US GAO (United States Government Accountability Office) (2010). States' and Localities' Uses of Funds and Action Needed to Address Implementation Challenges and Bolster Accountability. GAO-10-604. Washington, DC: US GAO.

Ugur, M. (2010). Institutions and Economic Performance: A Review of the Theory and Evidence. Munich Personal RePEc Archive No. 25909. Munich.

URA (Urban Redevelopment Authority) (2016) [website]. *About Us*. Retrieved from https://www.ura.gov.sg/uol/about-us.aspx (accessed 15 February 2016).

USAID (United States Agency for International Development) (2013). *Southern African Power Pool (SAPP) Energy Executives Discuss Power Market Expansion*. Retrieved from https://www.usea.org/sites/default/files/event-/SAPP%20Power%20Market%20Article.pdf (accessed 27 January 2016).

Van de Graaf, T., and Sovacool, B. K. (2014). 'Thinking Big: Politics, Progress, and Security in the Management of Asian and European Energy Megaprojects', *Energy Policy*, 74: 16–27.

Verduzco Chávez, B., and Sánchez Bernal, A. (2008). 'Planning Hydroelectric Power Plants With the Public: A Case of Organizational and Social Learning in Mexico', *Impact Assessment and Project Appraisal*, 26(3): 163–76.

Vilén, K., and Palko, T. (2010). Case Study Finland. Funding for Procurement of Innovations in the Public Sector. Helsinki: Ministry of Employment and the Economy.

Vogelsänger, J. (2012). Überprüfung des Bundesverkehrswegeplans: Teil Bundesfernstraßen. Retrieved from http://www.mil.brandenburg.de/sixcms/detail.php/587695 (accessed 16 February 2016).

Wang, S. Q., Tiong, R. L. K., Ting, S. K., Chew, D., and Ashley, D. (1998). 'Evaluation and Competitive Tendering of BOT Power Plant Project in China', *Journal of Construction Engineering and Management*, 124(4): 333–41.

Water Integrity Network, and Transparency International (2010). Integrity Pacts in the Water Sector. An Implementation Guide for Government Officials. Berlin: Water Integrity Network, Transparency International.

WEF (World Economic Forum) (2015). The Global Competitiveness Report 2015–2016. Geneva: WEF.

WEF (World Economic Forum) (2014). Strategic Infrastructure. Steps to Operate and Maintain Infrastructure Efficiently and Effectively. Cologny: WEF.

Wegrich, K., and Štimac, V. (2014). 'Coordination Capacity', in M. Lodge, and K. Wegrich (eds), *The Problem-solving Capacity of the Modern State: Govern-*

ance Challenges and Administrative Capacities. Oxford: Oxford University Press, 41–62.

White, A. J. (2012). 'Infrastructure Policy: Lessons From American History', *The New Atlantis* 35: 3–31.

Wildavsky, A. B. (1964). *Politics of the Budgetary Process*. Boston: Little, Brown and Company.

Williams, T., and Samset, K. (2010). 'Issues in Front-end Decision Making on Projects', *Project Management Journal*, 41(2): 38–49.

Wise, R., Wegrich, K., and Lodge, M. (2014). 'Governance Innovations', in Hertie School of Governance (ed), *The Governance Report 2014*. Oxford: Oxford University Press, 77–109.

Worldbrt.net (2015) [website]. *Yichang BRT*. Retrieved from http://www.worldbrt.net/en/cities/yichang.aspx (accessed 13 January 2016).

Zernike, K. (2012). 'Report Disputes Christie's Basis for Halting Tunnel', *The New York Times*, 10 April 2012: A18. Retrieved from http://www.nytimes.com/2012/04/10/nyregion/report-disputes-christies-reason-for-halting-tunnel-project-in-2010.html (accessed 15 February 2016).

Zhou, B. (2013) [website]. *Because We Can*. Retrieved from http://harvardpolitics.com/world/because-we-can/ (accessed 15 February 2016).

Zürn, M., Wälti, S., and Enderlein, H. (2010). 'Introduction', in H. Enderlein, S. Wälti, and M. Zürn (eds), *Handbook on Multi-level Governance*. Cheltenham: Edward Elgar, 1–16.

About the Contributors

Dorothée Allain-Dupré is Senior Policy Analyst at the Organisation for Economic Co-operation and Development (OECD) in the Public Governance and Territorial Development Directorate. She leads work on multi-level governance of public investment in the Regional Policy Division and has worked extensively on issues linked to regional development, decentralisation, as well as local and national public management. She holds a Master in Public Policy from Sciences Po (Paris, France) and a Master in European Studies from the University of Sussex (UK).

Rolf Alter (PhD, Göttingen) is Director for Public Governance and Territorial Development of the OECD in Paris. Prior to joining the OECD, he was an economist at the International Monetary Fund. He started his professional career in 1981 in the German Ministry of Economy and is currently member of the Global Agenda Council of the World Economic Forum and of the Advisory Group of the WEF Global Risks Report.

Helmut K. Anheier (PhD, Yale) is President and Dean of the Hertie School of Governance. He also holds a chair of Sociology at Heidelberg University and serves as Academic Director of the Centre for Social Investment there. Previously, he was Professor of Public Policy and Social Welfare at UCLA's Luskin School of Public Affairs and Centennial Professor at the London School of Economics.

Juan Garin is a consultant and researcher on infrastructure governance, planning, and regulation for the OECD. He is also Associate at NormannPartners, an international strategy consulting firm. He was previously Director of Consulting at Oxford Analytica, a leading political and economic analysis firm. Garin teaches courses on business-state relations and political risk at business schools including the Saïd Business School (Oxford University) and McDonough School of Business (Georgetown University).

Matthias Haber (PhD, University of Mannheim) is Research Scientist for the Governance Report at the Hertie School of Governance and leader of the governance indicators team. His research beyond that for the Governance Report team examines how conflict emerges within political parties and what consequences intra-party heterogeneity has for electoral and legislative outcomes.

Gerhard Hammerschmid (Dr. rer. soc. oec., Vienna University for Economics and Business Administration) is Professor of Public and Financial Management at the Hertie School of Governance and serves as honorary academic head at the Institut für den öffentlichen Sektor e.V. He has been

Visiting Professor at the Copenhagen Business School and the Australia and New Zealand School of Government and Director of the Hertie School's Executive Master of Public Management programme.

Ian Hawkesworth (MSc, London School of Economics) is Head of Public-Private Partnerships and Capital Budgeting at the Public Governance and Territorial Development Directorate, OECD. In this capacity he manages the Network of Senior Infrastructure and PPP Officials and is responsible for related country-specific reviews, advice to governments, and comparative studies. He is a contributor to the G20 Infrastructure Investment Working Group that seeks to develop and coordinate global policy issues on infrastructure. Prior to joining the OECD he was Head of Section at the Ministry of Finance of Denmark.

Claudia Hulbert is a consultant expert in local finance. Formerly of the OECD Public Governance and Territorial Development Directorate, she regularly collaborates with the OECD and has contributed to several publications related to subnational finance, public investment, fiscal consolidation, and fiscal policies. She graduated from the University Paris Dauphine with a Master in International Economics and holds a Bachelor in mathematics from the University Pierre and Marie Curie.

Sonja Kaufmann (MA, University of Potsdam) is Research Associate for the Governance Report. Before joining the Hertie School of Governance, she worked at the Berlin Social Science Research Center and the Free University's Collaborative Research Center 700, researching on various aspects of new forms of governance.

Genia Kostka (PhD, University of Oxford) is Professor of Governance of Energy and Infrastructure at the Hertie School of Governance. Her research and teaching interests are in energy governance, public policy, and political economy, with a regional focus on China. Before coming to the Hertie School, she was Assistant Professor at the Frankfurt School of Finance and Management and a strategic management consultant for McKinsey & Company in Berlin.

Margaux Vincent works as a consultant for the OECD on issues related to multi-level governance and subnational finance. Before joining the OECD, she completed a Master in Economics at the University Paris-Dauphine and is currently finalising a dual degree in European Affairs at Sciences Po Paris and in Political Economy of Europe at the London School of Economics.

Kai Wegrich (Dr., University of Potsdam) is Professor of Public Administration and Public Policy at the Hertie School of Governance. Prior to this position, he was a Tutorial Fellow at the London School of Economics and a Senior Researcher at RAND Corporation in Berlin and Cambridge. He is European Editor of *Public Administration* and co-editor of the book series on 'Executive Politics and Governance' (Palgrave). His main research interests are regulation, executive politics, and public sector reform.